Teenage Sex and Pregnancy

TEENAGE SEX AND PREGNANCY

Modern Myths, Unsexy Realities

Mike A. Males

Sex, Love, and Psychology Series
Judy Kuriansky, Series Editor

 PRAEGER

AN IMPRINT OF ABC-CLIO, LLC
Santa Barbara, California • Denver, Colorado • Oxford, England

Library of Congress Cataloging-in-Publication Data

Males, Mike A.
   Teenage sex and pregnancy : modern myths, unsexy realities / Mike A. Males.
      p. cm. — (Sex, love, and psychology series)
   Includes bibliographical references and index.
      ISBN 978–0–313–38561–2 (hard copy : alk. paper) — ISBN 978–0–313–38562–9 (ebook)
1. Teenagers—Sexual behavior—United States. 2. Teenage pregnancy—United States.
I. Title.
HQ27.M345   2010
306.70835—dc22   2010009113

ISBN: 978–0–313–38561–2
EISBN: 978–0–313–38562–9

14 13 12 11 10   1 2 3 4 5

This book is also available on the World Wide Web as an eBook.
Visit www.abc-clio.com for details.

Praeger
An Imprint of ABC-CLIO, LLC

ABC-CLIO, LLC
130 Cremona Drive, P.O. Box 1911
Santa Barbara, California 93116-1911

This book is printed on acid-free paper ∞

Manufactured in the United States of America

CONTENTS

SERIES FOREWORD

Mike Males is angry and he is not afraid to express it. He is angry that society seems to have bought into the relentless hype that teens are oversexed and that they engage in irresponsible sex. In contesting this point of view, the award-winning author presents compelling arguments and backs up his points with solid references from reliable sources. His passion for his subject figuratively jumps off the pages of his book.

In chapter after chapter, Males takes on the charge that teens are into debauchery, promiscuity, sexual pathology, and early pregnancy, among other accusations. As a media psychologist and sexologist myself who understands that television today is driven by a good debate, Males is perfect for the fight. After years of surveys published about the subject, it strikes me that professionals and the public are never too sure about the exact statistics concerning teen sexuality and also that results are constantly interpreted with contradictory implications—that youth sexual behavior and pregnancy rates are getting more out of control, or that they have leveled off, or that they have, at best, shown trends toward improvement. Males takes on this rollercoaster with conviction. As such, he makes a very important contribution to the field of sexuality—and to culture today!

I am no stranger to the controversy over whether youth are too wild and sexual. As a radio call-in advice host for over two decades, I have had thousands of young people call me with their sexual questions, which I included in chapters on "hooking up," "giving it up," and wondering "am I a freak?" in my book, *Generation Sex: America's Hottest Sex Therapist Answers the Hottest*

Questions About Sex. While there are hundreds of examples that are indeed shocking—including those about engaging in blood rituals, betrayals, and bondage—there were also thousands of questions from teens who wanted to act responsibly.

Over so many years as a media sexologist, I am familiar with many of the myths about sexuality, which makes me resonate with Males's arguments. One particularly distressing myth—that talking to kids about sex makes them go out and do it—formed the basis of an attack that my radio broadcasts would make kids more sexual. Fortunately, research showed the opposite: talking about sex does not make kids go out and do it, and even more impressive, those who were already active were more motivated to be safer about their activities. All this offers a solid foundation for Males's efforts to address myths about teenage sexuality and set the record straight.

Males's strong point of view is refreshing. He is not just defending a generation, he is educating all generations—about how to put teen sexuality into perspective. As a result, his book needs to be read by all advocates and professionals, by all media and the public, and even by youth themselves.

Dr. Judy Kuriansky

INTRODUCTION

Checking the evening television offerings in San Jose, Costa Rica, on a visit to Latin America a few years ago, I discovered *Dos Rombos*.[1] Its talk show format featured Spanish psychologist-actress Lorena Berdún chirping about all things sex, prefacing the evening's regularly scheduled explicit sex-toy update. Berdún's gay co-host, assorted celebrities, and pop experts that delivered commentary were backdropped by ubiquitous teenagers, some looking no older than 14, indulging in inter-gender bantering in the studio audience, participating in graphic discussions on stage, and contributing two-thirds of the call-ins. Their exuberant presence made the show's sardonic title—"Two Rhombuses," parodying the television symbol for "unsuitable for minors"— the popular talk show's unsubtle in-joke.

Further south in a hotel in Medellin, Colombia, where I was researching articles on the war on drugs, I ran across a local news channel's reporter-at-large feature, "El Sexo en Medellin." Effervescent female videocammers recorded on-the-street comments from locals on their sex lives and opinions. From serious teens as young as 13 to giggling elders bereft of hair, the on-camera revelations were appealingly candid, recounting the sizzling rewards and miserable failings of the opposite—and occasionally, same—sex from each side's well-stocked ammunition store.

These were mainstream, commercial channels broadcasting in prime-time hours. In Latin America, a region North Americans may think of as conservative and stilted, teenage sex is publicly accepted as a part of life. In Quito and Riobamba, Ecuador, where the drinking age nominally is

18 and blissfully unenforced, teens comprised an active element of the night-life and bar scene. Internet cafes and their unfiltered computers were often managed by unsupervised high schoolers and even children. No net-nanny software protected the 12-year-old girl and her 10-year-old brother showing me how to set up my account at their family's store. Intercity South American buses showed movies, including ones with uncensored R-rated language and sex scenes. I did not see parents engaging in frantic efforts to shield their children.

In Ensenada, Mexico, a port city with an active drug trade and tourism industry, I saw kids around 13 or 14 emerging at midnight from a theater showing what we label R-rated movies. There appeared to be nothing odd about it, as Mexican movie ratings are advisory.[2] They merely suggest that children ages 11 and younger should not watch movies rated "B" or worse. According to Mexico's B rating, youths 12 and older can handle movies containing explicit violence, sex, nudity, and drug use as long as it is not extreme or degrading, which seems to allow quite a lot.

For example, the B-rated movie, *High Art*, I watched on prime-time, uncensored Ensenada television shows hot sweaty sex, both heterosexual and lesbian (the latter involving a teenager), extensive cocaine sniffing, heroin shooting, nudity, and the legendary F-word (in its various Mexican Spanish translations) repeated dozens of times. There seemed to be very little time of this movie (I felt it necessary to watch it all, for research purposes) in which the characters were not high, having sex, or both. In the United States, this film is rated R (a hard R, I suspect), which means those under age 17 legally require an adult chaperone to see it.

As those who visit and reside there know, Latin American countries display wide varieties of urban life, but sexual codes are hardly lax. Traditional morality, often enforced against the got-lucky man by the offended girl's burly brothers and father, is far from rare. There is religious disapproval of abortion as well as sex outside of marriage. A museum in Costa Rica takes pains to explain that human fetuses on display in jars are not the products of the "crime" of abortion. However, religious views do not dictate state policy. For example, prostitution is legal and regulated, though prominent signs at airports (in English, interest-ingly) sternly warn against carrying drugs or sexually exploiting children. It is not the Summer of Love.

BACK TO THE CIRCUS . . .

What I was not finding in supposedly conservative Latin America was the hostile combination of puritanism and voyeurism that authorities and news media in the United States reserve for bullying the young. Back in the United States, I saw "experts" announcing (as they do every few years) an unheard-of "junior high sexual revolution." A parade of authors and "experts" unreeled licentious tales of teen, preteen, and preschool sex, as identical in horror and titillation as they were bereft of evidence.[3] Is there some expert-media plot to *convince* sixth graders that everyone their age is having sex? Major research institutes assigned employees to—wait for it—*count* the *number* of times "sexy" or "boob" or "doing it," or any kissing, hugging, flirting, or even the mildest allusions to sex occurred or were hinted at or otherwise *insinuated* on popular television shows.[4]

This ludicrous tee-hee inventory was scaled along some kind of screen-sex metric to produce real-sounding numbers to buttress alarms of 50 percent or 70 percent (or whatever) "increases in sex on TV" ... which instigated clown-ishly unscientific studies claiming even mild TV-program innuendoes incite millions of teen pregnancies ... which triggered clarions by TV news outlets ever-eager for chances to replay (that is, advertise) their networks' prime-time steam ... which afforded shocked reporters and experts another opportunity to gush outraged pieties to the effect that America was discovering, for the record-breaking twenty millionth time, that some people under age 25 do have sex.[5] How would America's delicate souls, apoplectic over the tepid scenes in *The O.C., Gossip Girl,* and *Friends,* survive *Dos Rombos,* prime-time Japanese anime, or the graphic BBC teen dramedy, *Skins?*

Then there was the big-time Federal Trade Commission report gasping over the "problem" that—again, wait for it—teenage movie audiences were exposed to *G-rated promos* for R-rated movies.[6] *The New Yorker*'s sophisticated movie critic is aghast that the bare-knuckle boxing movie *Fighting* is rated PG-13 ("approved for young adults and kids?" "How do you pull that off?") before noting with relief that "the movie's language is chaste."[7] (Please, sir, stay out of Mexico.) The official government position under ex-President George W. Bush, through an unholy alliance of its Abstinence Clearinghouse and Centers for Disease Control, was that schools should teach that men's and women's gender roles are sacred and biologically inalterable, that sex outside of marriage can cause suicide, that condoms are ineffective, and that abortion often leads to sterility.[8]

Libraries were blowing millions of dollars badly needed for necessary library materials like encyclopedias, History Channel documentaries, and beanbag chairs to install intrusively futile Internet censorware under the dic-tates of a panicked Congress that designated unfiltered computers a national emergency.[9] Promptly, I read of another lobby raising the panic sequel that innocent children wandering libraries were being polluted by "secondhand porn" glimpsed as they passed by adults' screens.[10]

America's latest resurrection of pre-pilgrim Puritanism does not represent normal taste or caution. As we will see, some neopuritans claiming a liberal mindset may invoke "healthy sexuality" abstractions, but in practice they hold that teens and young adults should not have sex, not talk about sex, and never even *think* about sex except in the context of adult-approved, sex education abstinence-pushing regimes. As Hillary Clinton shuddered about daughters going all the way, "Don't do it until you're 21, and then don't tell me about it."[11] Any evidence that teens have sex or even think or talk about sex on their own is depicted by authors and commentators as proof of the corrupting power of popular culture and media to provoke young people to the unspeakable.

THE ENDLESS PANIC

In the United States, inflamed panic and real danger bear only a passing acquaintance. *Dateline NBC* incessantly replays its "To Catch a Predator" series, depicting hordes of perverts lurking online in every community to seduce, abduct, rape, and otherwise harm children and teens.[12] Yet, despite the insistence that its sting operations are saving kids from assailants, the show cites vanishingly few cases in which such attacks *actually have occurred*.

Indeed, a University of New Hampshire study of law enforcement records nationwide turned up only a tiny number of children or teens who were assailed, raped, or kidnapped by someone they met online[13]—a finding that "To Catch a Predator" mysteriously fails to mention. The show's reporter-pervert confrontations inadvertently suggest the reason: these sad-sack "predators" are too inept to fool even the loneliest third grader. A moronic *Atlantic* magazine article, harking to the happy future day when teens will be banned from going online unless supervised by adults over their shoulders, trembles with fear of Internet predator and corruption perils it nowhere documents.[14]

But wait . . . the real crisis is teens preying on themselves! Next came revelations that teenagers are mobile child-porn dispensers. Panic erupted in city after city over "sexting" (teens sending even mildly sexy messages and pictures privately over cell phones) absent any evidence of harm beyond the occasional overstretched anecdote. School principals and police confiscated private phones, engorged to uncover naked pubescent pictures and hot little whisperings to saddle young offenders with lifelong branding as a sexcriminal.[15] (How about stamping a big red "**i**" on their foreheads?) *Time* magazine's inexcusably sloppy reporting ignited days-long national media splashes berating what turned out to be a nonexistent "teen pregnancy pact" in a Massachusetts resort town.[16]

Reviewers of the movie *Precious* described the title character, raped and impregnated at ages 11 and 14 by her abusive father, as illustrating "teen pregnancy."[17] (Yes, in 2009, pregnancy resulting from father-daughter rape is called *teen pregnancy*.) Strangely, the National Campaign to Prevent Teen and Unplanned Pregnancy—the quasi-public agency set up to candy up teenage sex and pregnancy to benefit its constituent interests—does not recommend *Precious*. Incest is too rough to suit the National Campaign's political needs. Rather, at this writing the Campaign's Web site[18] links a clip from the ABC television series *Cougar Town* (a show featuring older women chasing younger men, good for them!) because of a sex "talk" by a cougar mom directed at teens. (I am guessing "the talk" didn't include, "Hey, son, nail the young'uns like mommy does!") Commentators that included the National Campaign[19] continued, 15 months after the deed was discovered, to unburden incessantly mean-spirited speculations about the motherhood of former vice-presidential candidate Sarah Palin's teenage daughter Bristol. (None of them actually knew her.) If media staying power is the gauge, Bristol's must be the most important reproductive act in American history. Major televison networks time the seconds consumed by a paparazzi-videoed kiss by teen singer Miley Cyrus ("seven . . . eight . . . nine," the reporter exclaims in hushed tone, as if Apollo were being launched), preparatory to the host's own tongue-clucking.

America's austere commentariat perceived serious hazards in little Miley. When the then-15-year-old draped herself in a full-length sheet in *Vanity Fair* (less revealing than what you would see at the beach) or casually palmed an ice cream cart umbrella stand while singing at the MTV Music Awards, media prigs hollered "slut!" and "pole dancing!"[20] *For God's sake.* Did they seriously hallucinate millions of girls awaiting "Hannah Montana's" doomsday code to get fertilized? I watched bubbly Miley's little MTV act. It was not even in the same *galaxy* as strippers' pole dancing (so those who have seen a real one tell me). Here is your first clue: Miley *didn't strip.* Strange, as New York University law professor Amy Adler lamented in the *Columbia Law Review*, how the zeal to see obscenity in every teenage pose and aside infects us all with the squinty pedophile leer in which "everything becomes child pornography."[21]

Then, Lord help us, there were the evangelicals carrying on the worldly traditions of reverends Jimmy Swaggart of self-named Ministries and motel-prostitute rendezvous; Jim Bakker of secretary adultery and hush money fame; Billy James Hargis of the American Christian College and bisexual tryst; on and on, right into the second Bush administration's new "sexual purity movement" emblematized by Pastor Ted Haggard of the New Life megachurch and methamphetamine-laced male prostitute fondness. The greater the religious fundamentalists' power, the scarier they got.

Washington, D.C.'s "C-Street Family" cult serving key Congressmen, governors, and other leaders of both parties magically reinterpreted the Scriptures to affirm the privilege of the wealthy and powerful to demonstrate their exaltation as God's "chosen" by indulging in earthly corruptions, especially flesh and manna. A leader of Washington's power-cult, David Coe (son of C-Street ayatollah Doug Coe), was quoted by *Harper's* magazine consulting editor Jeff Sharlet[22] that he would excuse "Family leaders" he referred to as "the 'new chosen'" even if they "rape . . . little girls." Horrifying? A disgrace? Hardly. The more the righteous Right fed off its stalwarts' refusal to embrace the purity they preached, the more its abstinence crusade conveniently aimed holy demands at teenagers to remain virgins or, if sullied, to re-virginize. It is as if Jesus really said, let he who is with plenty of sin cast a boulder at those whores. "Scandal does not destroy American fundamentalism," puzzled Sharlet in *The Family*. "Rather, like a natural fire that purges the forest of overgrowth, it makes the movement stronger." If teens took seriously the message of Washington's new Ministry of Godliness, their unblinded eyes would see fornication as angelic and chastity as the mark of the Almighty's contempt.

Then there was Carrie Prejean.[23] At the 2009 Miss USA pageant, first runner-up Prejean discombulated everyone with her response when asked by pageant judge Perez Hilton whether she believed same-sex marriage should be legalized. "Well, I think it's great that Americans are able to choose one way or the other. We live in a land where you can choose same-sex marriage or opposite marriage," stammered Prejean, incorrectly. "And, you know what, in my country, in my family, I think that I believe that marriage should be between a man and a woman." Now, other than getting facts muddled, what was wrong with Prejean's affirming that same-sex marriage choice was "great" but she was partial to opposite-sex marriage? That is not only her right, it is more liberal than President Barack Obama's position. But Hilton, who is gay—and also a gossip-whore who tosses "slutty," "nigger," and "faggot" at his blog-targets— branded Prejean a "dumb bitch" whose answer "cost her the crown."[24] Genuine advocates of gay marriage such as San Francisco Mayor Gavin Newsom and the lesbian, gay, bisexual, and transgender (LGBT) gay-rights lobby criticized Hilton and defended Prejean's right to state her views.

No matter. Prejean bolted for the right-wing media, cutting an anti-gay-marriage ad and claiming liberal anti-Christian persecution violated her free speech rights, though she seemed quite unmuzzled. Then nude pictures of her surfaced, followed by lawsuits by and against Prejean (one alleging unpaid loans for her breast implants), and her termination by Miss USA. Next appeared a Prejean sex tape featuring autoerotic talents she claimed was just one she made as a naïve teenager for an ex-boyfriend, then new evidence that she really made at least eight sex tapes as recently as two years ago. More upward ratcheting of right/left hollerings ensued. All most odd. The Right's heroine was a siliconed sex-tape model against whom the Left was clucking purse-lipped moral disapproval. Had Prejean vigorously defended gay marriage and been bitch-tasered by a conservative homophobe, the moral-outrage hurricane would have raged just as blustrously, only left to right.

AMERICA'S HOT TROTTING "VIRTUOCRACY"

Is it coincidence that the sternest railers against teenage immorality seem unable to lead moral lives themselves? As *Newsweek* pointed out in the

1990s, modern "virtuecrats" are not expected to be virtuous themselves.[25] *Time* even suggested that morally compromised politicians like President Clinton could redeem their own tarnished family values by demanding strict morality from teenagers. Each new revelation of yet another pious politician philanderer, whoremonger, and sex-scandal briber only added to suspicions that champing for teenaged chastity is a cover-up for personal sleaze.

The sex scandals of Bill Clinton's White House and Newt Gingrich's Congress—two grand marshals in a bipartisan parade of tinpot-banging, family-values philanderers—are history, swept aside by more recent politician indiscretions. Just in the past year at this writing, we have had senators playing restroom-stall foot-solicitation, consorting with D.C. madame Heidi Fleiss, indulging in sordid affairs with their video documentarists, and ponying tens of thousands to bribe mistresses. Tough-talking governors recast "hiking the Appalachian Trail" and "Love Client Number Nine" as national risqueities.[26]

And those godly House types. Among the many scandals, a bipartisan one-two punch was particularly stunning. In October 2008, conservative Representative Tim Mahoney (D-Florida), who campaigned that "restoring America's family values begins at home," admitted he had paid a congressional staffer $121,000 to avoid a sexual harassment suit after he had an extramarital affair with her, and then fired her. Mahoney had replaced ultra-conservative Representative Mark Foley (R-Florida), who was caught sexting (real sexting, not the made-up kind) at teenaged pages.[27]

From now on, why not cut the lag time between morals-preaching and caught-sinning by just *assuming* that everyone who publicly invokes righteous morals (especially when sermonizing youths) is confessing to wretched personal sin? In Newt Gingrich's assertion of "a clear distinction between my private life" (the one filled with adultery, marriage abandonment, and ethics scandals) and his hellfire public stances (the ones championing punitive morality standards for the young and poor)[28] needs to be erased.

While many may consider my detailings of the sexual misconduct of family-values politicians, media celebrities, and other luminaries as unscholarly *ad hominem* and *feminem* attacks, I argue that they are of supreme relevance. Those who seek to profit personally and politically from judging others' morals open up their own lives to scrutiny. If the sanctimonious cannot live by their own righteous standards, who are they to demand that the rest of us (including teenagers) act better than they do? Worse, the inability to manage personal sin motivates harsh morality politics. The punishing puritanism of Fox News pundit Bill O'Reilly, comic Bill Cosby, former House Speaker Gingrich, former Clinton chief of staff Dick Morris, former president Clinton, evangelical leaders, and dozens of other arch-virtuecrats dwells in the same individuals whose own sex lives ranged from questionable to off the charts.

There is a kind of personality—which I will call "healthy"—that sees its own human foibles as reason to be *less* judgmental toward those of others. There is another kind of personality—which we seem to install in high office and enshrine in the commentariat by the dirigible load—that views its own monumental screwups as righteous reason to harshly punish similar or lesser screwups of the rest of us, particularly the young. Elites who regard their self-awarded exemption from high moral standards as license to lead glorious missions to bring the hammer down on the lowly are evil and dangerous.

O'Reilly, for example, scoffed without evidence that an abducted and sexually abused 12-year-old boy had "enjoyed himself" in captivity.[29] Very well. Perhaps, as a 2004 lawsuit the Foxter paid millions of dollars to bury alleged, O'Reilly enjoyed sexually harassing subordinates with lewd too-much-information banter and hardcore phone calls detailing how that little brown Balinese woman admired his manly endowment.[30] Comedian Bill Cosby disgorged ugly sexual comments about black teenaged girls and supported the police shooting of accused petty thieves (for stealing "pound cake," in his weird example). Surely, then, the cops should have shot confessed gigolo Cosby after a young woman accused him of drugging and sexually assaulting her.[31]

Why is there such adulation of pop-clowns lecturing teens on moral behavior? Cosby—the esteemed "Father of the Year" who diddled and quite possibly fathered a child with a woman not his wife—inexplicably became a family-values icon for liberals and conservatives alike after some incoherent rantings about the way ghetto-dwellers talk and name their kids, including a particularly gross aside on the black girl's "crack." Dr. Laura Schlessinger (of unwed pregnancy, shacking up, marital infidelity, nude Internet photos, and bitterly alienated family)[32] and Dr. Phil (of bad marriage, professional reprimand, and multiple lawsuits and ethical controversies)[33] deliver stern lectures on morality, especially to teens. Geraldo Rivera, the man-slut who boasted of having sex with "thousands of women, literally thousands" (though many he named denied it)[34] and then shamed a 14-year-old girl on his show as "a sexual slut just like her sister" before a national television audience,[35] now sniggers amiably with Fox's O'Reilly about modern young people's low morals.

Switch from conservative Fox to liberal MSNBC, and we find Donna Rice (the once-bikinied concubine whose loveboat and no-tell-motel affair with former Senator Gary Hart coitally interrupted the latter's 1988 presidential campaign) railing against Internet porn and supposed epidemics of online predators seducing children.[36] Switch to CBS, and what do I see as this is written? Oh, Dave, say it ain't so. Letterman, who badgered DWI-plagued Nicole Richie with moralizing on "what's wrong with young Hollywood," now is confessing indiscretions—*lots* of indiscretions—with staff interns.[37] Did you learn nothing from Bill-and-Monica's troubles or *Grey's Anatomy*?

Somewhere in the Tiger Woods scandal some priss must have fretted that millions of Blasian teenagers were primed to score cocktail waitresses in order to boost their golf scores (and vice versa). Breaking news! Forget the M-rated video games and Internet sites; should *Disneyland* be adults-only? A new expose[38] by a journalist and former Magic Kingdom photographer brands Florida's Disney World a real-life "hotbed of sex and drugs," featuring acid-dealing Winnie-the-Poohs, Jammin' Jungle porn stars, Dale the Chipmunk sluts who punched employees' prized SOP (Sex on Property) cards, and—of course—Mouse fetishists. The next day, there was the national news story of a Phoenix, Arizona, high school teacher suspended for taking her choir, which had played at the presidential inauguration, to a Hooter's restaurant, where the waitresses wear "somewhat revealing attire."[39] Everyone knows senior high students cannot handle "somewhat." Lighten up, Paradise Valley School District. At least she did not take them to Disneyland! Or a golf tournament. Or Congress. Or church.

But seriously... why do Americans reward preacher-philanderers and worship at their "bully pulpits"? What can they possibly teach young people except how *not* to act? How are American teenagers—already growing up in families with 50 percent divorce rates,[40] in a country whose adults have among the highest unplanned pregnancy and sexually transmitted disease (STD) rates in the developed world—supposed to interpret their elders' puritan-libidinal narcissism that combines rank grownup indulgence with thundering protect-our-children sermons? Of course, a society whose grownups sport statistics on a variety of fronts that are the shame of Western countries, in which one famous sexual idiocy marches after another, would strive to *blame* its problems on teenagers and preteens. President Obama—who was advertised to bring "change"—may lament "tales of... teens engaged in endless sexual escapades" (by his books' tales, his sexual escapades continued from teen years well into adulthood), but the real immorality is America's official surrender to easy-scapegoat politics and culture war clichés.

HOOKUP AMERICA

Still, all these grownup antics have got to be messing with the kids, right? Tom Wolfe is the dean of distilling sweeping cultural mantras from hip regalings of fringe bizarrities—sixties acidhead frolics, Black Panthers meet Jewish radical chic, astronaut foibles, deadly wrong turns in the ghetto. In *Hooking Up* (2001),[41] Wolfe waxes as florid as ever on "the lurid carnival" comprising the new radically sexualized America:

> Every magazine stand was a riot of bare flesh, rouged areolae, moistened crevices, and stiffened giblets; boys with boys, girls with girls, bare-breasted female

bodybuilders, so-called boys with breasts, riding backseat behind steroid-gorged bodybuilding bikers, naked except for cache-sexes and Panzer helmets, on huge chromed Honda or Harley-Davidson motorcycles....

This is prime Wolfology. Naturally, he can't stay away from teens:

Meanwhile, sexual stimuli bombarded the young so incessantly and intensely that they were inflamed with a randy itch long before reaching puberty.... From age thirteen, American girls were under pressure to maintain a façade of sexual experience and sophistication. Among girls, "virgin" was a term of contempt. The old term "dating"—referring to a practice in which a boy asked a girl out for the evening and took her to the movies or dinner—was now deader than "proletariat," "pornography," or "perversion." In junior high school, high school, and college, girls headed out in packs in the evening, and boys headed out in packs in the evening, hoping to meet each other fortuitously. If they met and some girl liked the looks of some boy, she would give him the nod or he would give her the nod, and the two of them would retire to a halfway-private room and "hook up."

"Hooking up," Wolfe told us, mystifies today's innocent parents who *never* did (or do) any such thing. But now . . .

Among the children, hooking up was always a sexual experience, but the nature and extent of what they did could vary widely. Back in the twentieth century, American girls had used baseball terminology. "First base" referred to embracing and kissing; "second base" referred to groping and fondling and deep, or "French," kissing commonly known as "heavy petting;" "third base" referred to fellatio, usually known in polite conversation by the ambiguous term "oral sex;" and "home plate" meant conception-mode intercourse, known familiarly as "going all the way." In the year 2000, in the era of hooking up, "first base" meant deep kissing ("tonsil hockey"), groping, and fondling; "second base" meant oral sex; "third base" meant going all the way; and "home plate" meant learning each other's names.

Right. Wolfe's stuff is not the sort for which you can demand evidence. It seems unfair to point out that the Centers for Disease Control (CDC)'s national survey found 94 percent of American girls under age 14 (the ones Wolfe contends found virginity contemptible) called themselves virgins,[42] or that the latest CDC statistics find pregnancy[43] and consistently measured STD[44] rates at *all-time lows* among teens, far lower than 30 to 40 years ago when today's supposedly nonhooked parents were teens. Wolfe's apocalysm in *Hooking Up* seems a non-sequitur given his similarly dire commentaries about past generations that, say, dropped acid on freeways and banged teen girls in crab-crawling yurts.

As polemic, Wolfe's is fun; as research, it is shit. It is scary that Wolfe's rhetorical drive-by forms the genesis for later, supposedly scholarly treatises. La Salle University sociologist Kathleen Bogle even opens her own 2008 book, also titled *Hooking Up*, with Wolfe's "keen" cultural observation on modern teens' revised baseball scorecard.[45] A silly piece by the *New York Times Magazine*'s Benoit Denizet-Lewis (who describes himself as a "sex addict") lamented the passing of "teenage romance" and alleged some scary new "hookup" culture is driving a scourge of loveless promiscuity, even suggesting that Hooter's restaurants impose age limits on customers.[46] More and more, I suspect commentators (well, perhaps not Wolfe) are exploiting teenagers as vehicles to soothe their own sexual excesses.

However, one sentence of Wolfe's did strike me as delineating the real tripwire setting off larger cultural alarm: "Teenage girls spoke about their sex lives. . .without the least embarrassment or guile." Wolfe seemed deeply troubled by the fact that when asked by news reporters, " 'How did you lose your virginity?' Girls as well as boys responded without hesitation, posed for photographs, and divulged their name, age, and the neighborhood where they lived."

Armageddon! That many modern young women (many more, no doubt, than in the past, Mae, Dorothy, and Isadora notwithstanding) are shockingly unembarrassed to talk publicly about sex and fail to cower beneath the old "stains and stigmas"—the ones Wolfe and many others would like to see restored—seems to underlie a great deal of the offense and fear. Not only did traditionalists find girls' greater frankness at younger ages offensive, they interpreted it as proof of a new age of rampant promiscuity. In traditional wolfpack-speak, girls who talk about it are girls who do it. The idea that a young female could repertoire the standard profanities and talk about sex unashamedly without doing the lacrosse team during study hall baffles older generations. It does not seem to matter that the wild scares and save-the-kids remedies do not turn out to be justified by any reasonable examination of information available.

Wolfe occupies the ozone of cultural chronicling, but he does get gut visceralities right. Like other commentators, Wolfe really was deploring the new sexual frankness by white, upscale women, as his references to college girls, baseball euphemisms, European notions, and suburban Internet games betray. If Wolfe was referring to black girls or poorer cohorts, his commentary would cease to be seen as incisive. Today, the public discussion of teen sex and teen pregnancy refers almost exclusively to higher-class youth, not the kids downtown.

Are the talking heads' worrying that the low morals of rich kids are corrupting destitute urchins (quite the reversal of past fears)? This false egalitarianism overlooks a large matter. As Chapter 1 details, "teenage sex" and "teen pregnancy" do not exist as distinct teenage phenomena, but are straight-line functions of economic conditions and the sexual behaviors of adults. In particular, vital statistics reports show that rates of birth, unwed birth, abortion, and total pregnancy among teens are uncannily similar to those of adults around them by race, locale, era, and related demographic characteristics. That is a crucial reality, though admittedly far less titillating than watching talk show hosts like Tyra Banks and Larry King pressing Levi Johnston for the juicy details on the sex with Bristol. So, do Jaime, Bristol, and "Juno" contribute to a pop-culture climate that prompts poorer black and Hispanic *adult women* to get pregnant? How else can we reconcile claims that pop culture profoundly influences teen pregnancy with the fact that teens and adults have very similar pregnancy patterns?

THE SANCTIFICATION OF *I'M OFFENDED*

In a few months, the celebrity names and teen-panics-du-jour will change in America's bizarre politician, institution, church, and media-figure sexcapades. As celebrity basher Chelsea Handler declared after a particularly scandal-laden week in which more big icons bungeed off the infidelity cliff, "The hits just keep on coming."

Still, even toughened up by America's certifiable craziness about sex—or maybe jealous that I am apparently having less fun than evangelicals exhibiting hot new versions of "holy roller"—I was unprepared for a long, front-page me-column in the *Los Angeles Times.* "I've covered murders, grisly accidents, airplanes falling out of the sky and, occasionally, dirty politics," reporter Catherine Saillant's opening sentence vented. "But in nearly two decades of journalism, nothing has made my insides churn like seeing what my 13-year-old daughter and her friends are up to on MySpace.com."[47]

Really? What horror *could* her daughter and MySpace friends be perpetrating that was worse than people *dying*? It turned out that Saillant had uncovered some girls' crudities and bathing suit posings. Mom's account of the shattering trauma she suffered was deemed worthy of front-page placement by editors of one of the nation's premier newspapers. It won overwhelming praise from readers' posts and launched a speaking and media tour. It is widely reposted and cited by Internet critics.

I puzzled to comprehend what the apparently widespread middle-class outrage tapped by this column could be about. It clearly was not the usual paranoia about Internet predators; Saillant admits none beckoned in the months of her MySpace saga. It was not about real rape or violence or even mild threats. It surely was not about protecting her daughter's privacy; that ship sailed after Saillant revealed her daughter's name and a wealth of incidents and details of her private life on the front page of a major newspaper. It could not have been the bad words. Saillant proudly affirmed she is no prude.

As near as I can fathom from this article and the reaction, the overriding issue blotting out all others is that Saillant was *offended* in a deeply visceral way—not at any *tangible* harm but merely at the realization that *her own daughter* sometimes talked dirty and posted a picture giving the finger while using a fearsome, new Internet technology (as opposed to talking dirty using gym locker rooms, telephones, and post-it notes). No one had to demonstrate any real catastrophe—like people getting maimed and dying, that is. The biggest catastrophe in all the universe is: *I'm offended.*

Clearly many conservatives and liberals alike are deeply offended by the increasing sexual explicitness of popular culture and the intrusion of new technologies that deliver it. Many, from Family Research Council conservatives to Media Education Foundation liberals, translate their personal offense into remarkably similar insistence—based on remarkably little evidence—that pop-culture *must be* corrupting young people into greater promiscuity, sexual violence, and related ills. Look at how *offensive* it is!

There are gradations to the degree of offense at modern popular culture, of course. There are those who condemn the presentation of irresponsible sex, violent sex, and more explicit sex in newer television shows, music, films, games, and other media, including depictions of teenage sex that were not ritually followed by punishing lessons. Then there are the growing numbers of absolute puritans such as the Kaiser Family Foundation, Rand Corporation, Heritage Foundation, and authors such as M. Gigi Durham who insist that any mention of sex at all, even the mildest innuendo other than in approved educational regimens, damages young people. Durham, for example, branded a harmless television scene of three swimsuited teens in a hot tub as "casual sex" and a "threesome."[48] Rand trumped up baseless "studies" to insist even mildly sexy shows like *Friends* and *That 70s Show* impel millions of teen pregnancies.[49] Censorware marketed to libraries and parents promised to keep teens from any site about sex (including, in one case, the Middlesex, Connecticut, city Web site).

Meanwhile, just about any serious media insinuations of sex by anyone under age 20 as legitimate, normative, and even pleasurable draw outrage from Americans of all stripes. When Susan Wilson of Planned Parenthood of Northern New Jersey suggested a school curriculum that included the normality of teenage sexuality, virulent condemnation quickly ensued—including in liberal media, led again by *Atlantic Magazine*.[50] Prominent teenagers such as Cyrus, who revealed enjoyment of the *Sex and the City* series, were loudly castigated merely for admitting they think about sex at all. Those who contend today's neopuritans, even liberal ones, embrace any notion of healthy teenage sexuality should look at what they actually say.

Behind the neo-puritanism toward youth lies uglier sentiments. Every once in a while, American agencies let the shield slip and provide a glimpse of the raw hostility behind their attacks on young people, particularly ones with the temerity to have sex. At a conference in San Diego in 2000, when I served on The California Wellness Foundation's teen pregnancy advisory board,

I grilled a National Campaign to Prevent Teen Pregnancy consultant about the organization's utterly repulsive (even for it) "Scarlet Letter" ads. These featured "CHEAP," "DIRTY," "REJECT," "USELESS," "PRICK," and the like in big red letters superimposed over pictures of teenagers, with a small "sex has consequences" caption.[51] My question concerned when the National Campaign would be running ads with similarly harsh epithets over the pictures of Bill Clinton, Rudolph Giuliani, Newt Gingrich, Dick Morris, Henry Hyde, Geraldo Rivera, and other prominent sluts—who, after all, influence the climate by which teenagers come to understand sexual morality. Her answer (my paraphrasing): We would never stigmatize powerful politicians that way; just young people who cannot fight back.

REFIGHTING YESTERDAY'S WAR

By the 2000s, the standard 90-second volleying between dueling teen-sex foes in the news media had become a hollaback drill: Sex education! (SENDS . . . TEENS . . . DOUBLE . . . MESSAGES!). Give me abstinence-only! (DENIES . . . TEENS . . . LIFESAVING . . . FACTS!). For all the sound and fury lamenting teens having sex and/or babies, these issues get raised the way jousters raise lances. On the progressive shows and blogs such as *Rachel Maddow, Countdown with Keith Olbermann, Huffington Post*, and *Salon*, teen pregnancy's main utility seems to be to jab at former Republican vice presidential candidate Sarah Palin (she of loud morals and prego daughter), Democratic senators who oppose health care reform, corporate advertising, southern-state legislators, conservative lobbies, Fox News, and anyone else they are otherwise annoyed with who also supported abstinence-only.

Truth and fairness are no more provinces of the Left than the Right. MSNBC's Rachel Maddow declared that in Texas, where abstinence was righteously preached, "a teenager gets pregnant every 12 minutes."[52] (Understated, actually; figures from the Alan Guttmacher Institute[53] suggest it is every six minutes.) True, Texas has the fifth-highest teen pregnancy rate in the country, 20 percent above the national average. However, the problem is, next door New Mexico, whose sex education curriculum is not limited to abstinence-only, has the nation's fourth-highest teen pregnancy rate, 23 percent above the national average. As for Palin's gravid daughter, the sex-versus-abstinence arguers exploited Bristol's pregnancy as a prime example upholding whatever they advocated without mentioning that the Wasilla, Alaska, high school Bristol attended provided comprehensive sex education and abstinence classes. Though I am pretty sure no one cares, Guttmacher Institute figures show Alaska's teen pregnancy rate ranks thirtieth in the country, well below the national average, even as its native Inuit teens have very high pregnancy rates.

What do Texas, New Mexico, and Inuit youth have in common that Alaska white youth do not? A high rate of poverty, which is an issue progressives like Maddow used to talk about. But in privatized debate concerning powerless populations like youth, no one feels compelled to consider, let alone mention, inconvenient truths. Tom Wolfe keyed the national tone for a teen-sex discourse that long ago stopped being about teens.

Still, I do not mean to imply that everyone involved in the issue has become as cynical and deceptive as combatants at the national level. From Internet sites to school and storefront clinics, there are hundreds of reproductive health programs and information providers serving clients of all ages at low or no cost. They help teenagers obtain contraception and other services, including getting around cruel and dangerous efforts by policymakers to deny adolescents any assistance neopuritans worry might facilitate their having sex without suffering consequences. If right-wing bluenoses cannot have a little indiscreet whoopee without getting love children or blackmailed or sued, why should some swarthy kid get away with it?

The irony is that as the quarrelers debating sex-versus-abstinence education insist in rising stridence that teens will screw and reproduce and die from poxes by the millions if the hated other side wins, the proliferation of online and localized services has rendered what schools teach increasingly irrelevant. Not only are school curriculums becoming less important in young people's larger world of sex and contraceptive information, but politics at the national, state, and school-board level is rendering schools unreliable sources of sexual information. Teens are much better off consulting a variety of Internet sources (note: *variety*) and local health clinics than in depending on politically warped school classes to provide truthful and useful information. Teens who feel the need to have abstinence preached at their wholesome faces can find PG-rated sites to do that as well.

I do not pretend neutrality in the old-school quarrel. As detailed in Chapter 10, my doubt that what schools teach has any great effect on teen pregnancy rates in either direction should not be taken as indifference to the factual and moral atrocity that abstinence-only education represents. Abstinence-only (including abstinence-lite that pushes chastity while short-shrifting alternatives) is not only ineffective and misleading; it is morally objectionable. It is simply not true, as Congress's 1981 Adolescent Family Life Act (AFLA) insisted, that "abstinence from sexual activity outside of marriage" is "the expected standard" Americans observe.[54] Surveys, unwed pregnancy rates, STD rates, divorce rates, and other measures confirm that, as a class, American adults—most especially adults age 20 and older who cause the large majority of what we call "teen" pregnancies—do not follow any such standard. In particular, grownups in the "red" states from whence the most conservative lawmakers pushing abstinence-only hail, and which have the highest unwed pregnancy and divorce rates, are the least likely to follow marriage-only edicts. As detailed, brothel-loads of conservative politicians and religious moralizers feel no compulsion to follow abstinence-outside-marriage standards themselves. The AFLA's mandate to teach abstinence to the exclusion of all other issues trashes the Ninth Commandment against bearing false witness and Ecclesiastes's warnings against vanity. It allows grownups, especially the most compromised, to indulge pleasing pretenses about ourselves amid the rosy glow of sternly telling the kids to keep it zipped.

What kids learn from abstinence education, then, if they are paying attention at all, is how to lie about sex like a grownup. Witness the peculiar "teen panel syndrome" (as San Jose State University library science professor Anthony Bernier terms it), which refers to conference organizers selecting certain teenagers for the mandatory "teen panel" according to their reliability in denigrating their youthful peers while affirming adults' rights to engage in the same behaviors for which they denigrated their peers.

This, then, is why comprehensive, objective sex education uncluttered by phony values preaching and abstinence-slanted misinformation is necessary as a school curriculum. First, sex, reproduction, contraception, sexual health, and related issues are normal parts of biology and health disciplines and thus normal topics for instruction. Second, adults owe honesty to teens because we, as a society, have made teens a part of the adult sexual world. Of the girls under age 18 who gave birth in the most recent years reported, California's tabulations (the most comprehensive in the country) show the ages of fathers ranged from 13 to 62. Just 20 percent of the fathers were also under 18; half were 20 and older; and as many were 30 and older as were under age 16.[55]

There are around 4,500 births every year in California involving fathers 21 and older with mothers age 17 and younger—and births reflect just a fraction of all sexual behaviors involving teens with teens and teens with adults. Although teenagers may find better information sources online, schools have an obligation to guarantee that no young person lacks objective, useful information on the realities they face. The practical reality, with a few exceptions, is that adult-teen sex even with large age gaps remains acceptable, and the younger party usually will be blamed for any consequences.

THE "PRIVATIZED SOCIAL POLICY" DISEASE

Conservative and liberal neo-puritanism carries a big price. As sociologist Barry Glassner observed in *Culture of Fear*, "Americans are afraid of the wrong things" at the expense of concern about real problems.[56] A decade later, I would go a step further: made-up panics are *designed* to prevent discussion of impolitic realities.

The price of manufactured panics is that genuinely harmful crises go unaddressed. That 14 million American children and teenagers grow up in poverty, including six million in utter destitution; that social service investigations substantiate 200,000-plus cases of violent and sexual abuses inflicted on children and teens by their parents and caretakers every year; that massive tax and education budget cuts force millions of students into substandard schools and price them out of higher education, are real crises that win little sustained attention. Progressive groups in the teen pregnancy debate display little stomach for pushing strong social justice measures to reduce epidemic child poverty; their message seems to be that teen pregnancy will be solved simply by more sex education. "Pro-life" conservatives' fervor for the welfare of unborn children curiously dissipates once the children are born.

Today's unholy combination of panic and indifference recalls family historian John Demos's lament that Americans seem curiously "unable to care very much or very consistently about other people's children."[57] The few of us who have carefully analyzed the increasingly irrational fears hurled at America's young people in recent decades have documented that the climate of panic over youth extends far beyond apocalyptic reactionaries.

The teen-pregnancy furor on all sides makes less and less sense over time as it morphs into a commodity valued merely for its political and fundraising capital. It has become a cacophony of talking points refined by interest groups, and there is no official or institutional entity commanding attention for getting tough realities recognized. This is the face of what I call "privatized social policy."

Privatized social policy refers to the system in which social and health lobbies, agencies, programs, institutions, and their media outlets across the political spectrum are ceded "ownership" of the policy area they dominate. Competing interests, manipulating information to suit their proprietary needs, synthesize a set of common assumptions over time that are not based on their factuality or importance but their salability to funders, policymakers, and the public. Messages are refined through polling and focus groups into talking points repeated over and over like the commercial advertising slogans they resemble. New information, no matter how compelling, that threatens the messages in which the interest groups have invested is strenuously resisted.

Privatized social policy discussion begins with the designation of a powerless, feared outgroup to blame for social problems. Members of designated scapegoat groups are depicted not as individuals, but as a mass that thinks and acts in the same destructive ways. In past decades, these included racial, religious, and immigrant minorities such as the Chinese, Jews, or African Americans. As these groups gained power in the post-civil-rights era, scapegoating shifted to children and youth, who have proven perpetually easy to malign and sensationalize for the purpose of quick funding and popularity scorings.

The natural corollary in privatized social policy discourse is that powerful constituencies must be flattered. In this case, adults are praised as the morally offended victims and rescuers of teenagers from premature sexuality driven by salacious cultural images, peer pressure, and hormonal adolescent brainlessness. Discussion of remedies (see the National Campaign to Prevent Teen Pregnancy's parents' page,[58] for example) is limited to various combinations of chaste imprecation, remedial sex education, parents' "talking" to teens, and stern monitoring and discipline. That is, a set of soothing messages proven to "sell." The bottom line is that nothing disturbing to the mainstream constituencies that interest groups seek to flatter may intrude.

The most pleasing talking points refined by privatized interests, as in commercial advertising, involve creating new crises to solve, emotional appeals, self flattery, extravagant claims of success, and glossing over troubling complexities. For example, privatized social policy lobbies are loathe to point out that teenage sexuality is not a distinct, out-of-control epidemic, but uncannily parallels the sexual behavior patterns of adults around them. Lobbies seeking to preserve and promote their own popularity have quailed from emphasizing that America's economic system that rewards older age groups while relegating millions of children and teens to poverty promotes early childbearing as a rational life-course choice. Bummers like child abuse, family violence, underfunded schools, unaffordable colleges, and similar realities that might require grownups to reflect on our own morality and contemplate sacrifices are ruled unsuitable for discussion.

Because privatized policy discussion markets emotional images to shape the perception of social problems in ways that meet the needs of interest groups rather than the larger society, it produces monumental mistruths. Those dominating discussion in the United States have created, then problematized, a mythical issue called "teenage pregnancy" by relentlessly misrepresenting teenage behaviors as separate from adult values, adult sexual conduct, and the conditions to which adults subject youth.

The remainder of this book examines the consequences of allowing a cabal of profiteers, charlatans, and once-caring interests corrupted by today's coldly competitive politics to create a poisonous climate that maligns and menaces young people. Chapter 1 details three monumental fallacies these interests have concocted to misrepresent "teenage sex" and "teen pregnancy" as distinct "teenage" behaviors when, in fact, they fit squarely into adult-created conditions and norms. Chapter 2 chronicles the century-long "teen sex" debate in which arguments between liberal sex-education and conservative "traditional values" combatants, well established by 1915, have been recycled with only modest refinements to the present day. Chapter 3 closely examines widespread, grossly biased claims that teenage childbearing produces "social costs," which turn out to be small even in the worst cases and nonexistent by the best economic analyses. In fact, for certain poorer groups, the teen years represent the ideal time to have babies for a variety of reasons their privileged critics have ignored, as Chapter 4 discusses. Chapter 5 details the wholesale unhinging of the teen-pregnancy debate in the 1990s and 2000s in a political feeding frenzy that managed to discard every relevant factor in a tornado of mythmaking. Chapter 6 names names in the dissection of popular authors' and commentators' bizarrely ungrounded claims in today's Make-It-Up ethic surrounding teenagers and sexuality. The disturbing resurrection of racism and sexism implicit in today's teen pregnancy discourse is dissected in Chapters 7 and 8 in rarely examined pregnancy and sexually transmitted disease statistics by age, race, nationality, and income level (with the surprising conclusion that middle-aged, not teen-aged, behaviors are becoming the riskiest). Chapter 9 extends the examination of the culture-war distractions outlined above, including the fear-laden myths surrounding sex on television, popular culture, Internet predators, "sexting," "teen dating violence," "hooking up," and "Lolitas" and other fearsome legends. Chapter 10 details the research illuminating today's virulent battle over comprehensive sex education versus abstinence-only education that has sucked the air from every other important topic. Chapters 11 and 12 conclude with the warnings that President Obama's and other centrists' conciliatory emphasis on issues culture-war combatants "can agree on" is disastrous; rather, the critical need is for leadership that forces privatized social policy interests to confront the serious realities they have long suppressed and the dynamic new developments in America's emerging multiculture.

In short, this book reverses the lens. Officials, commentators, lobbies, and news media so far have escaped the same harsh scrutiny they have directed at their young targets. Here, they are going to get it.

Chapter One

THREE REASONS WHY "TEEN PREGNANCY" DOES NOT EXIST

Here is teen pregnancy, the short take. Teen birth, unwed birth, abortion, total pregnancy, and sexually transmitted disease (STD) rates closely parallel those of adults of their community, class, and era.[1] In fact, 6 in 10 men who impregnate teenagers are adults.[2] The younger the pregnant teen, the bigger the partner age gap and the more likely she was to have suffered family chaos, including sexual abuse and other violence.[3] In 2005, among females under age 20, 60 percent of all live births, 64 percent of abortions, 62 percent of fetal losses, and 61 percent of all pregnancies involved black, Hispanic, and other nonwhite minorities.[4] More than four in five involve impoverished and low-income teens.[5] Teenagers living in more affluent areas have very low pregnancy rates comparable to those in Western European countries.

Therefore, it should be impossible to discuss "teenage pregnancy" without raising the pivotal issues of adult sexual behaviors, adult fatherhood, family abuses, race, poverty, and lack of opportunity. Yet, *these are exactly the issues America's debate, by unanimous consent, takes off the table.* Modern American teen-pregnancy discussion rivals the War on Drugs for its evasion of every important reality—and with good reason. If its realities were admitted, teenage pregnancy would cease to be a profitable institutional commodity. The interests of the big players in the debate are best served by ferreting out perpetual excuses to rehash interest groups' emotion-laden talking points. Following is a very bad, very common example:

STATES REJECTING "ABSTINENCE-ONLY" FUNDING

CBS Evening News with Katie Couric, January 7, 2008:

> In the sexually charged world of teenagers, it can be tough to just say "no."
>
> "It's difficult to really be abstinent until marriage because it's a lot of different things pulling at you when you're a teenager," 16-year-old Kristen Brown explains.
>
> CBS News correspondent Sharyl Attkisson reports the forces pulling at America's teens include the tribulations of idols and icons from pop culture, like the recent news that Britney Spears's 16-year old sister is pregnant.
>
> All those influences have driven Congress and the Bush administration to push "abstinence-only" education. The government has provided states a billion dollars during the past decade for abstinence-only programs. But many say it just doesn't work, and they point to the teen birth rate's first rise in 15 years as proof.

I have seen hundreds of news and interest-group presentations like this, and I still wonder: Is this a joke? How could "the teen birth rate's first rise in 15 years"—that is, 14 years of massive decline followed by a tiny increase *only among older teen girls* and their mostly-20-age male partners[6] —constitute "proof" of anything? How did teenagers who got pregnant in 2005 and 2006 anticipate Britney's sister's 2007 pregnancy? Do America's experts, politicians, news reporters, editors, and other commentators seriously believe that black teens living in South Bronx, Hispanic adolescents in California's migrant camps, and other impoverished teens whose pregnancy and birth rates are *dozens of times higher* than more privileged youth rush to get pregnant because they hear Jamie Spears or Bristol Palin or "Juno" did?

Do reporters, editors, and the "experts" they quote *think* before they broadcast?

What we are seeing—and CBS's is just one moo amid the thousands of herd-journalism stories and commentaries on "teen pregnancy"—is a disturbing peek into the craziness to which privatized social policy leads. Trivial, popular, easy, and salacious themes drive out the vital, difficult, uncomfortable, and complex. I have participated in "teen pregnancy prevention" programs in which surveys and focus groups, not research and sound policy ideas, dictated what messages the programs presented. Getting programs funded in a highly competitive budget-cutting climate often revolves around finding out what the public and policymakers want the "problem" to be, what "causes" they find most comfortable to believe, and what "solutions" are easiest to sell.

As this book will document, CBS's glib frivolity delivered by a veteran anchor and senior correspondent, citing established interest groups, approved by national editors, and uncriticized by anyone I could find represent the consensus image of "teen pregnancy" that left-right lobbies want to serve as the foundation for their increasingly rarified debate. America's "teenage sex" and "teen pregnancy" furor bumbles along decade after decade, extending the century-old philosophical skirmish: sex education versus chastity lectures; old-fashioned family values versus MySpace hookup culture; permissively-raised, pop-media seduced kids versus chaste parents counseled by wise experts.

This is the twenty-first century. It is time we left the nineteenth century behind. "Teenage sex" and "teen pregnancy"* do not exist as distinct behaviors fitting their popular and official depictions. They are constructed crises, holdovers from America's regrettable tradition of stigmatizing nonwhite races, women, and other once-powerless demographics. Behind interest groups' poll-tested talking points, however, today's teen pregnancy framings often sink to ugly depths, fueled by degrading myths, recoded sexism and racism, and barely disguised vitriol of the type that would be branded hate speech if inflicted on any adult demographic. Public images of white, celebrity, and affluent young women and teenage males as the poster faces of "teen pregnancy" notwithstanding, the reality is that the large majority involve racial minorities, marginalized youth, and adult men—that is, realities revealing systemic failings rather than just a snotty-girl attitude problem.

TEEN SEX, PREGNANCY DO NOT EXIST?

Of course, some teenagers have sex, and a fraction of these teens get pregnant. So do Missourians, Rastafarians, and people whose last names start with C. Individuals born on Monday account for a shocking one in seven unwed pregnancies, abortions, and sexually transmitted diseases. We might as well single out any or all identifiable groups for stigma and intervention.

It is also true, *on average*, that babies born to mothers younger than 18 have worse outcomes than those born to mothers ages 18 to 34—but so do babies born to Louisianans, African, Native, and Hispanic Americans, low-income mothers of all ages and races, and Americans in general compared to parents in other Western countries. If it is age we are hung up on, then so do mothers and fathers age 40 and older, whose rapidly rising procreation is producing epidemics of exorbitantly costly maternal complications, babies born with chromosomal abnormalities (8 to 25 times higher than among mothers age 15 to 24), and long-term child deficits.[7] But when have you seen a national campaign to stigmatize and prevent middle-aged pregnancy?

Scientific rankings regarding which groups cause the most "social problems" by objective criteria would bring justifiable howls of racism, classism,

---

*I realize that installing quotes around "teenage sex" and "teen pregnancy" to denote their artificiality quickly becomes irritating. I'll dispense with the punctuation, though I contend that these terms are popular euphemisms rather than accurate descriptors.

regional bigotry, and ageism (against older parents). Economic analysis that apportions the gigantic taxpayer bailouts and public losses resulting from corporate malfeasance, costs of white collar crime, and the impact of over-consumption on environmental degradations such as climate change in the same way social-cost studies now apportion crime and welfare costs to teenage mothers would find the costliest babies on earth are those born to affluent, white American grownups.

When I contend teenage sex and teen pregnancy do not exist as distinct behaviors, I mean they are simply straight-line products of the sexual and reproductive behaviors of their societies in general and of the numbers of young people our private and public disbursement systems consign to poverty and deficient opportunity. European, Latin American, and Asian nations have seen sharply reduced rates of births by mothers younger than 20, more rapidly and to lower levels than occurred in the United States, due to their economies and social policies opening up more opportunities to young people and without our vitriolic attacks on teen behaviors.

To complete the adult-teen connection, approximately 450,000 of the 750,000 pregnancies among teenage females every year involve adult men age 20 and older. (As just one example of the primitive sexism of the terminology, no one calls the 100,000 or so annual pregnancies involving teenage males and women 20 and older "teen pregnancies.") More than 70 percent of births and at least 60 percent of total pregnancies among girls age 19 and younger involve male partners age 20 and older.[8] We might as well call it "adult pregnancy"—or, at least, "adult-teen pregnancy." Yet, no interest group publicizes statements such as, "The rate of American adult men impregnating teenagers is twice as high as is found among Canadian adult men and six times higher than among Japanese and German adult men. . . . " Rather, the presentation of teen pregnancy reflects both traditional sexism of blaming females for unwanted fertility and America's disturbing legacy of singling out society's *least* powerful groups—in this case, younger girls—to blame for social and moral problems.

How, then, did pregnancy among teenaged females, among all the potentially stigmatizable groups, wind up being singled out as a cataclysmic social problem, and why do we label an adult-teen phenomenon a "teenage" problem solely because of the age of the female? The answer, this chapter will argue, is not edifying: because we can. Since most adult populations have acquired the power to fight back against prejudice, young people represent one of the few scapegoats left for privatized social policy entrepreneurs safely to attack.

Is today's furor over "teen pregnancy" entirely contrived, then? In one sense, no. There are distinct adolescent reproductive health issues, just as there are for older ages. Adults could play a more positive role, but we choose not to. Fortunately, young people today have available a vast, largely unregulated Internet medium in which they can find information and communicate about sexual issues from a variety of standpoints. The rest of this chapter details the argument that "teen pregnancy" is not "teenage," but simply the predictable result of the adult-imposed conditions millions of teenagers face.

"TEEN PREGNANCY" IS STRICTLY AN ECONOMIC PHENOMENON

Marin County, California, has been regaled and ridiculed as the font of all things affluent, permissive, and New Age. Unburdened Cyra McFadden's 1977 satire, *The Serial*, on the vexations of parents in the redwooded paradise across the Golden Gate from San Francisco:

> What had got into Marin adolescents? Didn't they all feed them, listen to them, enroll them in the Mogul Ski Club? Straighten their teeth? Buy them stereos, wet suits and sailing lessons? Stay out of their sex lives and look the other way when they found their stashes?
>
> And look what came down. Debbie had straightened out, finally, but not until they'd bailed her out of a Mexican jail, dragged her away from the Haight twice, and spent one entire summer looking for her up and down the Mendocino coast before they finally found her living with some turkey in a yurt.
>
> Frank Gallagher had complained at Kate's dinner party the other night that their older son, a biofeedback freak, was now one big Alpha wave. And the Wilsons, Kate's other guests, were also having heavy problems: their Nancy, who was eighteen, hadn't been heard from since she dropped out of some fancy foreign exchange program because the Sorbonne "didn't have a crisis center."
>
> Sam thought it had something to do with the turmoil of the Sixties; hadn't somebody written a book about it? . . . He couldn't help being sort of curious about Harvey's new old lady, however. Wasn't she supposed to be fourteen or something and hooked on poppers?[9]

In the atrocious film version, heroic parents fled hedonistic Marin to the safety of Hammond, Indiana, where teenagers had no "human rights" and uptight moral values ruled. (And, the film fails to mention, where teens are much more likely to have babies than in Marin.)

Fulfilling one aspect of their image, Marin County teenagers do have lots of sex. Or say they do. California's 2007 Kidsdata.org Survey[10] ranked Marin 14 to 17 year olds as the second most sexually active in the state: 46 percent had engaged in sexual intercourse, compared to 20 percent statewide. (California's number-one teen-sex county? Need you ask? San Francisco, where 50 percent reported being nonvirgins.)

But do Marin's unusually sexy teens suffer epidemics of pregnancies and sexually transmitted disease (STD)? Not so much. At 12.6 per 1,000 females age 15 to 19 (all races, 2008), Marin's teen birth rate[11] is below the corresponding rates of Canada, the United Kingdom, and Norway and comparable to those of Germany.[12] The birth rate for Marin's 5,000 white teen girls ranks among the lowest in the world, less than half the rates of Denmark,

Switzerland, and Japan! While county abortion statistics are not available, U.S. white teenagers in general abort a lower proportion of pregnancies than teens in most other Western nations.

But Marin teens are even more impressive than their low birth rates indicate. Unlike European countries whose populations average over 95 percent white, nearly 40 percent of Marin's teens are nonwhite.[13] That is, Marin's low teen birth rates reflect a diverse youth population. And here the disparities begin.

Drive down the steep hill from Marin's lush suburban and leafy hillside neighborhoods, and you find county seat San Rafael's flatland east side, largely occupied by Hispanics. Here, teen birth rates average 20 times higher than for whites, similar to those in the Philippines or Costa Rica but still below the state average.

Motor another hour or so (traffic allowing) south along the 880 and the 580 east to the impoverished Central Valley, and a starker picture emerges.[14] In Stockton and San Joaquin County, Hispanic teens have birth rates 50 percent higher than Marin Hispanics, similar to rates found in rural Mexico. White San Joaquin teens have birth levels *nine times higher* than Marin whites.

Drive a couple of hours down I-5 to Bakersfield, and white teen births rise to 17 times higher than those of Marin whites, and Hispanic rates soar to levels well above Mexico's. But the highest rates by ethnicity are found in the adjacent county, Tulare, the state's most impoverished. Here, black teens' birth rates are nearly 50 times higher than for Marin whites and approach levels found in rural Guatemala. A similar disparity exists for whites. Where Marin's 5,000 white teen girls had just 11 babies in 2008, Tulare's similar number of white girls had nearly 200.

Copenhagen to Calcutta in a couple of hours . . . California's massive disparities are what we lump together as "teen pregnancy." Throughout history and all over the globe, poorer populations have had babies earlier in life.[15] As discussed in Chapters 3 and 4, that is because early childbearing makes sense for poorer people.

The Alan Guttmacher Institute (AGI)'s detailed 2001 study, *Teenage Sexual and Reproductive Behavior in Developed Countries*, found U.S. patterns also apply in Europe and Canada.[16] There are inevitable problems with the way AGI compares low-income and low-education status among the various countries. For example, young people's poverty at similar economic levels is much more concentrated and severe in the United States than in Europe. There are so many government-provided income, housing, health, education, vocational training, and related advantages conferred upon European youth, including poorer ones, compared to youth in the United States that even these discrepancies understate the effects of economic disadvantage. Still, the report finds strong associations between low socioeconomic status and high

Table 1.1   Around the World, Teen Birth Rates Track Poverty Rates

	Birth rate*	Poverty rate**
Marin County, CA (white)	2.2	4.2%
Marin County, CA (Asian)	3.8	13.7%
Marin County, CA (all races)	12.6	7.5%
San Joaquin County, CA (white)	20.2	10.2%
Marin County, CA (black)	27.8	30.0%
California (all races)	35.6	18.3%
Kern County, CA (white)	37.3	15.2%
Marin County, CA (Hispanic)	43.3	17.6%
Tulare County, CA (Hispanic)	77.2	40.9%
Kern County, CA (Hispanic)	90.3	37.3%
Tulare County, CA (black)	102.3	39.8%
International comparisons		
The Netherlands	3.8	6.5%
Japan	5.1	na
Sweden	5.8	4.3%
Denmark	5.9	2.7%
Germany	10.1	9.0%
Canada	13.3	15.6%
United Kingdom	26.7	19.1%
United States (all races)	41.2	22.2%
Mexico	68.5	27.7%
Guatemala	107.5	na

*All births to mothers younger than age 20 divided by female population age 15 to 19 for 2008 (California) or the most recent year.
**International poverty rates are the percentage of children living in families with incomes below half the nation's median income. They are not comparable to US poverty rates, which are still calculated from a 1950s formula that understates true poverty rates.
Source: California Center for Health Statistics (2010); World Health Organization (2009).

adolescent childbearing and pregnancy levels "in all five countries" studied:

- In Canada, an analysis . . . showed a strong association between low income and high adolescent birthrates and high STD rates.
- The association between socioeconomic deprivation and teenage pregnancy and childbearing is well established in Great Britain. . . . The risk of becoming a teenage mother is almost 10 times higher among women whose family is in the lowest social class than among those whose family is in the highest class.
- Researchers in France also have found that the teenage birthrate is highest in départements (administrative areas) in the north, where poverty and unemployment are highest. . . . Many adolescents who have a baby are reacting to problems in their family, including poverty and abuse.
- One study in Sweden concluded that pregnant teenagers are much more likely than teenagers who are not pregnant to be from broken homes and to be of low socioeconomic status.[17]

Indeed, young women with the lowest education levels were approximately 10 times more likely to have a baby as a teenager than those at the highest levels in all five countries studied.

Table 1.2 provides the most recent U.S. teen pregnancy rates (for 2005, at this writing). These data show that after decades of raging controversy, pregnancy rates among teens remain almost straight-line functions of pregnancy rates among adults of the same races. For populations with high poverty levels, such as African Americans and Hispanics, pregnancy and outcome rates among teens not only are much higher but are closer to those of adults than for races with low poverty rates, chiefly whites and Asians. Further, the legend that affluent teen girls cover up their pregnancies by getting abortions is not true; a lower proportion of white teen pregnancies end in abortions than for nonwhites.

A similarly parallel adult-teen pattern is evident when birth, abortion, and miscarriage rates for teens and adults by race and state are compiled. As predicted, the groups with the highest poverty rates have the highest pregnancy rates, though this relationship is not 100 percent consistent. Even at slightly lower poverty levels, Hispanics have slightly higher pregnancy rates, and considerably higher birth rates, than do blacks.

Table 1.2   U.S. Teen and Adult Pregnancies Per 1,000 Females by Race, Outcome, 2005

Outcome, 2005	Female age	All races	Hispanic	Black	Asian/ other	White
All pregnancies	Age 15–19	72.2	131.4	128.3	52.9	44.6
	Age 20–44	108.6	147.6	140.7	115.5	91.7
Live births	Age 15–19	41.2	83.0	62.6	26.6	26.1
	Age 20–44	71.0	100.4	67.5	74.4	64.4
Abortions	Age 15–19	19.8	25.2	48.2	19.0	11.4
	Age 20–44	19.5	27.8	52.6	21.7	10.3
Miscarriages	Age 15–19	11.3	23.3	17.5	6.7	7.1
	Age 20–44	18.1	19.4	20.7	19.7	17.0
Poverty rate	Age 15–19	18.8%	27.1%	31.2%	19.7%	13.7%
	Age 20–44	14.5%	23.4%	25.2%	14.0%	10.3%

Note: Rates for age 15 to 19 consist of pregnancy outcome involving females under age 20 divided by the female population age 15 to 19; for age 20 to 44, and all pregnancy outcomes among females age 20 and older divided by the female population age 20 to 44. "White" and "Black" are non-Hispanic. "Asian/ other" is mostly Asian American but includes some Native American, mixed, and other races.

Sources: National Center for Health Statistics (2009); Bureau of the Census (2009).

Little of this seems to matter to today's teen pregnancy players. For many years, U.S. interests used subterfuges to dodge the impolitic realities of the huge disparities in teen birth rates by race and economic class. Until recently, lobbies declared that most pregnant teenagers were white (which is true only if Hispanics were included with Caucasians as "white"). Later, interest groups spread the unfounded rumor that richer kids got pregnant just as much but disposed of their pregnancies via abortions, even though abortion tabulations showed vastly higher rates among blacks and, to a lesser extent, Hispanics, than among whites. In Washington, D.C., for example, birth, abortion, and miscarriage rates among black teens (who are among the nation's poorest populations) are around 25 times higher than among white teens (who are among the nation's richest).[18] In this case, a *10-minute drive* is like traveling, teen pregnancy wise, from Milan to Mogadishu.

A better case for discriminatory reporting can be made for sexually transmitted diseases, or STDs. (The more recent term is sexually transmitted infection, or STI; this book uses STD.) STD data are heavily tilted toward public clinics and health providers that disproportionately serve younger and poorer populations. Thus, official statistics understate STD rates among older, higher income, and white populations. Numbers from the Centers for Disease Control's latest *STD Surveillance* (for 2008, as of this writing)[19] and HIV/AIDS Surveillance (2004 through 2007)[20] are shown in Tables 1.3 and 1.4. They show:

- Chlamydia rates among African Americans are 12 times higher for those age 10 to 14, and eight times higher for those age 15 to 19, than among white teens.
- Hispanic teen chlamydia rates are three times higher, and Native rates three to five times higher, than for whites.
- Gonorrhea levels are *20 to 24 times higher* among black than among white teens.
- HIV and AIDS rates diagnosed from age 13 to 25 (indicating infection in teen or early-20s years) are a dozen times higher among blacks than whites, including levels that are 15 times higher among young black than among young white women.
- African Americans, just 12 percent of the youth population, account for half of all chlamydia, 6 in 10 HIV/AIDS, two-thirds of syphilis, and three-fourths of teen gonorrhea diagnoses.

The key issue, once again, is economic disparity. Affluent youth are much less likely to suffer STDs just as they are much less likely to get pregnant. Marin County provides a clear example. In 2007, the California Department of Health's survey reported STD rates among teens age 10 to 19 (indexed by combining the most common serious infections, chlamydia and gonorrhea) in affluent Marin were three per 1,000, or just one-third the state average.[21] Rates among Marin's under-15s were too low to estimate. In California's impoverished Central Valley, however, rates of gonorrhea and chlamydia among teens were four to six times higher than in Marin.

Table 1.3 Teenage Sexually Transmitted Disease Infections per 100,000 Population by Age, 2008

	Chlamydia		Gonorrhea		Syphilis	
	10–14	15–19	10–14	15–19	10–14	15–19
Both sexes						
Asian	11.1	493.0	3.0	58.2	0.0	0.8
White	22.6	849.3	3.7	107.0	0.0	0.9
Hispanic	61.4	2,809.3	7.9	204.2	0.1	3.4
Native	108.3	2,547.7	16.2	294.1	0.0	0.9
Black	279.2	6,651.0	90.6	2,237.2	0.7	19.1
All races	70.6	1,956.4	18.1	453.1	0.1	4.2
Female						
Asian	20.6	885.7	5.1	90.7	0.0	1.1
White	44.0	1,534.5	7.0	181.3	0.1	1.1
Hispanic	113.3	3,186.2	13.8	288.4	0.1	1.6
Native	205.2	4,792.6	27.2	456.5	0.0	1.9
Black	501.0	10,513.4	151.4	2,934.6	1.0	24.0
All races	129.9	3,275.8	31.0	636.8	0.2	5.3
Male						
Asian	2.0	124.2	0.9	27.7	0.0	0.5
White	2.3	199.3	0.6	36.6	0.0	0.8
Hispanic	11.9	637.5	2.2	124.9	0.0	5.1
Native	14.1	870.6	5.6	135.5	0.0	0.0
Black	64.3	2,889.5	31.8	1,488.6	0.4	14.1
All races	13.9	701.6	5.8	278.3	0.1	3.0

Source: CDC, STD Surveillance (2009).

Table 1.3 reveals another crucial pattern in what we call teenage sexuality: female STD rates are vastly higher than those of males. Gonorrhea rates, for example, are five times higher among girls age 10 to 14 and more than twice as high among young women age 15 to 19 than among corresponding boys and men. HIV/AIDS levels are higher among males, but only because most cases still involve male homosexual transmission. For cases involving heterosexual contact, female rates are double those of men.

The higher ratio of female-to-male STD cases diminishes with age. Higher rates are found in over-30 men than women for gonorrhea and, despite the lack of male screening, for chlamydia, in those 45 and older. Thus, greater female anatomical vulnerability to STD is not the main reason rates are vastly higher among young women ages 15 to 19 and, especially, ages 10 to 14, than among males their age.

Table 1.4   Teen and Young Adult HIV/AIDS Rates and Cases, 2004–2007

Race	Ages 13–19			Ages 20–24		
	Total	Male	Female	Total	Male	Female
HIV/AIDS cases (annual rate per 100,000 population)						
Asian	0.6	0.9	0.2	4.6	7.6	1.6
Native	0.8	1.0	0.7	7.2	10.3	4.1
White	1.1	1.3	0.9	8.4	12.9	3.7
Hispanic	4.3	5.3	3.2	27.8	40.2	13.7
Black	21.2	27.8	14.4	101.6	142.6	60.3
All races	4.8	6.0	3.4	25.3	36.4	13.8
HIV/AIDS cases (total numbers, 2004–2007)						
Asian	26	21	5	133	110	23
Native	22	13	9	94	67	27
White	774	468	306	3,436	2,699	737
Hispanic	885	567	318	3,233	2,486	747
Black	3,946	2,619	1,327	10,020	7,058	2,962
All races	5,653	3,688	1,965	16,916	12,420	4,496

Source: CDC, HIV/AIDS Surveillance (2009).

Interestingly, even under surveillance systems biased toward detecting STDs among young ages, white teenaged boys are among the safest from STDs of any group in society, with age 15 to 19 rates of chlamydia just one-half, gonorrhea one-third, and syphilis one-fifth the national average. However, white teen girls have considerably higher rates than average, and minority disparities are even more extreme. Among African Americans, chlamydia and gonorrhea rates are highest among females age 15 to 19, who suffer levels *five to 12 times* higher than among white female teens. Among black males age 20 to 24, levels are *eight to 30 times* higher than for white males that age.

Similarly, HIV/AIDS rates among blacks peak at age 20 to 24 at levels some 10 times higher among white males, and among black females age 20 to 24 at levels 15 times higher than among white females of the same age. Given the incubation period for HIV, diagnosis at age 20 to 24 would indicate many infections were contracted during teen years. These staggering disparities in STD and AIDS rates when gender, age, and race are compared beg for much tougher analysis than the Centers for Disease Control's simplistic slogan that "many young persons in the United States engage in sexual risk behavior and experience negative reproductive health outcomes."[22] This is like saying, "drivers run into things and experience wrecks." Indeed, the most striking feature is the huge escalation in rates as poverty levels rise. The common factor associated with high STD rates is not young age, but the fact that in aggregate and for each race individually, teens and young adults suffer poverty rates two to three times higher than middle-aged adults. STD rates are higher among black men in their 40s and 50s than among white boys age 15 to 19, and among black women in their 30s than among white girls ages 15 to 19.

There is another compelling, largely unmentioned factor in high STD rates among young females, and high HIV rates among young males, which buttresses the argument that "teenage sex" is not a "teenage" phenomenon: adults have sex with teens.

MOST "TEENAGE PREGNANCY" IS CAUSED BY ADULTS

This rather large complication has proven such a bummer for teen-pregnancy interests that, with few and fleeting exceptions, they have never been able to deal with it. One clear message I have learned from working on this issue for 20 years is that the interests involved, regardless of other differences, *only* want to talk about high-school and middle-school teens. Nineteen-year-olds and even 20 to 24 year-olds may be dragged in to boost "teen" numbers and make problems appear scarier, but lobbies really want the issue confined to adolescents.

Under the dictates of today's privatized social policy, interests controlling teen-pregnancy discussion *need* the issue limited to school-age kids who can be singled out for condescension and cure-alls too risky to aim at adults. As with "teenage sex," "teenage prostitution," "teen pregnancy," and "teenage motherhood," commentators blame what are really predominantly adult-teen events on their youngest female participants, even those who are obvious victims.

True, you can find the reality that 60 percent of "teen" pregnancies involve men age 20 and older—and that 70 percent of pregnancies among girls age 17 and younger involve adult males, not juvenile boys—acknowledged on the National Campaign to Prevent Teen and Unplanned Pregnancy's Web site . . . if you look really, really hard.[23] It is also quite likely that adult-teen sex is responsible for most, if not all, the large surplus of STD cases among teenage females compared to younger males. This is even more likely given that at least some young-male STD and HIV/AIDS cases result from male-male sex.

But the CDC and health authorities seem particularly squeamish about raising adult-teen sex. In the official fantasy, these are "teen" events that result from "adolescent risk taking." The blinding obsession with "teen age" that defines fixation on the pregnant female (19 years, 1,439 minutes old? Epidemic social problem! 20 years, 1 minute old? No problem!) somehow dissipates when the matter of the impregnating male arises. Just another reason to view the discussion as mired in nineteenth-century thinking.

Beyond the sexist hypocrisy of fixating on the teen age of the mother while dismissing the post-teen age of most of the fathers, the generally older age of the men involved in "teen pregnancy" has important implications for those seeking to understand its motivations (see Chapter 4). The older age of the male is a major incentive for early pregnancy for obvious reasons. Adult men usually possess more resources, rights, and independence than teens do (as well as mobility, which can prove a blessing or a curse). Girls from troubled, violent families, in particular, can and do escape via liaisons with adults.[24] There are both attractive features and added problems in older partners, as a number of studies have found.[25] Nor is this simply a female issue; about 25 percent of married teen males have wives older than 20, and a similar proportion of babies fathered by teen boys are by post-teen mothers. Indeed, in many ways, high school girls and boys are not sexual peers when it comes to outcomes such as fetuses or diseases. What a revolutionary concept for sex and abstinence education that would be.

One particularly ugly form of adult-teen contact consists of rape and sexual abuse. In our barbaric terminology, a 12-year-old girl raped and impregnated by her 40-year-old father (a scenario similar to the movie *Precious*) is perpetrating "teen pregnancy." Judith Musick surveyed 445 pregnant or parenting teens in her Ounce of Prevention program in Chicago and found that 61 percent of the sample reported having been sexually abused, and 65 percent of these victims reported abuse by more than one perpetrator. For many of the victims, the abuse was an ongoing situation: although one-quarter of the victims stated that the abuser had committed the act only once, 50 percent reported having been abused between two and ten times, and the remaining 25 percent reported being abused more than 10 times. The average age of first occurrence was 11.5 years, and only 18 percent of the abusers were two or fewer years older than the victims; another 18 percent were three to five years older, and 17 percent were 6 to 10 years older. The remaining 46 percent were more than 10 years older than their victims. Very large age differences were especially common among victims abused before the age of 14 years.[26]

Likewise, a 1992 study of hundreds of pregnant or parenting teens for Washington state's Alliance Concerned with School-Age Parents found more than 6 in 10 had histories of sexual abuse and rape, overwhelmingly by much-older assailants.[27] Similar findings were reported by other programs. An Alan Guttmacher Institute survey found 43 percent of girls who had sex before age 15 reported that their only experience consisted of being raped, and another 17 percent said that they had been raped and had voluntary sex. That is, just four in 10 of all "sexually active" girls age 14 and younger had voluntary sex only, and the perpetrators tended to be considerably older men, Guttmacher found.[28]

While childhood histories of sexual abuse and rape are realities for many if not most teen mothers, this is too rough a stuff for the National Campaign,

CDC, and other privatized interests to engage. Even voluntary adult-teen sexual liaisons seem to engender deep discomfort. Despite decades of U.S. marriage records showing that 80 to 90 percent of the grooms in marriages to teenage brides were 20 and older (including one-fourth who were 25 and older) ... despite decades of birth records, including near-complete tabulations from states like California and Maryland, showing two-thirds or more of the fathers of babies born to teenage mothers were 20 and older[29] ... despite large surpluses in STDs among teenage girls compared to teenage boys ... the official depiction of "teenage sex" and "teen pregnancy" is that it involves *only* teen boys with teen girls.

The CDC, the nation's top health agency, still refuses to admit the existence of child sexual abuse and of voluntary adult-teen sexual contact as contributors to the sexual health issues it labels as "adolescent." The CDC's latest press release as of this writing discussed teen-girl STD rates as higher than teen boys' rates only because "biological differences place females at greater risk for STDs than males."[30] That most of girls' (and some of boys') STD and HIV infections very likely result from sex with adults is an issue the CDC continues to bury under its useless doctrine of "youth behavior risk." This cliché indulges the privatized-policy pretense that the sexual behaviors of disfavored groups such as youths can be neatly walled off from behaviors among favored groups (adults, in this case). In that light, the CDC's press release also failed to acknowledge that high STD rates among young people result from policies to screen persons under 25,[31] resulting in severe under-diagnosis among older adults. A decade of skyrocketing rates of new HIV infections among adults age 35 and older should have led to expanded screenings—if health agencies can overcome their antiquated prejudices.

The primitive climate of denial fostered by privatized consensus that has resisted two decades of new information represents a severe impediment to understanding sexual health issues and particularly endangers young people. In 1992, I published an article in the *Journal of Sex Research*,[32] followed with updates in *Phi Delta Kappan*,[33] pointing to statistics indicating a large majority of the male partners of teen girls who gave birth were 20 and older. Shocking it was. A number of journals completely rejected the concept, as did many researchers and organizations involved in teen pregnancy prevention. There were speculations that girls must be overstating the fathers' ages and that huge numbers of "hidden" fathers must be teens. Questioning statistics is legitimate, but it should apply equally toward those depicting "teen pregnancy" as a teen-teen event.

To make a traumatic story short, Planned Parenthood researchers confirmed from multiple data sources in a 1995 *Family Planning Perspectives* paper that around two-thirds of the fathers in births by mothers younger than 20 (including half the fathers in births by mothers under age 18) were

20 and older.[34] This detail was thus confirmed a mere 80 years after teen sexuality first became a raging public controversy. Predictably, the next reaction was to insist this new fact was unimportant and perhaps dangerous to raise. Some minority men I worked with complained that raising the adult-father issue fed prejudices against black and Hispanic men as sexually rapacious. (Curiously, they had not expressed sensitivity about similarly prejudicial depictions of black and Latina teenaged girls and boys.) Critics of raising issue of adult-teen sex also worried that the statutory rape prosecutions would be exploited to put more dark-skinned men in jail.

In this last concern, the critics had a point. Some welfare reformers, led by former California governor Pete Wilson and a number of district attorneys, briefly talked of stepped-up prosecutions for statutory rape aimed at men fathering babies with teen girls, with the contradictory ideas of imprisoning them and collecting more child support from them.[35] These campaigns never went anywhere. For both practical and cultural reasons, holding adult men criminally responsible for "teen pregnancy" has proven a failure.[36] In California, even during the mid-1990s peak, only a few hundred prosecutions per year occurred amid the thousands of babies fathered by men 20 and older with girls 17 and younger (and the millions of instances of statutorily forbidden non-baby-making sexual contact).[37] Prosecutors I spoke with complained that the younger girls often flummoxed judges and juries by coming across as more mature than the older men being charged with taking advantage of them. In one controversial case, social service agencies and courts approved the marriage of an Orange County, California, 13-year-old mother to the 20-year-old father described as caring and gainfully employed, in the best interests of their baby. As in nearly all highly publicized teen-sex cases, the outraged kibitzers had never met the couple.[38] The notion that girls and their male partners might be individuals capable of maturity and responsibility is rarely considered.

However, the biggest stumbling blocks to moving teen-sex discourse into the modern era are the interest groups and news media, which remained hard-wired to beat up on school-age girls and preferred to focus on the male partners only when they also were teens. Worried efforts to shift attention back to teenagers ensued whenever American social-issue discussion threatened to include entities with higher social status—in this case, adult men. All that was needed to bury the "adult male" inconvenience was a scientific-sounding excuse. That came in the form of a 1997 Urban Institute "study"[39] that ranks among the most egregiously sexist, methodologically atrocious, and mathematically perverted I have ever encountered.

Urban Institute researchers first deplored *all* teenaged mothers under age 20, including 18- and 19-year-olds, married and unmarried, as unacceptably precocious. However, they continued, the adult fathers of babies born to these same under-20 women constituted a problem *only* when they (a) impregnated girls under age 18, who (b) they were not married to, who (c) were not more than five years younger than the fathers, and who (d) did not "abandon" the mothers. Bingo! The "older male" problem suddenly becomes "very small," the study proclaimed.

The study not only constituted statistical fraud, its misogyny was breathtaking. The Urban Institute authors at the study's outset declared that "regardless of the mother's age," men impregnating girls fewer than five years their junior (that is, a 20 year-old knocking up a ninth grader) "fits squarely within societal norms." The pregnant ninth grader is a problem, but the impregnating 20-year-old is socially acceptable. They then scolded all teenaged girls and women as old as 19 who *got pregnant* (in fact, all under-20 females who ever had sex) for choosing "to prematurely engage in childbearing and other adult behaviors." How could *Family Planning Perspectives* publish this atrocity that would have been backwards in 1897? It should have drawn outrage from feminists and teen-pregnancy lobbies who had declared their rhetorical support for "male responsibility" (which turned out, in the few cases where it was invoked at all, to mean responsibility by adolescent boys). I have often wondered where feminists (with a few notable exceptions, such as the University of Hawaii's Meda Chesney-Lind[40] and the University of Southern California's Karen Sternheimer[41]) disappear to when teenaged girls are being vilified in the crudest of sexist terms.

With the rare exception of sexuality education consultant Peggy Brick,[42] Planned Parenthood of Greater Northern New Jersey, and a few others that incorporated the adult-male issue into teen-pregnancy programming, the industry, media, and politicians comfortably re-wallowed in the ancient mire that "teenage sex" and "teen pregnancy" just meant horny kiddies with too much free time and TV watching. The national debate has returned to lecturing teenage girls and boys to avoid sex or to use contraception when having sex. In 2010, that is all that we have.

TEENAGE SEX IS JUST LIKE ADULT SEX

Even more than the economic and adult-teen aspects of teen sex and pregnancy, the uncanny parallels between teen and adult sexual outcomes are the most ignored factor of all. In fact, teenage sex is a closely controlled behavior, reflecting the sexual behaviors of adults around them. *Where and when adults have high rates of pregnancy, abortion, birth, unwed birth, STD, and HIV/AIDS, so do teenagers.* The chief complication is that high rates of poverty shift a population's sexual outcomes to younger ages, but the parallel with adult outcomes remains uncanny. There is also an interesting partial exception— the large, post-1990 decline in pregnancy among teens and young adults— that has been poorly analyzed, a research deficiency Chapter 5 dissects.

The pivotal adult roles, both in terms of the older age of most sexual partners in teenage pregnancy and the parallel nature of teen and adult sexual outcomes, reflect a crucial reality: under similar conditions, adults and teenagers behave in remarkably *similar* ways. As one sage put it on the University of California, Santa Cruz, radio station's "Sounds of Young America" program: "The world works exactly like your eighth grade prom."

Teenagers are not defiant rebels against, but conformists to, adult morality and sensibility. Sociologist Kristen Luker points out, "like teenagers, adult Americans get pregnant more often when they do not intend to, pass on more sexually transmitted diseases, and have higher abortion rates than almost any other adults in the industrialized world."[43] I fault young people for not having better judgment than to emulate us, but not enough to actually improve my own behaviors.

The close relationship between adult and teen sexual outcomes can be tested mathematically by a technique known as multiple regression. Regression analysis begins with an outcome (in this case, rates of teen pregnancy by race and state) and proceeds to show which of a number of potential causes are the most important in predicting the outcome. Reasonably complete and consistent statistics on births (both marital and unwed), abortions, and miscarriages, which add up to total pregnancies, were available by age of female and race/ethnicity (white, black, Hispanic) for 47 states and the District of Columbia.[44,45] Other relevant variables such as poverty rates, unemployment rates, percentage of population that is foreign born, state median personal incomes, school enrollment rates, school spending levels, percentage of children living in two-parent families, and marital status rates[46] were added to the regression analysis to pin down what characteristics go with high or low rates of teenage pregnancy.

The question this regression analysis sought to answer is: Are teenage pregnancy rates (including rates of birth, unwed birth, abortion, miscarriage, and total pregnancy) still associated with the factor of teen age once other factors (such as corresponding adults' rates of birth, unwed birth, abortion, miscarriage, and total pregnancies, and poverty, income, and other social characteristics) are included? Such questions have crucial policy implications. If teenage sexual behaviors simply reflect those of adults and fit into the continuum of larger American standards, then we should address teen and adult problems as *integrated*, not as separate, issues.

The results of the regression analysis were compelling. Normally, a set of variables that explains as much as one-fourth of the behavior in question are trumpeted as key finds; factors that account for as much as half are treated as a breakthrough. In this case, the variables accounted for an astounding 81 percent of the differences in teen pregnancy rates by race and state. Just two factors—the adult pregnancy rate and the youth poverty rate by race and state—were associated with 82 percent of variation in teen pregnancy rates. These two varia-bles accounted for 78 percent of the variation in birth rates and 90 percent of the variation in abortion rates. Adult sexual outcomes were the strongest predictor by far of teenage outcomes; poverty levels simply adjusted the prediction a bit.

When regression variables this strong are found, it is safe to say that teen-age and adult sexual behaviors under similar economic and social conditions *are one and the same.* We are not looking at two separate sexualities, the adult version of which can be accepted and encouraged while the teenage version is deplored and prevented. We are looking at the *same behaviors,* just as if we were comparing, say, sexual outcomes for Americans born in July with those born in August.

American society accepts nonmarital sex and, grudgingly, nonmarital preg-nancy for adults. The logical result is that nonmarital sex and pregnancy then become acceptable for teenagers and teenagers with adult partners. Selective moral imprecations affirming our adult right to sexual indulgence (despite clear consequences evident in statistics on unwanted outcomes) while con-demning similar behaviors for anyone under age 20 (or 21 or 25 or 18, or whatever age) do not work and should not work, as we will see.

Getting things this wrong about teen sex and pregnancy did not happen overnight. Many years of consistent warping of the facts, trends, and realities faced by young people went in to producing today's dung heap of unreality. The next chapters discuss how earnest, early 1900s movements concerned with the sexual health of young people devolved into cynical, early 2000s enterprises concerned with grownups who are interested in getting more money, good press, and elected.

Chapter Two

1915 ALL OVER AGAIN

At least seven U.S. presidents had sex with teenagers. James Monroe, Martin Van Buren, Andrew Johnson, Teddy Roosevelt, and Jimmy Carter impregnated their adolescent wives. Thomas Jefferson and John Kennedy had mid-life extra-marital affairs with teens aged 14 and 15, respectively. Those are just the ones we know about. Five U.S. First Ladies, from Elizabeth Monroe to Rosalynn Carter, were pregnant teenagers. The mother of the current president, Barack Obama, was an unwed, pregnant 17 year-old.[1] Quite the venerable history for what is now deplored as an "epidemic crisis" that offends America's fundamental morals, spits on our family values tradition, and creates massive "social costs."

Look in standard indexes such as *Reader's Guide to Periodical Literature*, and you find little mention of "teen pregnancy" prior to the 1970s.[2] While past generations accepted teenaged wives and mothers even as young as 16 or 17 (as long as their men were considerably older), they did not accept teenaged girls having any kind of sex *with teenaged boys*. Teenaged girls were (and, I will argue, still are) considered the territory of adult men, even men many years their senior.

Past generations did develop a few limits. A coalition of American educators, social workers, and other liberals known as the "child savers" discovered in the late 1800s that young females were not so benignly protected by family and society as assumed. They won several reforms, including "age of consent" laws at which young girls could consent to sexual contact with men.

These early laws specified that a girl consenting to sex had to be at least 10 to 12 years old in most states, with a few specifying ages as old as 14 or 16. In Delaware, the age of consent was seven, based on ancient English laws setting the age of a squire.

Why were these reforms seen as necessary in a pastoral America now mythologized as chaste, family valuing, and child cocooning? Feminist Anna Garlin Spencer, in a 1913 article, was one of many pointing to the massive numbers of teenage prostitutes in the 1800s and early 1900s. In New York City, one survey found, there was one prostitute for every 19 men in the city's population, four in 10 prostitutes were age 16 or younger, and one-fourth died from disease or violence every year.[3] Another study found that one in 200 women in Chicago in the early 1900s was a professional prostitute. Opponents of consent laws, such as the editors of *Medical Age*, berated the power of "the licentious, designing *demi mondaine*, many of whom are under the age of eighteen" to seduce innocent males and then have them charged with criminal offenses.[4] Even today, efforts to hold adult men responsible for having sex with and impregnating teenaged girls incurs reactions ranging from outrage to distinct unease.

Psychologist G. Stanley Hall, author of the 1904 classic *Adolescence*, and a host of young rebels such as Max Eastman and Margaret Sanger championed a franker approach to sex out of fear both of adolescent sexuality and as part of a larger movement toward women's equality and independence from mandatory motherhood.[5] Behind liberal health and equality agendas lay the darker shadow of eugenics and its pseudo-scientific veneer. Not only was presumed sexual degeneration among white teenaged girls seen as dragging the entire race down to the animality of savage darker cultures, reformers worried, high rates of childbearing among poorer classes threatened to swamp polite society with "low grade stock." President Theodore Roosevelt warned that low fertility among whites would lead to "race suicide."[6] Hall's theories merged fears of youthful and inferior-race lustiness into his concept of "adolescent races," a vague notion that justified imposing controls on the sexuality both of white teenaged girls and non-Western-European populations.[7]

Prior to the advent of social hygiene movements of the early 1900s, married teenaged girls were assumed to be the property of older husbands and unmarried ones asexual, while boys were presumed either sexually innocent or uncontrollable. The presumption of teenage innocence persisted despite the first national vital statistics reports beginning around 1915 that showed 200,000 babies born to mothers younger than age 20 every year (90% fathered by men older than 20, and one-third by men 25 and older), including 1,000 by mothers 14 and younger.[8] (My 25-year-old grandfather's marriage to my 16 year-old grandmother in 1912, beginning a 70-year marriage, would be considered predatory today but then was routine.) Studies found thousands of young prostitutes in urban areas and diagnoses of hundreds of thousands of STDs among teens every year. The curiously contradictory American view of teens as both innocently pure and savagely libidinal, the latter unleashed once teachers or cultural images reveal the existence of sex, underlies the argument to this day that sex education and media images usher youths into dangerous precocities.

The insistence of early social hygiene and later sexuality education advocates that it was really ignorance that promoted disease and unwanted pregnancy directly challenged prevailing views. One issue politely ignored by all sides to this day is that teenage sex is not an insular, age-bounded phenomenon; adult men of all ages (and a smaller number of adult women) engage in sex with teens via voluntary, coerced, forced, and purchased means. The myth that teens are protected by a benign larger culture and best kept naïve to shield them from their own base urges remains the real danger.

SEX-EDUCATION WARS

It is not surprising that the first efforts at formal sex education classes in schools emerged in Chicago, then a center of social reform.[9] Chicago's school superintendent at the time, Ella Flagg Young, proposed a three-lecture series to gender-segregated high school classes and less explicit talks to middle school and elementary school students by local physicians covering basic physiology, hygiene, and venereal disease (VD) prevention. Though questionnaires found students survived the lectures untraumatized, conservative Chicagoans and religious leaders succeeded in dumping the school "smut" program by 1915.

While sex educators warned of rising pregnancy and crippling venereal diseases abetted by the "conspiracy of silence" regarding health information, traditionalists led by Anthony Comstock, who successfully pushed anti-obscenity laws, demanded that adolescents be kept sexually "innocent" and crusaded against sex education for planting prurient ideas into pristine teen-age minds. Though proposing sharply differing solutions, social hygienists and morality crusaders were in surprising agreement on the nature of the crisis.[10] Like puritans, sex educators denied any romantic or healthy aspect to adolescent sexuality. Rather, they saw their roles as deploying a cocktail of hygiene information, scare tactics about VD and pregnancy, and morals imprecations to suppress sex *between teenagers* in all forms. Advocates and opponents lapsed into a common language that blamed prostitution and VD crises on the lurid commercializations and societal temptations of the 1910s and 1920s corrupting innocent, reckless youth. They just as carefully avoided asking why so many thousands of prostitutes earned gainful livings in a sup-posedly chaste, married society, or why most female VD cases were being diagnosed among married women. In any case, the rise of sex education ignited a century-long, perhaps eternal, war. The talking points of the two sides were set in stone from the beginning. All the next eight decades would bring was toning up the message.

THE FIFTIES: THE "TEEN PREGNANCY" DECADE

Teenage pregnancy and motherhood peaked in the 1950s amid the postwar Baby Boom, when nearly 1 in 10 girls age 15 to 19 gave birth every year and nearly *half* of all new brides in the country were under age 20. That four-fifths of these were "legitimized" by often-short-lived marriages did not cover up the high rates of high schoolers' sex. Notions that the past was more moral— what one sociologist historian called "the myth of an abstinent past"—were belied by cold statistics of the time, which were much less complete than those tabulated by today's more sophisticated surveillance systems. Sociologist Phillips Cutright's 1972 study in *Family Planning Perspectives* found the mysterious disappearance of staggering numbers of pregnancies originally reported by physicians in the 1940s and 1950s, suggesting high abortion and other fetal loss rates.[11]

Did abortion's illegality prior to the Supreme Court's 1973 *Roe v Wade* decision mean fewer abortions occurred? Not by the best analyses. An unusually graphic three-part article on "one of our most shocking social evils" appeared in the *Saturday Evening Post* in May and June of 1961, revealing that "every day, thousands of American women risk their lives to be rid of unwanted, unborn children." Author John Bartlow Martin's research cited public health authorities' estimates of 750,000 to 2 million illegal abortions in the United States every year, and teenagers figured prominently. "The choices open to a pregnant high-school girl are abortion, disgrace, or reluctant and often disastrous marriage," he stated. Many women seeking abortions "have suffered childhood deprivation, divorce, spontaneous miscarriage, severe emotional disturbance and other sociomedical traumas."[12] These are not traits we associate with the 1950s. That ignoramuses today presenting themselves as "experts" can find publishers to issue books insisting that younger teens never had sex in the pre-1960s years remains a travesty.

DISCOVERING OLD EPIDEMICS

Then, abruptly, the Baby Bust arrived. The teenage birth rate plummeted by 40 percent, from 98 per 1,000 females age 15 to 19 in 1957 to 58 per 1,000 in 1975.[13] Similar plunges in young-age parenthood globally accompanied liberalized contraception (especially the marketing of the Pill in 1961), abortion (legalized in various states in the mid-1960s and nationally by

Supreme Court's *Roe v Wade* decision in 1973), and, most importantly, grow-ing educational and career opportunities for women. One would have thought, then, that if teen pregnancy and motherhood were not considered problems in the 1950s or before, they certainly would not be at much reduced levels in the 1970s. But the massive drop in birth rates during two decades of official inattention went largely unnoticed as the furor over youthful sexuality intensified.

While opponents of sex education later would hold up pictures of Woodstock to deplore the degeneracy they blamed on permissiveness and sex education, they failed to mention that 1960s teens grew up during the 1950s, when "the majority of adolescent 'revolutionaries' had never heard an official word about sex in the schools."[14] In fact, sex education later proliferated as a belated *response* to the sexual liberalizations of the 1960s.

"Nowhere was sex education taken up with more vigor than in the California public schools," historian Jeffrey Moran reported in his excellent *Teaching Sex.*[15] Modern sex education had been implemented in San Diego's schools since World War II, and other school districts followed suit. Governor Edmund Brown initiated the Governor's Commission on the Family in 1966 with a specific mandate to develop courses in family life education. These courses approached sexuality with a surprising frankness, and some included a scary new aspect—"dialogue-centered discussion" among students on the reality of adult sexual behavior. Anaheim, California's, sex education curriculum, for example, encouraged ninth graders to understand "the divergence between actual behavior and personal and societal moral codes." Students debated sexual intercourse before marriage, pro and con—did it promote "integrity in relationships" and "broadening of human sympathies," or "duplicity in relationships" and "exploitation of others"? Did it weaken or enforce "sex roles?"

As can be imagined, a war quickly erupted between Orange County's reli-gious conservatives and sex educators, repeated in other school districts with active programs, such as San Mateo's. Informed by the Christian Crusade's pamphlet, "Is the Schoolhouse the Proper Place to Teach Raw Sex?" and fiery orators such as the Rev. Gordon Drake, the godly learned of sex education teachers stripping naked and models having sex for the edification of young students, classes conducting explicit condom (which Drake called "condrum") demonstrations, children sent into dark closets for "exploration," boys raping teachers after incitement by sex lessons, schools abolishing separate boys' and girls' bathrooms to eliminate "inhibitions," phony lists showing rape and pregnancy becoming top school problems, teachers advocating bestiality and incest, schools showing X-rated films to students and assigning hardcore porn, children vomiting from the grossness of sexual demonstrations, and every other perverted horror that sex-obsessed minds could invent.

In this book, I frequently criticize liberal and left-wing interests defending sex education and contraception programs for succumbing to sensational, nonfactual, and prejudicial arguments. At the same time, however, the larger context in which these dubious liberal/left tactics incubated must be recognized. For decades, advocates who sought to teach even limited information about sexual health and disease prevention have endured the most vicious, hysterical, often certifiably psychotic attacks by extremists; fanatic attacks that, as the 1980s and 1990s revealed, were proving successful.

Sex education proponents, brandishing carefully designed curriculums and evaluation components, were appalled by the unabashed eagerness of opponents to troop to microphones to rage against unimaginable, fabricated horrors that never happened anywhere. Indeed, I witnessed shocked school trustees and legislators trying to discern what school, what teacher, what class, and when the outrages testified to actually occurred, quickly exposing the tales as wild embellishments or made up wholesale. "Hardcore pornography" turned out to be a Judy Bloom book in the school library. "Forced sex" was a student book report on *Catcher in the Rye*. Many seemed to reference England's famous Summerhill ultra-free school or the fictional *Harrad Experiment* novel of radical college co-edities. I do not know if anyone ever documented those famous condom-banana lessons; too bad there were not more of them. Sex education advocates learned it was useless to demand documentation from opponents, but the fearful did not seem at all chagrined by their inability to verify their lurid tales. They simply bellowed new ones.

Presaging the coming "culture war," sex education opponents were not about "facts." They believed they were called to a holy mission, as the Christian Crusade's Billy James Hargis (yes, the same reverend dismissed from his ministry for bisexual trysts with his students, including "All American Kids" choir members) orated, to fight off the National Education Association's "cleverly contrived plan" to "destroy the traditional moral fiber of America and replace it with a pervasive sickly humanism" akin to "communist slavery."[16] Any tactic, including the basest of lying, was justified to win.

The intensity and irrationality of 1970s anti-sex-education panic had little to do with the target and everything to do with widespread fears generated by America's newly visible racial diversity, technological advances such as television and global communication, the rise of vocally aggrieved minority cultures, the chaos in traditional institutions such as marriage, and the demise of insular, segregated communities—all summed up, then as now, as "the Sixties." Extremists, however organized and screaming, were not really the problem. The real villains were moderate lawmakers, school trustees, and voters who caved in to their lunacy. Watching the circus of sex-ed horror regalers—including their seeming delight in publicly repeating the most obscene language and explicit descriptions of sex acts from which they claimed to want to protect children (except those in hearings audiences)—I expected school board members and legislators to listen politely, then do their duty for the public and student interest. What I saw was that the capitulation of moderates and some liberals was killing rational discussion of teenage sexuality and how schools might make modestly beneficial contributions.

Liberals, some envious of the satisfying nature of morality crusades, others itching to give the far Right a taste of its own nasty vilification, still others just tired of losing to paranoid rantings, increasingly embraced falsification and fear tactics of their own. The tragedy of post-1990 unreality was foretold as sex-education wars degenerated into a two-way brawl that buried the interests of the young under the interests of the interests.

To defend sex education from heated, often hysterical right-wing attacks, liberals such as SIECUS, Planned Parenthood, and Senator Edward Kennedy created and publicized the image of an "epidemic" of teenage pregnancy that only sex education could quell.[17] The myth of a teenage pregnancy epidemic, which allowed progressive interests to invoke stern health and values education to tame wayward kids, was ideal for burnishing Democrats' nouveau-puritan image. It proved a disaster for American social policy and the young, and it later morphed into a political disaster for Democrats as the country grew more conservative in the 1980s and 1990s.

The real trend during the 1970s was that falling teenage pregnancy (and certainly birth) rates coincided with sharply falling poverty rates, burgeoning educational opportunities, and increased contraceptive availability—that is, fruits of the most liberal government policies. Instead of highlighting these successes, progressives joined the Right in creating the image of teenage sex as an erupting, subcultural "epidemic" completely alien to responsible, mainstream adult values. Perhaps efforts to defend sex education and reproductive health services to foster healthy adolescent sexuality would not have resonated with the public or policymakers in any case, but the liberal attack on teenage sex wound up being just as scurrilous as the Right's.

A decade before Charles Murray popularized his *Losing Ground* thesis that welfare causes illegitimate births that drive poverty that drives welfare, 1970s Democrats such as Senators Daniel Patrick Moynihan and Ted Kennedy and former Health Secretary Joseph Califano, Jr. were perversely claiming that poverty was caused by sexual irresponsibility, primarily among those of dark pigment.[18] Moynihan charged that high rates of birth among teenagers were the reason blacks were poor. After all, African Americans had been liberated on paper for almost a whole decade since the 1964 Civil Rights Act following a mere 300 years of slavery, displacement, and harsh legal discrimination.

For the next two decades, mostly white, affluent, liberal interests—quailing from addressing race directly—took aim at the "epidemic of teenage pregnancy." From far Right to far Left, from the Family Research Council to

Planned Parenthood, the basic assumptions about "teenage" sex and fertility were the same. Whether dumb, promiscuous, and immoral (Right) or dumb, promiscuous, and under-sex-educated (Left), both sides conspired to malign teenage girls as being knocked up by hormonal teenage boys in record numbers due largely to adolescent foolishness.

THE ELDERS STRIKE BACK

That said, the icier political incentives of post-1970 America still strike me as inadequate to explain the vehemence and irrationality of the attacks on young people, centered on teen pregnancy, that accelerated into 1990s anti-welfare campaigns. Why, suddenly in the 1970s, did a number of American politicians and interest groups suddenly ignite a virulent culture war by pronouncing "teen pregnancy" an "epidemic" and "major social problem" when past, much higher rates of "children having children" were not considered a problem? There were four contexts that I will argue rocketed teenage sex, pregnancy, and motherhood into political and media prominence.

The emergence and rising alarm over "teenage pregnancy" and motherhood in the 1970s reflected both admirable reproductive health advocacy for adolescents, whose sexuality was finally being recognized, and opportunistic exploitation of growing anxieties over increasing minority visibility, younger men's usurpation of older males' sexual territories, and the "unladylike" flood of young women into higher education, careers, leadership, and other public, formerly male-dominated roles. These initiatives and fears have merged into the bewildering maze of contradictions, myths, and omissions characterizing "teen pregnancy" discussion today. As Chapter 3 details, fear triumphed.

The first and most important development, in my view, was the persistence of racism in a climate in which direct racist expression was becoming taboo. Prior to the civil rights era of the 1950s and '60s, American officials, institutions, and news media regularly blamed powerless demographic groups, including the delicate and corruptible female, for vexing problems. As minorities organized and gained more power in the post-1960 era sufficient to punish their detractors at the ballot box and cash register, however, a "demagoguery vacuum" developed. Conservatives, in increasingly coded terms, argued that minority races, immigrants, homosexuals, poorer people, liberated women, and a radical younger generation posed a threat to mainstream society. As the backlash against civil rights movements in favor of traditional values popularized conservative messages in the 1970s, liberal politicians and newly created agencies sought values issues of their own.

It is not surprising, then, that moderates and liberals discovered that fear of the "generation gap," carrying new racial and gender undertones, was the ideal catch-all for their own "values" campaign. After all, past depictions of teenage sex and pregnancy had involved Elm Street white girls. The 1959 film *Blue Denim* presented the classic image of the insecure, white high school boy (the film begins as he misses a crucial shot at a basketball game) out to prove his manhood with the neglected, promiscuous white high school girl. (Spoiler alert! Wised-up fathers ally to rescue wayward girl from shady abortionist.) Fifties films, including *Teenage Devil Dolls, Girls in the Night, Girls Under 21, So Young So Bad, Under Age, Girls on the Loose, Jailbait, Delinquent Daughters,* and a hundred others starred busty white girls fornicating (off camera) out of control.

The chief purpose of family life education, though rarely stated so baldly, remained the same as it was in earlier decades: to deter middle- and upper-class white girls from emulating the loose morals of members of the underclass— and especially, to avoid emulating them *with* members of the underclass. The extreme sensitivity over even the mildest intersection of race and sexuality was underscored by the abrupt 1957 cancellation of disc jockey Alan Freed's popular TV show for showing black singer Frankie Lymon dancing with a white girl.[19]

The 1970s replaced older images of innocently "wayward youth" with more hostile depictions by politicians, lobbies, agencies, and media reports that teenage drinking, drugs, crime, violence, sex, pregnancy, alienation, suicide, and a host of other youthful misbehaviors had ballooned into crises. These crises were described in terms strikingly similar to those deployed in previous eras to stigmatize African Americans, Latinos, Chinese, poorer Catholics, Jews, and other minorities. This was not just traditional generational tension, but an increasingly organized, evolutionary attack on the young buttressed with growing legal punishments, restrictive policies, and divisive theories and measures to separate youth from adult akin to now-discredited racial segregation.

What changed? By the mid-1970s, it was becoming disturbingly evident that births by teenage mothers were heavily concentrated among minorities, not the nice-girl whites of popular depiction. California's pioneering racial tabulations in 1977 found 6 in 10 teenage mothers were Hispanic, African, Asian, Native, or "other" nonwhite Americans. In urban areas, high and rising proportions were visibly darkly complected. Later tabulations would confirm these racial disparities, contributing to a coded political narrative that teenage mothers (hint: dark ones) were "not like us"—that is, they represented a value system alien to middle America's—spurring redoubled efforts to prevent the epidemic from menacing middle-class (white) girls.

Race was not the only demographic concern, however. The second fear, rarely mentioned, was that teenaged boys were invading the teen-girl territory previously reserved for adult men. In 1975, vital statistics reports showed that males under age 20 fathered an unprecedented 40 percent of all births by teen girls. That represented a huge, uncomfortably sudden increase from the corresponding estimates of 20 percent in the 1950s and 10 percent before World War II. In tandem, the percentage of teen mothers' babies fathered by men age 25 and older had shrunk from one-third throughout the early 1900s to fewer than 10 percent by the 1970s.[20]

The teen-boy revolution was unmistakable. From 1950 to 1970, the fatherhood rate of teenage boys rocketed from 37 per 1,000 to 55 per 1,000—up 49 percent.[21] The postwar boom in earnings and education had boosted the income, business, and property ownership potential of younger men so that many could provide for families. The rapid growth in high school graduation and college enrollment had produced a generation of 1950s and 1960s males and females who, both socially and educationally, were sexual peers for the first time. They were discovering each other just as the birth control pill and new freedoms were facilitating more interfacings. Meanwhile, older, less educated men of the 1960s, though still wealthier than younger men, seemed hopelessly tied to the obsolete, distant past. The famous generational self-identification of sixties kids, on campuses, in jobs, and in cities, was associated with more peer-teen sex and offspring in anecdote and statistic alike.

Not only were teen boys occupying more teenage girls, they were horning in on women in their early twenties. In 1950, males under age 20 fathered just 65,000 babies with teen girls and 10,000 with women aged 20 and older. By 1970, teen boys' sirings had soared to a quarter million, including 220,000 with teen girls and 30,000 with older women. Meanwhile, fatherhood by older men—especially among whites—had actually dropped. Men age 25 and older, in particular, were rapidly being pushed out of the reproductive party, with overall fatherhood rates dropping by nearly 30 percent.

In sum: two big evolutionary alarm bells were going off in the 1970s. Not only were there more young fathers who were darker in color, but even among whites the avuncular Robert Young and Hugh Beaumont were being supplanted by mustachioed Meathead and even younger and hairier usurpers. The image of pimple-faced adolescent boys increasingly out-competing grown men for evolution's juiciest reproductive prize—the nubile, virginal, fertile adolescent female—is the sort of development that viscerally troubles the patriarchs. Along with racial fears, then, anxiety over teenage girls having sex—and worse, reproducing—with *teenage boys* fueled the teen-sex and teen-pregnancy panics.

This theory is buttressed by the puzzling paradox of American interests' near-complete disinterest in the older-father issue even as concern over teen mothers burgeoned. The short-lived fervor for statutory rape prosecution in the 1990s and the quixotic panic over older-male Internet predators in the 2000s did not evidence fear of adult men so much as a temporary interest in obtaining child support payments from poorer men pursuant to welfare reform and panic that modern youth, especially girls, were enjoying excessive freedoms enabled by Internet technology.

Clearly, dominant interests wanted the issue confined to teenaged girls without the potential distraction, perhaps even backlash, involved in including adult men. The menace is really *high school boys* knocking up teenage girls. The coming triumph of the "social cost" arguments over the once-vibrant adolescent sexual health imperative as the driving force setting policy on teen pregnancy in the 1990s and 2000s further suggests the power of established interests' anxieties over minority-race and underclass demographics.

BEFORE WE LEAVE THE SIXTIES . . .

Conservative anger toward the 1960s, even if misdirected and often hypo-critical, was not entirely unfounded. A third trend was that from the 1950s to the 1970s, crime, violence, drug abuse, violent deaths, divorce, unwed births, venereal disease, and other problems also rose rapidly. One could argue these trends, which have been depicted as occurring only among young people, would have provided grounds for concern about teen pregnancy and childbearing and, especially, younger, darker fatherhood. The problem is that these dissipating trends occurred with equal vigor among older ages—a fact never discussed in any account, to my knowledge.

For example, drug abuse deaths among teens rose from around 30 in 1955 to nearly 750 by 1970 (a big increase, even if we accept that the 1950s num-bers were drastically undercounted). Ignored was the fact that drug deaths among Americans ages 30 to 59 rocketed from 990 in 1955 to 3,250 in 1970.[22] Crime rose among all ages, including a leap in serious violent and property felonies, including murder, among Americans age 40 to 49—the Greatest Generation—from 55,000 in 1960 to 90,000 in 1975, a per-capita increase of 60 percent. Though still not as lethal as they had been in the 1930s, rising American dangers in the 1960s were televised sensationally.

In addition, the rate of unwed births doubled from 11.9 per 1,000 unwed females age 15 to 19 in 1950 to 22.6 in 1970. During the same period, however, unwed birth rates rose from 15.2 per 1,000 women age 20 to 44 in 1950 to 28.4 in 1970—an identical trend. That is, even as overall births were plummeting, the number and proportion that occurred among unmarried couples was rising sharply.[23]

Similarly, gonorrhea and syphilis rates nearly tripled among both teens— from 425 diagnoses per 100,000 teens aged 15 to 19 in 1965 to nearly 1,300 in 1975. But similar growth took place among adults aged 20 to 44 (311 per 100,000 in 1955; 1,004 in 1975).[24] Abortion rates rose sharply and similarly during the 1970s among both teens and adults, mainly due to increased reporting after legalization. Divorces per 1,000 marriages more than doubled from the 1950s to the 1970s in similar fashion among all age groups, from supposedly stern elders to no-longer-high-school-sweethearts.[25]

The 1960s featured not what demographers call a "cohort effect" (that is, trends confined to one age group or population group), but a "period effect" in which all populations display similar trends during a certain time period. The image of stern elders facing a revolutionary "new morality" of the 1960s young was a flat lie. This reinforces my argument that youths were simply made the scapegoats to allow older powers to evade potentially troubling scrutiny of trends affecting Americans in general. Indeed, "teen" was rapidly becoming a euphemism for "nonwhite."

THE INSTITUTIONALIZATION OF PUBLIC ANXIETY

Another 1970s development underscoring this point was the advent of government agencies (and their semi-public and private disciples) chartered to address social problems made visible by the revolutions of the 1960s. Sociologists coined the term "moral entrepreneurs" to characterize bureaucracies such as the National Institute on Drug Abuse and the National Institute on Alcohol Abuse and Alcoholism in tandem with the growing roster of institutions, private programs, and academics deploring teenage drinking, drugs, pregnancy, mental illness, and a host of largely manufactured crises to compete for dwindling 1970s funding.[26] The fact that most of the excesses of the 1960s were ebbing on their own in the 1970s, particularly among younger ages, was an inconvenience to politicians' and agencies' campaigns—especially since reductions in teen pregnancy and birth rates appeared to have been in response to liberalized opportunities that provided new education pathways for poorer young women rather than to behavioral interventions. If liberals were going to save behavior education, social programs, and agencies, some deception would be required.

Whatever their bleak political options, sex-education advocates' use of scare tactics to defend their programs against irresponsible right-wing attacks bolstered the conservative pendulum swing in the 1980s. If there really was an "epidemic" of teen pregnancy as liberal groups were alleging, conservatives argued after Republicans won the White House and Senate in 1980, then sex education and liberal indulgence of adolescent sexuality must be failures.

Congress passed the first Adolescent Family Life Act (AFLA) providing federal funds for abstinence-only education in schools in 1981 as part of a budget compromise supported by liberals such as Kennedy because it earmarked two-thirds of its funding for support services for pregnant and parenting teens.[27] But the conservative juggernaut against teenage sex was now out of control. Programs such as Teen-Aid and Sex Respect were proliferating into thousands of schools. A central tenet was to eschew traditional school curriculums that emphasized science and biology in order to push chastity "values." These included falsehoods that contraception, particularly condoms, failed at high rates and that male/female roles were naturally established at birth and altered only by yielding to sinful temptations. Too late, Moran noted, SIECUS and sex education backers realized that founding the promotion of sex education in the "constant demand for sexual crises to solve and urgent need for evidence of behavioral change" had backfired.[28]

The Clinton administration's 1996 welfare reform act leaped beyond the 1981 AFLA to mandate that $50 million in annual federal funding must be used by states for the "exclusive purpose" of promoting teenage abstinence until marriage; no money could go to curriculums that in any way discussed contraception.[29] *Abstinence* was a conservative doctrine, but it took a Democratic administration to enact *abstinence-only*. Liberals would have a great deal more evidence for their next, more successful campaign posing the 1980s HIV epidemic as the crisis proving the need for sex education and condom availability, a campaign endorsed by President Reagan's surprisingly progressive surgeon general, C. Everett Koop.

By the late 1970s, clear information was available to show that "teen" pregnancy, motherhood, and STD (and, later, HIV/AIDS) overwhelmingly afflicted poorer populations and involved mostly adult, not peer, partners. However, neither sex educators nor their right-wing abstinence promoters showed much interest in incorporating these pivotal realities of "teenage sex" and "teen pregnancy" into their 90-year-old political battle. Instead, both sides tacitly agreed not to talk about them amid increasing furor over what schools teach and what "messages" are sent to teens regarding sex.[30]

Chapter Three

BABY PRICING AND THE NEW EUGENICS

From its inception a century ago, the birth control and family planning movement has presented Jekyll and Hyde faces. The movement's contribution to the liberation of women from perpetual childbearing, families from mistimed children, and societies from rising fertility beyond what environments could absorb must be regarded as one of the crowning achievements of health science and politics. A truly optimistic trend has been the "demographic transition," in which rising prosperity produces falling birth and death rates, promising a safer, less starvation-edged future.

The sinister face of family planning and birth control is eugenics—that is, efforts to improve a society's "population stock" by preventing the births of babies of disfavored populations. "Negative eugenics" is defined by Merriam-Webster's Medical Dictionary as the "improvement of the genetic makeup of a population by preventing the reproduction of the obviously unfit."[1] "Positive eugenics" consists of encouraging the fit to breed.

Early family planning leaders expressed eugenics goals. "Birth control must lead ultimately to a cleaner race," declared Margaret Sanger, pioneering contraception advocate and founder of Planned Parenthood, in the early 1920s. "Eugenics is . . . the most adequate and thorough avenue to the solution of racial, political and social problems."[2] Planned Parenthood points out that Sanger also affirmed "the principles that a woman's right to control her body is the foundation of her human rights," "created access to birth control for low-income, minority, and immigrant women," fought the repressive

Comstock laws banning information about sexuality and contraception, and established the first family planning networks. As for Sanger's advocacy for eugenicist policies,

> Planned Parenthood Federation of America finds these views objectionable and outmoded. . . . However, attempts to discredit the family planning movement because its early twentieth-century founder was not a perfect model of early twenty-first-century values is like disavowing the Declaration of Independence because its author, Thomas Jefferson, bought and sold slaves.[3]

By the same token, it is doubtful that all but the most extreme conservatives today would identify with their famous puritan forbear, Anthony Comstock, who boasted of destroying millions of books and causing suicides. Sanger's work ultimately was endorsed by such African-American elder statesmen as W. E. B. Dubois and Martin Luther King.[4]

Sanger's views were very much in line with progressive scientific thinking of the early twentieth century that embraced new medical technologies and intelligence testing as tools to improve the quality of the American population through selective immigration, education, and family planning policies. Many intellectuals and professionals then held what we now would consider racist views on eugenics alongside liberal views on sexuality. American Psychological Association president H. H. Goddard spearheaded a movement to deport "mentally defective" immigrants and demanded that the "feeble minded" as demonstrated by psychometric testing be forcibly prevented from breeding. In particular, Goddard deplored the fiscal "charges upon the state and community"—that is, the "social costs"—caused by allowing "inferior" parents to bear children and perpetuate "the menace of moronity" from generation to generation.[5]

The dominant scientific view of the time held that sexuality education, contraceptive provision, abortion, and sterilization could reduce or eliminate reproduction among lower-class and "feeble-minded" populations at the same time it optimized the timing of fertility for middle- and upper-class couples. Family planning could improve human stock across populations, within races, and within families. The Supreme Court even endorsed negative eugenics in its famous "three generations of imbeciles are enough" decision (*Buck v. Bell*, 1927), upholding a Virginia law requiring sterilization of the mentally "unfit" for "the protection and health of the state."[6]

The next half century brought a withering attack on eugenicist notions of branding entire classes of people and their babies as inferior. Nazi Germany's experiments in medical genocide added to the discrediting of negative eugenics. Voluntary family planning remained an entirely different issue; medical advances in contraception and legalized abortion would help individual couples time pregnancies and reduce childbearing risks. However, the notion of deploying family planning to cleanse the population of inferior children based on broad demographic classifications was rightly seen as too vulnerable to temporary political prejudices supported by bad science.

Or was it? Fast-forward 50 years. By the 1980s, groups promoting family planning that included adolescent health had expanded substantially across the country. Every major urban area and many smaller ones provided access to accurate information and confidential, high-quality reproductive health services. At first, family planning advocates measured success in terms of reducing poor health outcomes. Indeed, maternal and infant mortality, babies' complications, and other sexual health problems had declined rapidly as services improved.

By the mid-1980s, however, an uglier trend was emerging in some segments of the movement, employing the same prejudicial language and grossly biased "science" of early-century eugenicists. New eugenics lobbies (which certainly do not term themselves as such) at the state and national levels began emphasizing the "social costs" of teenage motherhood. This chapter explores the misuse of research and the political deception involved in selectively exploiting social-cost notions to produce arguments against teenage childbearing that are virtually identical to the nineteenth century's racialized eugenicist arguments. New eugenicists do not mention race directly, but it looms large when the demography of the group targeted is considered.

EUGENICS RETURNS

Early studies by the Urban Institute in the 1980s claimed to quantify the "tremendous financial and social costs . . . of teenage childbearing" as a new lobbying argument for funding program efforts to stop all teenage motherhood.[7] Inconvenient details, such as the Urban Institute's finding that even by its grossly biased method, most teenage mothers did not generate social costs, were ignored by all. No longer was adolescent health the dominant goal; new eugenics lobbies measured success solely by whether the numbers of babies born to teen mothers declined. As "teen pregnancy" became a political hot button in the 1990s and 2000s, many lobbies misused social-cost studies to justify funding pitches by the bottom line of a balance sheet: the cost of preventing any random teen's baby versus the actuarial cost of that teen's baby, calculated from the presumed average cost for all teens' babies as a group. Baby pricing—highly selective baby pricing—in short.

By new eugenics logic, teenage mother Rosalynn Carter's first child, Jack Carter, would be seen as a social costly baby who should have been prevented in exactly the same fashion as every other baby whose mother was one second or more under 20 years of age at the time of birth. Likewise, Barack Obama, born when his mother was 18 years old; or, if your politics lean the other way, Newt Gingrich, whose mother was 16 at his birth. That is, a nuclear physicist/lawyer, a U.S. president, and a House Speaker all would have been branded as societal burdens whose birth should have been prevented. As for their former teen mothers, Obama's (who earned a Ph.D. in anthropology); Gingrich's (who soon wed a career military officer, a marriage that lasted 50 years until his death); and Rosalynn Carter (who some might say did all right) could be presumed to have destroyed their lives with thoughtless early reproduction.

That is just the first problem with eugenicist thinking: the "fitness" of an individual parent is not predictable from the characteristics of his or her larger demographic class. Likewise, the "average worth" or "social cost" of a class of children, even if fairly and accurately calculated, ignores the vast range of potential and achievement among children of both "fit" and "unfit" parents. Jesus's mother, by best historical account, was a dark-skinned, homeless immigrant who was around 14 years old at his birth and attached to an unemployed young man. By contrast, Hitler's mother was a 28-year-old married Caucasian from an established, devoutly religious family. However, individuality does not matter to eugenicists. Their parent-fitness criteria have always favored the characteristics of wealthier classes and assigned higher values to their children. The misuse of social-cost studies by modern eugenics lobbies, detailed below, is the inevitable result of this bias.

What should be ringing alarm bells are the prejudicial criteria by which the babies of teenage mothers are selectively classed as "socially costly." Why not quantify and rank the worth of *all* classes of children, then? What are the social costs of African-American babies compared to white, non-Hispanic babies? What are the social costs of childbearing by mothers over age 35 (that is, Sarah Palin's choice, rather than Bristol's); or of middle-aged fatherhood? A 2009 study by Oxford University researchers published in *Nature Genetics* reiterated that as the quality of a man's sperm decreases with age, his risk of fathering a child with serious health problems increases. Fathers aged 40 and older were six times more likely to have a child with autism and twice as likely to have a child with schizophrenia as men who became fathers before age 30. Learning disabilities and related problems among children of older fathers have been documented in long-term studies.[8]

If social classes are pitted, what would the social cost of each baby born to wealthier white parents be if affluent whites, as the class comprising nearly all corporate executives and directors, were charged with the hundreds of billions of dollars corporate crime, welfare, and bailouts cost taxpayers and the economy every year? What if the "carbon footprint," an index of environmental damage that is much larger among richer than among poorer people, was assigned as a social cost to babies born to affluent parents? Conversely, if teenaged mothers are judged socially costly because, on average, their children grow up to be poorer than children born to older mothers, what would the "social benefits" be of the low-cost labor that the poorer classes supply to the economy? As detailed below, when examined across a broad spectrum of variables, the problems ascribed to teenage mothers and their children turn out largely to be those suffered by poorer women in general. The new eugenics is the same as the old.

While many may be offended by my equation of today's teen-pregnancy prevention advocates who cite the "social costs" of teen motherhood with the racist arguments of early-century eugenicists, note the main principle unifying the two: that the demographic "average" may be used to evaluate the "worth" of *every* individual in that group. If, on average, babies born to dark-skinned, or immigrant, or 17-year-old mothers can be shown to have outcomes *as measured by selected indexes* that are worse than those of babies born to white, European-origin, or 28-year-old mothers, then the value of *every* baby born to each of these respective groups can be quantified from the group average.

This new-eugenics principle that babies can be priced and ranked by their demographically averaged "social cost" is nightmarish enough. Recall the justifiable outrage many liberals expressed when sociologist Charles Murray suggested that more babies born to African, Hispanic, and Native Americans (compared to East Asian and European Americans) represented "dysgenic" trends that reduced the quality of the American population.[9] Recall how enraged a chunk of conservative Americans became at the baseless suggestion that President Obama's 2009 health care reform plans included "death panels" to dispatch old and unfit members. When it comes to *our* hides, no judgments as to "worth," please.

ECONOMIC MALPRACTICE

Beyond the notion of redlining certain infants, more conceptual atrocities loom in how we choose to define social costs when calculating the potential worth of a class of babies. In a climate of prejudice created by political pressures to produce compliant cost-benefit calculations, "social costs" *will not be fairly calculated.* The crude biases dominating social-cost studies of teen motherhood involve selecting measures that emphasize only those costs attributable to the targeted group while ignoring their benefits; ignoring costs imposed by more favored groups in society; and blaming personal choices while ignoring external conditions.

Early social-cost studies of teen motherhood such as those conducted by the Urban Institute recapitulated nineteenth-century travesties. They compared the welfare payments, education levels, child health, and so on of teen mothers *straight across* with those of teens who did not have babies or with mothers in their twenties and found (presto!) that teen mothers generated gargantuan social costs. Yes, if one compares outcomes of children born to mothers living in Southside Chicago with ones living on the Lakefront, large differences will be found. That also was true a century ago, when such disparities were blamed on inferior-race motherhood. Back then, the University of Chicago School of social scientists' famous 1920s mappings showed crime and other problems tracked the severe social disadvantages characterizing transitional urban neighborhoods, not racial or immigrant qualities.[10]

Indulging the same fundamental error as 1900 calculators who graded fit and unfit babies along race and class hierarchies, modern social-costers ignored the fact that teen mothers were vastly poorer than teen non-mothers and non-teen mothers *before* they had babies. Both failed to consider whether poorer child outcomes were due to external conditions rather than innate character.[11] Recognizing this problem, some researchers inaugurated studies comparing various mother and child outcomes of teen mothers with those of their childless teen sisters or cousins, with much-diminished and inconsistent results. For example, researchers led by University of Pennsylvania sociologist Frank Furstenburg initially found teen motherhood generally forecast lower incomes and worse child outcomes,[12] while those led by University of Michigan health scientist Arline Geronimus found teen mothers and their children fared no worse or even a bit better than their non-parenting teen counterparts.[13] Birth-order effects and the differing conditions in which girls were raised at different times in the same families continued to beg the question of whether the baby or a unique set of external stresses that predicted teen motherhood was the true culprit. Interestingly, Furstenburg's most recent, long-term study of 300 teenage mothers in Baltimore directly challenged claims, including by President Obama, that teenage motherhood is the chief cause of poverty:

> Early childbearing was not the main cause of the economic difficulties these women faced in their lives, and did not trap them in welfare dependence for the rest of their lives. Having a child as a teen, which most policymakers believe to be a powerful source of disadvantage, had only modest effects on their educational and economic achievement in later life, after taking into account their economic circumstances prior to becoming pregnant. The teen mothers in Baltimore did better than most observers would have predicted in continuing their education, and did not fare substantially worse than their counterparts who postponed parenthood until their twenties.[14]

When more comprehensive, longer-term social cost studies began to find that teen motherhood really was not that costly, the next step for officials and interest groups was to misrepresent the studies. The most serious example was the Robin Hood Foundation's distortion of the first study of the long-term costs and benefits of teen motherhood it had commissioned as a centerpiece of the fledgling National Campaign to Prevent Teen Pregnancy's 1997 press conference on the "public costs of teenage childbearing." Robin Hood understood the rules. The foundation already had denounced teen mother-hood as "pervasive and damaging" to poor communities. It had faithfully adopted the political debate's limited moral horizon: even if teen mothers were "disproportionately concentrated in poor, often racially segregated communities characterized by inferior housing, high crime, poor schools, and limited health services" and many "had been victims of physical and/or sexual abuse,"[15] Robin Hood did not challenge government authorities to confront these devastating conditions—ones, as we will see, that underlay the vast bulk of the "social costs" that studies misattributed to teenage motherhood.

Rather, all agreed, only those costs that could be assigned to teen mothers' behaviors and only remediations directed at changing their behaviors would be considered. The social-cost parameters chosen—earnings, taxes paid, use of social and welfare programs, poorer educational achievement, higher rates of incarceration—were already biased against the poor. This choice of factors would guarantee the conclusion that virtually all childbearing by low-income parents, not just teenaged ones, generated "social costs." If Robin Hoods' and National Campaign's guiding principle was that only affluent parents should have children, why not state that directly?

Consider how differently a social-cost analysis would turn out if factors unfavorable to richer parenthood were chosen instead. For example, Congressional economists have estimated the annual costs of corporate crime at $250 billion (in 1997 dollars); repeated tax-funded bailouts for banking and loan industries in 2008 and 2009 alone totaled hundreds of billions of dollars.[16] Corporate executives and directors overwhelmingly are white and affluent. Using the same social-cost assumptions applying population-level welfare and tax expenditure estimates for teen mothers to apply hundreds of billions of dollars in annual corporate corruption and bailout costs to white parents, each white baby born generates an average of tens of thousands of dollars in social costs every year. The social costs of more affluent whites having children would dwarf the paltry $7.3 billion Robin Hood now blames on teen motherhood annually.

For another, climate change is ranked by the United Nations as among the most potentially disastrous global crises. Greenhouse gas emissions, especially the byproducts of carbon-based fuels, causing climate change are substantially higher among individuals with larger homes, more and larger vehicles, more driving, and greater product consumption. Each child born to an affluent parent, on average, contributes vastly more to greenhouse gas accumulation than a child born to a poorer parent, a serious environmental cost widely pre-dicted to trigger massive social costs such as the need to relocate entire cities, industries, and agricultural areas. If eugenicists assigned all teen mothers, col-lectively, the costs of welfare, imprisonment, and other public expenses attributable to some of the children born to teen mothers, then doesn't fairness dictate that we assign to all white and affluent parents the full costs of bailouts, corporate crime, pollution, climate change, and other social and public costs attributable to their offspring? Class bias is another way in which today's social-cost evaluations of teen childbearing resemble the eugenics "studies" of a century ago.

Robin Hood commissioned UCLA (now Duke University) economist V. Joseph Hotz and colleagues to evaluate the economic issues in teen motherhood. Hotz's landmark 1997 study was hailed by other top researchers, such as Harvard social policy professor Christopher Jencks, as the best ever. The details of Hotz's updated, 2005 study are examined below.[17]

Hotz's model differed from those of previous researchers in two big ways. First, his team looked not just at the initial years after birth, when all families incur high costs, but also at how former-teen mothers were faring 10 to 20 years later. Second, his study compared mothers who had babies before age 20 not to all young women or to random samples based on broad demographics, but to poorer young women who had *intended to have babies during teen years but had miscarried* and who then had their first baby after age 20. This "natural experiment" produced two sets of teen women whose poverty and background characteristics, unlike those used in previous studies, turned out to be remarkably similar. Thus, Hotz's design focused on exactly the question at issue: is it having a baby as a teenager, or the previous circumstances of the mother regardless of age, that generates social costs?

Hotz and colleagues' findings were surprising. Over time, former teen mothers actually earned more money, paid more taxes, and saved taxpayer costs compared to similarly situated young women who became mothers later. Further, teen mothers were just as likely to graduate from high school or obtain equivalent GED credentials and just as likely to wind up with male partners. Meanwhile, similarly situated young women who waited until their twenties to have babies were saddled with caring for young children into their late twenties and early thirties, reducing their earning potential at the very time they could have commanded higher wages.

Hotz's findings, in my interpretation, were devastating to official depictions. Hotz and colleagues suggested that teen motherhood actually represented a rational, long-term investment by which poorer young women from harsh family backgrounds achieved greater stability, attracted public and personal resources, and, within a decade, were earning more money and taking less public assistance than their counterparts who waited to have babies. Such a finding applied only to the poorest young women; early motherhood would be costly for more affluent teens planning higher education and careers—exactly the advantaged classes from whence blossomed so many of those who condemned the "costs" of poorer teens' offspring.

The strongest implication of Hotz's research was that if official America wanted fewer teen mothers, the best policy was to reduce the severe poverty that made teen motherhood a sensible, long-term economic choice. Hotz's 1997 findings called into question the very existence of a National Campaign to Prevent Teen Pregnancy and the massive, bipartisan political and institutional campaigns exploiting the issue. Right before the National Campaign's star-studded press conference slated to announce the huge "public costs" generated by teen moms, their own study, the best done to date, had seriously undermined their case.

The National Campaign, Robin Hood Foundation, Urban Institute, and others at the party could have declared Hotz's startling findings worthy of further analysis and suggested potential changes in policy away from stigma and prevention and toward investment in poorer families. Not a chance. The official view was politically precast; the academics they hired were supposed to produce "research" to support it. As punishment, Hotz was disinvited from the press conference and reception.[18]

So, Robin Hood's executive summary report (the only one anyone reads) buried Hotz's unwelcome findings and selectively presented *only the costs* that teen mothers generate *during the initial years after giving birth*. Hotz's finding of long-term benefits was obscured. Robin Hood's deceptive cost numbers presented in *Kids Having Kids*' colorful executive-summary charts became the basis for disciples around the country. For example, California's Public Health Institute presented state lawmakers with cost-benefit analyses of teen-pregnancy prevention programs for every legislative district based on this fraudulent metric.[19] Spend x on funding this client's prevention program, and then save an even larger y for every teen's baby not born, the logic went. That is how crazy privatized social policy's baby-pricings had become.

IS TEEN MOTHERHOOD A LONG-TERM INVESTMENT?

As researchers considered more complex factors and tighter research controls, even those insisting teen motherhood generates unacceptable social costs found their case, still loudly proclaimed in public forums, harder and harder to sustain scientifically. The best example is the Urban Institute's own 2008 update of *Kids Having Kids*.[20]

Even if we accept the Urban Institute's biased factors, its 2008 study of teen childbearing suggested "social cost" is not much of an issue. Publicly, Urban Institute authors claimed that "teenage motherhood costs taxpayers about $7.3 billion annually in social-program costs, including foster care and incarceration, as well as diminished taxes from lower-earning and lower-spending teenage parents and their children." This total, even taken at face value, was a pittance when the costs of other groups such as the elderly, home mortgage tax deductors—or unneeded fighter plane programs—were considered.

But even this cost estimate is questionable. The Urban Institute's authors admitted their study demonstrated no simple relationship between early parenthood and subsequent health, wealth, or wisdom. Instead, the volume's 21 contributors found, many personal and economic factors combined to influence the quality of life of teen parents and their kids. While "assessments of health, cognitive ability, and behavior" predictably showed that children of teen mothers scored lower than children of older mothers, there was an important caveat:

> Much of the difference disappears, however, when researchers control for such background factors as a teen's education, her mother's education, and whether she grew up with both parents. . . . When social, economic, and demographic factors are controlled, many findings diminish or go away, which suggest that improving a mother's educational and social circumstances would contribute to better outcomes for children.[21]

Here we go again.

Likewise, in the case of teen mothers' supposedly spawning future criminals and thugs, a common claim in the 1990s, The Urban Institute found that controlling for the prior poverty and disadvantaged backgrounds of teen mothers all but wiped out the disproportionate odds that their children would be incarcerated. Even using a biased control (imprisonments of older versus younger children of the same former-teen mothers, which overlooked birth-order effects and the fact that mothers get better off economically as they age), the Urban Institute found "the age of the mother has less of an effect on delinquency than other differences in the circumstances facing the children of young teen versus nonteen mothers."

In terms of earnings and taxes paid, the report concluded that teen mothers actually do a bit better than older mothers:

> Women who become parents before age 18 have about $1,600 more in net annual income from all sources, including public assistance, than would be expected if they delay childbearing until age 20 or 21. Women who become parents at 18 or 19 have average net incomes about $300 higher than expected if they delay childbearing.[22]

The Urban Institute's last conclusion was based largely on Hotz and colleague's updated 2005 study,[23] which found "no statistically significant effect of early childbearing on the probability that teen mothers obtain a high school level education—either in the form of a regular high school diploma or GED—relative to what would have happened to these women if they had delayed their childbearing." Further, teen mothers actually wound up working more hours and earning more money than did their later-motherhood counterparts: "Over the ages of 21 through 35, teen mothers earned an average

$7,917 per year. In 1994 dollars . . . teen mothers would have earned an average of 31 percent less per year if they had delayed their childbearing," the study found. Hotz's findings in the key area for which the study had been commissioned, the consumption of welfare by teen moms, was also startling:

> From age 18 until around 22, the estimated effects of teenage childbearing are positive, indicating that teen mothers were more likely to be on public assistance and receive larger amounts of transfers from these programs than if they had delayed their childbearing. For these younger ages, the estimated effects are statistically significant only for the annual amount of benefits received in the form of public assistance. However, from around age 22, the estimated effects reverse in sign, implying that teen mothers actually reduced their participation in and amount of benefits received from these public assistance programs compared to what they would have done if they had delayed their childbearing.

Indeed, that was the factor that had been overlooked. The short-term "public costs" of teenage motherhood—the only issue previous studies concerned themselves with—simply reflected the start-up costs of raising an infant. As teen mothers' children aged, required less care, and generated lower medical costs, the mothers were able to go to work (at 20-age rather than teen-age salaries), earn more money, pay more taxes, and get off public assistance. Meanwhile, the poorer women who waited until their twenties to have babies were now experiencing the high cost of infants and young children, were unable to work as much, and were more likely to be on welfare. "Our research casts doubt on the view that postponing childbearing will improve the socioeconomic attainment of teen mothers in any substantial way," the study concluded.[24]

The National Campaign's Saul Hoffman's refutation of Hotz's study for the updated *Kids Having Kids* claimed that more recent cohorts of teen mothers age 16 and younger did generate public costs.[25] There are serious problems with Hoffman's update, however. The worst is that he reported no statistically significant effects, which meant that no conclusions could be drawn from his analysis. Absent explanation, the failure to present such standard tests indicates the results would not have favored Hoffman's conclusions. Second, even the nonsignificant effects he suggests—that more recent teen mothers do generate social costs—may be due to welfare reforms and policy changes in the 1990s. The National Campaign presented only Hoffman's meaningless analysis on its Web site, claiming teen motherhood had generated public costs of $161 billion from 1991 through 2004 and inviting state and local programs to prorate these costs to teen birth numbers in their areas.[26] So much for the National Campaign's scientific credibility.

The famous "social cost" issue not only is a bust once appropriate standards are applied, it resurrects the worst racial and gender biases of a century ago.

Even if we accept at face value National Campaign's "social cost" claims, the $7 billion to $9 billion per year for teen mothers' babies is only a fraction of, say, the cost of the home mortgage interest deduction ($95 billion per year and rising rapidly), the treasury's third-largest tax loophole that allows homeowners to deduct from their taxes the interest paid for up to $1 million in mortgage indebtedness.[27] If taxpayers can help mostly well-off homeowners pay off their loans, why is it such a terrible burden to pay a modest amount to help some of the poorest children in society?

WHAT ABOUT FATHERS?

Finally, we have to ask another tough question privatized social policy interests too easily slide by: why are we blaming mothers for babies' social costs? For all age groups in 2007, the Census reported that 53 percent of custodial parents due child support—including two-thirds of poor parents and half of non-poor parents—received only partial payment or no payment from absentee parents; one fourth received nothing. Five of six custodial parents due child support were mothers. In another confirmation of Boomer family instability, 40 percent of those parents due child support in 2007 were age 40 and older, up from 25 percent in 1994.[28]

Why, then, isn't a "national campaign" buttressed by institutional crusades and emotional media coverage established to stigmatize the irresponsible sexuality of deadbeat parents, virtually all of whom are adults and 85 percent of whom are men? Such campaigns gain temporary traction here and there, but you can judge their effectiveness and public impact by searching your TV listings: how many stories and programs deal with "teenage sex" and "teen pregnancy" and how many with "deadbeat adult fathers?" Once again, the imperatives of privatized social policy intrude. The reason campaigns to hold adult men responsible for sex and fatherhood with teens are quixotic and largely futile is the irresistible pull exerted by privatized social policy's need to scapegoat the most powerless party. This repulsive tradition has no place in a modern, diverse America that pretends to racial and gender equity.

At a time in which hundreds of thousands of qualified high school graduates await space to open up in colleges and universities and student debt is pricing lower-income students out of higher education, the official notion that poorer young people should put their lives on hold indefinitely until government attitudes improve remains dominant. The obsession with the age of the mother, the foundation of eugenics, is clouding progressive judgment. If having babies at a young age makes long-term economic sense for poorer people, it makes no sense to argue they should not do it simply because politicians and interest groups prefer to ignore systemic inequalities. There are more good reasons some teens have babies, detailed in the next chapter.

Chapter Four

MARIE ANTOINETTE WOULD HAVE LOVED THE NATIONAL CAMPAIGN

During my late-adolescent tenure as a hamfisted construction worker in Mexico, I helped rebuild a fire-gutted scrapwood home perched atop a windy mesa outside Tijuana for a destitute campesino family of mom, dad, grandma, a couple of aunts, and seven or eight or a dozen children depending on the time of day. As I unloaded supplies, I noticed a pixie girl, around five or six years old, watching with intense curiosity. Eager to extend my high school Spanish, I labeled our modest inventories for her as I stacked them: "clavos, seis, ocho, diez," "techuelos," "papel de brea," "carton de yeso," and so on, which she seemed to be cataloguing like an inventory technician. I later realized this tiny girl's job, crucial to the functioning of her household, was to *know where everything was*. At night, when only a sputtering cooking fire dimly illuminated the remote barrio with no electricity and few lanterns or flashlights, her role was to fetch whatever anyone needed. Her job assignment must have derived from a GPS mind, for over the two-week construction project, she scampered to retrieve our lost hammers, sorted nails, and ferreted out a vital plumbline we forgot we had brought.

Children in poor families, unlike their wealthier counterparts, are not money-sinkholes. Poor kids do not cost their parents $15,000 per year to raise (the U.S. Department of Agriculture's estimate for families with $70,000+ household incomes). In this Tijuana barrio, like in American migrant labor camps and inner-city apartments, children contribute valuable services to their families and teens provide monetary value from employment. Children and adolescents represent vital workers, eyes to watch the even younger, grownups when grownups are gone or imprisoned or debilitated, and security for aging parents . . . which in indigent families, begins as early as the thirties.

We have seen that all over the globe, poorer populations have more babies earlier in life. However, other forces are at work than just children's services to poorer families. In ethnically conflicted cities—Jerusalem, Belfast, Johannesburg, Los Angeles, or Paris and its suburbs, for examples—the minority population (Palestinian, Catholic, Hispanic, and Algerian, respectively) has a substantially higher birth rate at younger maternal ages than does the affluent, dominant population (Israeli, Protestant, White, and French). Are poorer people simply behaving irrationally? Their more privileged critics may talk as if poorer pregnant teens recklessly tossed away full-ride Harvard scholarships, an attitude reflecting the centuries-old Antionettism of those for whom higher education and well-padded careers were provided as birthrights. "Many young women have told me that while they did not actively seek to become pregnant, they were not disappointed with the result," reported the director of Santa Fe's La Familia Medical Center of the teens who came from "broken families" and faced bleak futures,[1] echoing a point I heard from Chicago's Judith Musick and many other providers who actually talked to teens.

Depicting teenaged motherhood as the product of adolescent delusion and ignorance while denying the benefits teenage motherhood confers on poorer populations evidences the class biases and cognitive limitations of experts who persist in refusing to acknowledge the few options available to millions of disadvantaged American young—as well as a craven refusal to challenge the low moral standards of those in power who allow such conditions to persist. As sociologist Kristin Luker put it after an iconoclastic investigation of teen pregnancy, "early childbearing does not make young women poor; poverty makes women bear children at an earlier age."[2]

What, then, might the benefits be of having babies during teen years? First, as noted in the last chapter, the public costs of teenage childbearing have been drastically exaggerated by self-promoting eugenics lobbies. In reality, early childbearing may be better termed an investment by poorer young women.

Second, as the example that began this chapter illustrated, poorer children's labor contributes economically to family income and aging relatives' support. Childbearing during teen years enables low-income mothers, who tend to raise children in extended families, to maximize grandparents' and older relatives' assistance in childraising before the health problems associated with aging set in.[3] It also enables older children to assist parents and grandparents in raising younger ones.

Third, repeated studies have found that far from being terrified, upset, and ashamed as they are often portrayed, teen mothers and pregnant teens typically show improvements in morale and health. For example, a 1990

Washington University/Harvard University study of 2,100 teenage women found that "many of the problems of adolescent mothers are, in fact, those that are associated with the social and economic disadvantages of adolescents who have high rates of pregnancy, and thus, may not be due to child-bearing per se." While most teen mothers came from "unstable family backgrounds," researchers found that "significantly fewer of those youths who are rearing children have recent (within the past year) symptoms of conduct disorder, alcohol or drug abuse or dependence, and depression, as well as suicidal thoughts, than their peers. . . . The adolescent mother, in contrast with the sexually active adolescent who is not a mother, feels better about herself and engages in fewer overt undesirable behaviors." The reason? Teen mothers have achieved "independence" from past family abuses, family instability, and associated destructive influences.[4] In another typical study, a California pediatrics team interviewed and clinically tested 352 pregnant teenagers and found huge drops in cigarette smoking, alcohol use, and drug use compared to their pre-pregnancy behaviors.[5] As with long-term economic benefits, the health and behavior benefits of teen pregnancy for disadvantaged girls have been ignored by teen-pregnancy prevention movements and social-cost accountants.

Finally, as the example of divided cities indicates, poorer populations increase their *political power* via higher birth rates at younger maternal ages. This is a big reason—openly acknowledged in embattled foreign cities but rarely admitted in the United States—that lower-class fertility has always frightened powerful groups. Exhortations by leaders of the dominant population to provoke more births have failed; richer people view children beyond one or two as economic liabilities. Whether through democratic franchise or physical presence, the dominated equalize with the dominators by the weight of numbers. As I heard a Latina spokeswoman quip at an immigrant rally in California, "I'm afraid our strategy isn't, 'we shall overcome,' but 'we shall overwhelm.'"

PERSUADING TEENS THAT SEX IS AWFUL

Is non-reproductive sex also of benefit to teens? This issue has been banished by today's rigid rules, in which instant condemnation rains on those who suggest that some teens might actually enjoy and derive benefits from sex. When Susan Wilson (formerly of New Jersey's Network for Family Life Education) suggested that teens could engage in responsible and pleasurable sexual conduct, or when York University (Toronto) literature professor Peter Cummings suggested leaving alone teens who engage in "sexting" and sensual expressions with each other, or when 15-year-old singer Miley Cyrus said she liked watching HBO's *Sex and the City* and would play a small nonsexy role in the movie version, howls of anger ensued from liberal *Atlantic* magazine[6] to right-wing Fox News pundit Bill O'Reilly.[7]

Lobbies highlighted the National Longitudinal Survey of Adolescent Health's 1996 finding that 25 percent of girls and 8 percent of boys age 14 to 17 who were "sexually active" reported being depressed within the past week, compared to 8 percent of girls and 3 percent of boys who were not sexually active. "Sexually active" was defined as "ever had sexual intercourse." The National Campaign to Prevent Teen Pregnancy reported in 2000 that 63 percent of sexually active teens age 12 to 17 regretted having had sex and wished they had waited until they were older, compared to 32 percent who did not.[8]

The inference the National Campaign and others touted was that having sex, even once, *causes* depression and regrets in teens—and therefore, enforcing virginity must make teens happier. The surveys do not present evidence for that cause and effect and ignored other explanations, as discussed later. Satisfaction, particularly on conservative Web sites such as Heritage Foundation's, that teen sinners made themselves miserable was palpable.[9]

More cruelly, researchers and agency reports persist in their bad habit of lumping together youths who have experienced rape, sexual assault, coerced sex, and prostitution with those whose sexual liaisons were purely voluntary. The younger a teen reported having "had sex," the more likely the "sex" was a rape. As noted, a Guttmacher Institute survey found that 43 percent of girls who had sex before age 15 reported that their only experience consisted of being raped, and another 17 percent said they both had been raped and had voluntary sex.[10] The 2007 Youth Risk Behavior Survey found 9 percent of teen aged 15 to 19 reported their first sexual experience was a rape, and one in five teens that age had been raped at least once. Given that fewer than half of teens that age had ever had sex at all, the proportions who were rape victims were even more troubling.[11] These findings are consistent with those of surveys of pregnant and parenting teens discussed in Chapter 3.

Since the small percentage of teens these groups deplored for "having sex" at very young ages included (when teens were asked) a high proportion who were raped, usually by older men, such tactics maximized the negative findings about teen sexuality that lobbies seem to covet. Yet, none of the surveys I found differentiated between rape (or coerced sex, survival sex, and prostitution for that matter) and purely voluntary sex. We might expect teens whose "sexual activity" had been violent or otherwise involuntary would find that experience depressing and regrettable. The callousness of privileged commentators who enjoy the luxury to ignore youths' histories of molestation and sexual violence does not mean teenagers can ignore these realities.

Today's anti-teen-sex climate is so pervasive that rare are the researchers willing to study why teens actually have sex as opposed to why officials and experts say they do. The official view is that teens have sex only for bad reasons: because of enticing media images, peer pressure, hormones, limited brains, and other misguided compulsions. In such a climate, researchers who find teens expressing positive attitudes about sex and their sexual experiences often feel compelled to slant their results in a negative manner—and if they do not, media reports will.

For example, Web MD reported a University of California study of 619 teens, 275 of whom had intercourse or oral sex during their ninth or tenth grade years, under the headline, "Teen sex may take emotional toll. Girls especially vulnerable to negative emotional aftereffects."[12] Web MD's headline and article were not fair characterizations of the 18-month study published in the February 2007 *Pediatrics*.[13] In fact, the study found teens aged 15 and 16 were quite positive about their sexual experiences. Directly contradicting those who claim teen sex inexorably leads to regret, depression, and even suicide, only 2 percent (among teens who had both oral sex and intercourse) to 4 percent (for those who had only oral sex) said their experiences had been *entirely negative*. In contrast, an astounding 61 percent (oral sex), 86 percent (intercourse), and 96 percent (both) said at least one aspect of the sex had been positive. Even though researchers gave teens only half as many positive as negative options to choose from, 8 to 20 times more felt their experience had been entirely positive. Most reported *both* positive experiences (led by pleasure, feeling good about oneself, and making one's relationship better) and negative ones (led by much lower levels of feeling used, feeling bad about oneself, and feeling regret).

Web MD's headline, then, should have been, "Teenagers generally report positive experiences from sex." That most sexually active teens could think of at least *one* negative consequence, as defined by the researchers, not only failed to negate their generally positive reactions, it indicated a healthy ability to recognize the complexity of sexual experience. What sexually active adult has not experienced some bad results (remember the famous "Hite Report" of yore?)?

Similarly, a study of sexual attitudes among 637 ninth graders by Indiana University and University of California researchers found that teens valued intimacy the most, followed by social status and sexual pleasure.[14] Girls, unsurprisingly, valued intimacy more, and sexually experienced teens reported valuing the intimacy and pleasure sex brought them more than sexually inexperienced teens expected. Again, these do not seem all that different from adult motivations.

On the other side of the issue, another University of California study of 612 high-school-age teens over a two-year period found *abstaining* from sexual activity carried a number of negative consequences that increased over time.[15] While nearly all teens reported both positive and negative consequences of abstaining, the "positive consequences ... dramatically decreased over time" while the "negative consequences ... steadily increased." Teens who abstained from sex increasingly felt less proud of themselves, less responsible, more left out, and more at odds with partners the longer they went without it. I suspect a lot of grownups could sympathize. Another study of 580 California teenagers aged 14 to 15 found those who either previously had sex or intended to in the near future were a lot more likely to have experienced (or to expect) positive results from sex such as pleasure, improved relationships, and feeling good about themselves than did teens who were virgins and expected to remain so. The two groups did not differ much in their appreciation of the risks of inter-course, such as disease or pregnancy, only in how they weighed the risks versus the benefits.[16]

The most reasonable conclusion, as it often turns out to be, is that teenagers are *individuals*. A garage full of studies reveals the wide diversity of teens' atti-tudes, expectations, and behaviors regarding sex. Large percentages do not have sex during adolescent years. Of those who do, it appears that a large majority of teens whose sexual experiences did not consist of rape found them enjoyable, even if including some downsides. Very few found consensual sex entirely negative. The reason that about half the number of teens have sex during high school years is—sit down for this shocker—because they thought they would like having sex, and it turns out a large majority did. The reason the other half, give or take, do not have sex is because they saw more benefits to retaining their virginity.

Unfortunately, acknowledging teenage individuality threatens the interests governing discussion of the issue who have attempted to impose strict, one-size-fits-all opprobrium on any teen having sex. I can not imagine any sexuality education curriculum acceptable to school boards in all but the most radical enclaves daring to explore pleasurable, relationship-building, and positive feelings resulting from school-age teens engaging in sexual activity—benefits sexually active teens find obvious.

In that vein, it may be puritanical American attitudes that are harshly con-demning of teen sex, rather than having sex per se, that causes regrets among some teens. Europeans (other than in the United Kingdom, whose views land somewhere between the United States and the Continent) tend to view ado-lescents as individuals, with true risk behaviors the object of state concern and non-risky behaviors tolerated, even approved.[17] Pierre-Andre Michaud, chief of the Multidisciplinary Unit for Adolescent Health at Switzerland's University of Lausanne Hospital and a leading teen sexuality researcher, noted that "in many European countries—Switzerland in particular—sexual intercourse, at least from the age of 15 or 16 years, is considered acceptable and even part of normative adolescent behavior."[18] Joan-Carles Surís, head of the research group on adolescent medicine at the University of

Lausanne, added, "The main difference is that in the States sexual activity is considered a risk. Here we consider it a pleasure." It appears most sexually active U.S. teenagers would agree.

The official American position—liberal, conservative, in between—is that no one under age 20 should ever have sex of any kind. For those who disagree with my characterization that the left-right position toward teenage sex is so absolutist, see how many positive references to real teenagers having real sex you can find by major players on any side in the debate. Then, note the universal deploring that reflexively greets survey findings that any teenagers at all say they have sex—even older teenagers, even the mildest contact. Note also how surveys showing any decline in the numbers of teenagers saying they are sexually active are greeted with left-to-right approval and efforts to grab credit.

TOUTING IRRELEVANCIES

Insistence that teenage sex is motivated by mass external pressures rather than individual, internal considerations is politically useful as well. In a lengthy November 3, 2008, *New Yorker* article, writer Margaret Talbot introduced the seemingly puzzling reaction by conservative Republicans to news that their vice presidential nominee's unwed 17 year-old daughter, Bristol Palin, was pregnant:

> Many liberals . . . expected the news to dismay the evangelical voters that John McCain was courting with his choice of [Sarah] Palin. Yet reports from the floor of the Republican convention, in St. Paul, quoted dozens of delegates who seemed unfazed, even buoyed, by the news.

Talbot interpreted this seeming paradox with an explanation that fits political zeitgeist:

> Social liberals . . . tend to support sex education and are not particularly troubled by the idea that many teen-agers have sex before marriage, but would regard a teen-age daughter's pregnancy as devastating news. And . . . social conservatives . . . generally advocate abstinence-only education and denounce sex before marriage, but are relatively unruffled if a teen-ager becomes pregnant, as long as she doesn't choose to have an abortion.[19]

I think a more careful analysis would show the dichotomy Talbot postulates understates the hypocritical way both sides exploit teen sex and pregnancy. Even a glance at right-wing Web sites shows mainstream conservatives do indeed deplore teen pregnancy and have supported the most punitive welfare and abstinence measures aimed at teenage mothers. However, they make quick-turn, cynical exceptions when their *own* conservative heroes and heroines are caught violating the Commandments, including their beloved vice presidential candidate's teen-daughter pregnancy. Similarly, a large proportion of liberal commentators, especially left-wing culture-warriors, harshly condemn all forms of teen sex, as is detailed throughout this book. One need go no further than the Clinton administration's and congressional Democrats' strong support for abstinence-only education, or SIECUS policy spokesman William Smith's testimony to a congressional committee in 2008 that a major goal of "comprehensive sex education" is to "help more young people abstain and delay sex."[20]

This seeming conservative/liberal dichotomy is not a moral or cultural divide, as Talbot postulates. In the practical, political world, teen sex and pregnancy are simply commodities available for expedient manipulation as needed to bludgeon the other side and gain political advantage. There is no ethical "principle" at work here.

It is true that there are a few on the Left, outside the mainstream, who fit Talbot's description. For example, in a remote section of the National Campaign Web site, I do find a favorable commentary by Liz Sabatiuk on a British pamphlet called *Pleasure*, which modestly discussed the positive side of masturbation (and still raised a hullaballoo). However, a few comments here and there by those rarely included in mainstream discussion do not offset the barrage of condemnation and failure to cite the favorable aspects of teen sex that characterize interest-group, author, and media discourse.

Worse, adults' personal difficulties seem connected to a growing meanness toward young people. Consider Westwood One's August 2, 2006, edition of *The Radio Factor*, in which the host Bill O'Reilly lambasted kidnapped, raped, and murdered 18 year-old Jessica Moore for "wearing a miniskirt and a halter top with a bare midriff." Likewise, of the abduction, confinement, violent abuse, and sexual abuse of Shawn Hornbeck, 15, over several years by a violent predator, O'Reilly opined this—all without an iota of evidence—on Fox News: "The situation here for this kid looks to me to be a lot more fun than what he had under his old parents. He didn't have to go to school. He could run around and do whatever he wanted . . . there was an element here that this kid liked about his circumstances."[21]

What warped thinking could motivate O'Reilly's despicable speculations? I can speculate, too. I suggest O'Reilly's gratuitous meanness reflected his effort to excuse and distract attention from his own sordid sexual transgressions sworn to in public court records—ones he, unlike victimized teenagers, had the lucre to pay millions of dollars in lawsuit settlements to flush away. To wit: on October 13, 2004, O'Reilly was sued in the Supreme Court of New York by Andrea Mackris, a former intern to President George W. Bush and then a producer at Fox News.[22] Mackris's lawsuit alleged that the married O'Reilly, her supervisor, made unsolicited, explicit comments to her, including repeated references to phone sex, vibrators, offers to have threesomes with her and her college friend, his numerous sexual dalliances and fantasies, his affinity for pornography, and explicit sexual stories (my favorite among the many was the "little brown woman" in Bali who was "amazed" at his prodigious endowment, which he elsewhere specified as his "big cock"), and, further, that he masturbated during many phone calls purportedly made to discuss her job and future career. These acts, the suit alleged, constituted criminal sexual harassment, since O'Reilly had supervisory authority over Mackris. "At all times . . . Defendant O'Reilly has held himself out to be a morally upright, independent political pundit," the suit deadpanned. Mackris provided excruciatingly detailed and lengthy quotes indicating she had recorded some conversations. O'Reilly complained the suit was a "shakedown" but paid, according to several press reports, $2 million to $10 million to settle it,[23] considerably more than the standard "make it go away" sum.

Wow! This sounds like exactly the kind of celebrity salaciousness a "culture warrior" network like Fox News normally would be hot to spread all over the screen (maybe via its famous "ambush journalism"). After all, O'Reilly had no problem digging into obscure young people's sex lives, as in *Sexting Shocker*, or *The Birds, the Bees, and CellPhones* in which he disgorged "outrage" at certain teens' audacity in sending sexy text messages to each other.[24] (Perhaps O'Reilly thinks they should be proposing threesomes during masturbatory phone sex instead.) Nor did MSNBC's sleazy *Caught on Camera*, one edition of which breathlessly peeps at teenagers' purported videos, or a host of other network and newspaper teen-sex splashes. Nor O'Reilly's May 22, 2009, show calling for a national investigation (by someone) of a few of teen singer Miley Cyrus's mildly sexy and patently nonsexy pictures and music videos he found sexually arousing.

Yet again, the double standard the news media reserves for its own stars' sex scandals compared to its fascination with "teen sex" reflects the power of the players, not their behaviors. Few teens have the privilege to lawyer up, negotiate a sex-suit payoff, then announce, as did O'Reilly, that his "ordeal is over" and "I will never speak of it again." This is exactly backwards. If anyone's sexual conduct should be investigated and detailed in national media features, it is that of the "values" types—the Bill Cosbys, the Dick Morrises (that former get-tough-on-teen-sex Clinton deputy, devotee of expensive prostitutes, and now Fox News commentator[25]), and other media stars and politicians who profit handsomely from posing week after week as moral leaders with a license to condemn lesser souls. The extremism and irrationality of O'Reilly's and other culture-war crusaders' self-righteous attacks on teenagers make their own records of morality relevant to discuss. The rise of the culture-war Left blaming corporate advertising and media for teenage sex has joined ongoing right-wing fears of minorities and youth to advance a unified agenda in which the positive aspects of youthful sexuality can barely be whispered.

THE KINDERGARTEN CROSS-DRESSING AGENDA

Gay young people are at the nexus of the culture war. The Center for Disease Control (CDC)'s 2009 survey found 4 percent of males and 8 percent of females age 15 to 17, and 5 percent of males and 14 percent of females age 18 to 19, reporting they had some kind of "sexual experience" with same-sex partners. What it was—hand-holding? golden shower?—was not specified. Among girls under age 18, both the prevalence and the proportion of sexual experiences consisting of same-sex contact appears two to three times higher than among boys.[26] (I would be amazed if that finding has not made it into some licentious hypocrite's prime-time bellowing.) As for real outcomes, the CDC reports that in 2006, approximately 2,900 men aged 20 to 24 were diagnosed as HIV/AIDS-positive from having same-sex relations, 10 times the number of men and 3.4 times the number of women aged 20 to 24 who contracted the disease from heterosexual sex.[27]

Thus, a rational sex education curriculum would include information on same-sex contact, but "gay teens are often left out of sex education," the GLBT Teens Web site laments.[28] Given charges by conservatives such as Thomas Sowell that sex education advocates intended to make "propaganda for homosexuality . . . one of the hallmarks of American education" and Robert Simonds, president of the National Association of Christian Educators, to promote "homosexual/lesbian recruitment of children in the classroom,"[29] even staunch sex-ed backers have proven reluctant to raise the topic. Congressional efforts led by Republicans and conservative Democrats sought to deny funding to schools whose classes "would tend to denigrate, diminish, or deny the differences between the sexes as they have historically been understood in the United States" (whatever that meant) and to prohibit government benefits for anyone who held that homosexuality could be "an acceptable alternative lifestyle."

A major example conservatives cite of gay penetration into classrooms was clarioned in a May 7, 2002, *Fox News* reporter-outrage on the "homosexual agenda in the schools:"

WASHINGTON — Jesse's Dream Skirt is causing a stir in California. For one, he's a little boy wearing a skirt.

Second, he's part of an elementary school plan designed by activists pushing for acceptance of the transgender lifestyle.

But Jesse is just one of the more outrageous examples of the "gay agenda" infiltrating the public school systems across the country today, according to a group gathered at a Washington seminar on Monday.

Standing before a picture of the be-skirted Jesse, Robert H. Knight, director of the Culture and Family Institute, said parents are not being told the truth about what their young children learn in school today. "If most parents understood the depth of the homosexual agenda in the schools," he argued, "there would be a revolution."

> Knight joined representatives of other groups in denouncing what they called a massive effort on the part of groups like the Gay, Lesbian and Straight Education Network (GLSEN) to promote the homosexual lifestyle, using "diversity," safety and anti-discrimination programs as a stalking horse.[30]

The *Fox* story and fear-lobby materials failed to make it clear the menacingly swirly Jesse was *not a real boy in a real school*. He and his Dream Skirt were fictional characters in a 1979 story suggested by a gay rights group for inclusion in school curriculums. None of the outraged protesters I could find alleging public schools' deep homosexual agenda named any schools that had adopted the story and its "kindergarten cross-dressing" message in the three decades since. Or why, to borrow from Monty Python, it couldn't be construed as an alien plot to turn children into Scotsmen.

No matter. Beskirted Jesse revealed a master plan to "lure a whole generation of young people to explore 'alternative' sexual behavior" and "discover their 'gay side'" so that "radical homosexual activists . . . will have a whole new generation of young, willing sex partners," Concerned Women for America charged.[31] The paralyzing rage right-wing lobbies—not just fringe groups, but mainstream conservatives—hurled at a picture of a small boy in a skirt (like fearsome sodomites Bert & Ernie, Spongebob, and Tinky Winky) was just another face of anti-sex-education and homophobic groups' toxic lunacy.

Fear of the "homosexual agenda in schools" would prove so potent that organizers of referendums to repeal or ban gay marriage found from surveys that their zingiest talking point was that legalization would open the door to schools teaching "gay lifestyles" to students. How this would transpire was never made clear. Schools in gay-legal Vermont, Massachusetts, and Iowa had not turned schools into Man-Boy-Love bathhouses. Regardless of relevance or veracity, however, the baffling argument that schools are champing to queer up your kid resonated with a large chunk of liberal and moderate voters. In California, the same electorate that supported Barack Obama for president over John McCain by a 61-percent-to-39-percent margin passed Proposition 8, which banned gay marriage. A similar result occurred on Question 1 in Maine in 2009, a state that also had voted overwhelmingly for Obama. To date, every state that has voted on gay marriage, from Mississippi to Oregon, has rejected the idea by margins far exceeding those conservative voters alone could muster.

Why do even moderate Democratic voters fear schools might teach homosexuality to students? It should be remembered that for all their rabid disagreement on gay rights, liberals and conservatives share *a common attitude about children and teens*. From leftist culture-warriors such as the Media Education Foundation to moderate institutes like Rand Corporation to far-right lobbies like the Parents Television Council (see Chapter 6), the view is that young people will seek out the most objectionable image the media, advertisers, or schools present to them and rush en masse to ape it in the most self-destructive way possible. Those who believe a Victoria's Secret ad will turn girls into spiky-heeled sluts share a remarkably similar mindset with those who believe a school health curriculum with a few paragraphs on homosexuality will convert teens into Ross Matthews flameboys.

Fortunately, these attitudes seem to be changing with startling rapidity. CNN's exit poll found 61 percent of California's voters under age 30 voted to affirm gay marriage in the 2008 election, including 67 percent of young whites and 59 percent of young Latinos. In contrast, just 45 percent of voters age 30 and older and 39 percent age 65 and older supported gay marriage rights.[32] Estimates for young African Americans were not reported separately, though older blacks overwhelmingly opposed gay marriage. Polls in Maine likewise showed voters under 30 strongly in favor of gay rights as older voters were strongly opposed.[33]

In such a climate, any public school that discusses homosexuality or gay behaviors with open-minded recognition of the diversity of lifestyles—let alone one that presents objective information affirming benefits and not just risks—is likely to face national condemnation and punishment. The constriction of public discussion of teens and sex, especially gay sex and varied lifestyles, into a constant drumbeat of negativism, alarm, and propaganda demonstrates again that the wide-open Internet is a far better venue to promote modern sex education than compromised legislatures and schools. The apparently widespread and visceral fears harbored by many Americans and fanned by interest groups on all sides has now culminated in a complete unraveling of discussions of teenage sex and pregnancy in the 1990s, the subject of the next chapter.

Chapter Five

THE "TEEN SEX" DEBATE UNHINGES

By the 1990s, teenage sex and teen pregnancy had entered the realm of cultural icon, like the Marlboro Man and Barbie, available for whatever molding suited various interests. For the record, from 1990 to 2005, births among married teenagers and adults of all ages plummeted sharply,[1] along with abortions and total pregnancies.[2] These are crucial trends, particularly in their unexpected patterns, and analysis would have yielded vital insights into real (as opposed to iconic) cultural trends and the potential for more realistic policies. Do the drop in teen pregnancy and rise in unwed births among all ages largely reflect the march toward family doom, as conservatives allege, or are they necessary shifts accompanying women's expanded roles of society and the demise in traditional careers?

Among teen-sex lobbies, these questions mattered less and less. In previous decades, right-wing anti-sex-education troops had floated all kinds of lurid tales. Even so, I argue, information issued by the Alan Guttmacher Institute (AGI) and Planned Parenthood remained largely cautious and reasoned. For example, former AGI director Jeannie I. Rosoff acknowledged in 1990 that "most of the programs we have had have been preaching sex education" even though "we now know increasing knowledge does not necessarily affect behavior." The claim that sex education is the remedy for teen pregnancy persists, she said, because "sex education is something we know how to do."[3] Indeed, reviews of decades of research found "none of the dozens of studies by sociologists, psychologists, and educators has discovered that sex education has a significant effect in either direction on adolescent rates of intercourse, use of contraception, and rates of unwanted pregnancies and births."[4] Later claims by both sexuality and abstinence advocates that newer studies, often by partisans, do find effects for their favored approaches should be met with a great deal of skepticism, as detailed in Chapter 10.

Liberals' more reasoned approaches to sexuality and sex education had failed in the political arena. Now moderates and liberals, swept into office in the Clinton era, fed up with losing to hysteria, joined conservatives in abandoning truthfulness, opening wide the floodgates of bipartisan distortion and formalizing the triumph of privatized social policy as a wholly owned subsidiary of the culture war.

THE DEMISE OF PROGRESSIVE SOCIAL ADVOCACY

Chief among the liberal capitulations to conservative ideology was the Clinton administration's acceptance that overly generous welfare, principally the now-dismantled federal Aid to Families with Dependent Children (AFDC) program, had subsidized a new epidemic of unwed mothers who wantonly disdained men because the government bestowed big checks for spewing "illegitimate" babies. Sociologist Charles Murray, in *Losing Ground* (1984),[5] advanced the thesis on the Right that welfare was driving rising unwed motherhood, and in the 1990s liberals, led by President Bill Clinton, announced that Murray was "essentially right." The consensus villain would be teenage mothers, even though they comprised only a fraction of unmarried mothers.

In particular, Clinton's "Democratic Family Values" crusade popularized the patent fiction that generous welfare was spurring rebellious teen girls to have babies so they could move out from under wise Mom and Dad's strict morals to set up their own dens of immorality.[6] Abstinence advocates, led by Clinton himself, urged teens to wait to have sex until they were married. The president's Welfare Reform Task Force formed in 1994 urged public campaigns and welfare restrictions against teen mothers. Clinton's kickoff address, to black high schoolers in Washington, D.C.'s destitute Anacostia district, won swooning press coverage—*The Nation*'s Alexander Cockburn was a scathing exception[7]—as it adroitly spelled out just who was spawning the "epidemic."[8] The press reverberated with cloned articles branding unwed teen mothers as the genesis of all social ills. ABC News's Diane Sawyer (the fortunate daughter of a wealthy judge) confronted teen mothers as selfish and lacking moral values.[9] The newly formed National Campaign to Prevent Teen Pregnancy launched a crusade to stem the "epidemic." It was nasty stuff, and the loudest demands for "personal responsibility" often emanated from politicians and other commentators whose own personal records fell far short of responsible.

Factually, just about no research supported the joint "Democratic Family Values" and Republican "Contract with America" consensus that emerged in the mid-1990s to blame and punish teenage mothers. All one had to do to demolish the welfare-breeds-breeding argument was to assemble a spreadsheet presenting AFDC and welfare payments by state and era alongside unwed birth rates, percentages of births to unwed parents, and whatever other indexes were of interest. They consistently showed that the *higher* the rate of welfare benefits (in real dollars, or as a percentage of the state's median income), the *lower* the rate of unwed births and births by teen mothers.[10]

For example, in 1990, Connecticut offered a welfare package (AFDC, food stamps, school lunch program, and Medicaid) to low-income families that totaled $10,300 per year, while Mississippi's welfare package totaled a paltry $3,400 per year. So, did Connecticut teens rush to bear bastard spawn to cash in while Mississippi teens clapped their knees together? Just the opposite. Mississippi's teen birth rate was 2.5 times higher than Connecticut's. Further, unwed parenthood had risen over the previous 25 years as AFDC payments in real dollars fell sharply.

Nor did anyone provide credible evidence for another key tenet of the Clinton-era "personal responsibility" platform: that AFDC and other programs benefiting poor children incite teens to get pregnant to move away from home. A 1990 Congressional Budget Office report found that fewer than 4 percent of mothers under age 18 lived on their own away from older adults, and those who did were unable to live with parents due to abuse and family troubles.[11] The cruelty of the Democratic-Family-Values/Contract-with-America bipartisanship was delineated in a 1994 Government Accounting Office report, *Can They Go Home Again?*, which found no evidence that welfare induced teen mothers to leave home, and a Center for Law and Social Policy analysis concluding that forcing the small number of independent teen mothers back home would effectively force "a minor teen mother to return to an abusive environment."[12] Even Murray himself, in a remarkably analytical 1994 research update, admitted he was largely wrong: welfare *doesn't* cause much unwed or teen procreation after all.[13] Clinton's free-living teen welfare queen of 1995 was as much a figment as Ronald Reagan's black welfare queen.

The refusal to talk about adult fathers remained vehement and bipartisan, from Clinton's profoundly limited Health and Human Services Secretary Donna Shalala (who would only speak ill of "teen girls" who "become pregnant") to Republican welfare reform leader, then-Representative Clay Shaw of Florida, who argued for punishing teen girls who "sleep with someone" and "get pregnant." On both sides of the aisle, I found (and the press reported) that by "personal responsibility," Congress and the White House meant only by teenagers—that is, girls and, occasionally, boys.[14]

No one in power much cared what "research" was finding. The entire 1990s attack on teen mothers was founded in demonstrable falsehoods, many preposterous. The Clinton-Republican "Personal Responsibility and Work Opportunity Reconciliation Act of 1996" passed the Congress handily and went about its bipartisan mission of replacing the tide of illegitimacy with tough new government sanctions to uphold traditional marriage. How did that work out? Not like anyone planned—but again, barely anyone cared.

From 1990 to 2005, the rate of teen pregnancy did decline sharply to the lowest level since the first statistics were compiled in 1973. Most celebrated by all interests was the 50 percent decline in the rate of births by mothers younger than 20 to the lowest level since around 1940. All sides, from abstinence promoters to sex educators to welfare reformers and especially the National Campaign, rushed to claim credit for it.

But, as Table 5.1 shows, there was an unexpected aspect to the decline that no one seemed eager to admit, let alone own: *the entire* decline in teen births occurred among *married* teen women.[15] In 1990, the Centers for Disease Control reported, 41 percent of married teen women gave birth; in 2008, 24 percent, a record fertility decline in a very short period.[16] In raw numbers, 360,000 unwed teens had babies in 1990; in 2008, 383,000. Similarly, in 1990, 805,000 unwed adult women age 20 and older gave birth; in 2008, 1,345,000. Meanwhile, births by married teens dropped by 115,000 and births by married adults dropped by nearly 400,000.

This was not supposed to happen! How did massive, coordinated campaigns by abstinence, sexuality education, welfare reformers, and the mass media

Table 5.1   Teen Birth Rates Declined from 1990 to 2005, Then Rose Slightly

	Births Per 1,000 Females		Birth rate per 1,000 teens		Number of births	
	10–14	15–19	Married	Unwed	Married	Unwed
1990	1.4	59.9	410.4	43.8	172,838	360,645
1995	1.3	56.8	319.5	43.7	124,936	387,179
2000	0.8	47.7	276.8	39.9	99,924	377,585
2005	0.7	40.2	292.5	34.9	69,312	352,003
2008	0.6	41.1	241.7	37.1	57,996	382,779
Change, 1990–2008	−58%	−31%	−41%	−15%	−66%	+6%

Source: Ventura, Abma, Mosher, & Henshaw (2009). Births for 2008 are from just-released update: B. E. Hamilton, J. A. Martin, and S. J. Ventura (2010). *Births: Preliminary Data for 2008*. National Vital Statistics Reports, 58:16 (April 2010).

aimed at promoting marriage and reducing "unwed teenage childbearing" wind up being followed by a huge drop in *marital* childbearing? Married teen mothers averaged 18.5 years old, with husbands around 22 years old—pretty much the Jimmy Carter-Rosalynn Carter model and not exactly the teens the abstinence-until-marriage folks had in mind.

WHY ARE MARRIED TEENS HAVING FEWER BABIES?

Traditionally, teenage women got married, mostly to adult men, to establish a household and to get pregnant or "legitimize" a pregnancy. Yet, census figures showed teen marriage was changing rapidly. Rising numbers of married teens did not live with their spouses, not because of separations but developments possibly related to employment or education. Mothers age 20 and older also trended away from marital childbearing, also for reasons not entirely clear.

The plummet in births by married teens provided a rich area for research . . . yet, none of the groups I am aware of chose even to acknowledge it. Nowhere does the National Campaign's Web site mention the astonishing drop in annual marital teen births, from 173,000 in 1990 to 58,000 in 2008 even as unwed teen births increased by 22,000. My contacts with a few luminaries in the field indicated just about no interest, and the reason was painfully obvious. None could figure out how this unexpected trend could contribute to their agendas, and so for their purposes, it did not exist. "Unexpected" generally equates with "threatening" in the privatized social policy world. It would be very difficult to explain why abstinence-until-marriage, school sexuality, welfare reform, and other anti-teen-pregnancy measures proved an astounding 35 times more effective in deterring childbearing among the married teens they did not target than among the unwed teens on which prevention measures were concentrated.

Nor would it be easy for interests, despite vigorous official efforts to strengthen marriage, to explain why strong trends toward unwed parenthood *continued unabated* among both teens and adults. In fact, one would think welfare reformers, social policy interests, and culture warriors had united to *destroy* marriage. Given the contrary realities evident in solid vital statistics reports, all interests squared their shoulders and . . . resolutely ignored reality. This was yet another crucially important trend that privatized social policy interests simply were not positioned to deal with. Thus, interests dominating "teen pregnancy" discussion effectively banished unwanted realities from media discussion—not by overt conspiracy, but simply because no one would profit from talking about them. Unmoored from rational, scientific discussion, the teen-sex and teen-pregnancy debate has continued its post-1990 drift toward narrowness, unreality, and meanness.

THE RISE OF BAD "RESEARCH"

When the history is written as to why late twentieth and early twenty-first century social science research went so badly wrong, the self-reporting survey may be singled out as the flawed method behind the madness. So, let us examine this notoriously weak, easily biased research tool that has become the workhorse of supposedly scientific commentary on youth. When the statements lobbies and news reports make about teens are based on any investigation at all, it nearly always consists of surveys.

Yet, I doubt any objective scientist could explain what overamped surveys really tell us. Interest groups and media reporters do not seem to care whether 1 percent or 91 percent of young people admit to whatever behavior is being surveyed, or whether the scary behavior consists of sending an email emoticon or jumping into a twenty-way orgy. If 6 percent of girls under age 14 say they have had sex, *all* girls are branded the "Sex at 13 Generation," as one celebrated Christian book title put it. No one seems to care that how many teens tell surveys they are having what kind of sex today compared to whatever teens of the past said they did has nothing to do with levels or trends in teen pregnancies, abortions, diseases, rapes, or anything else important.

To measure behavior in a population accurately, a sample must be carefully constructed to represent the larger population studied. In a self-reporting survey, respondents in the sample are given a series of questions to answer about their own behaviors. Even if they correctly understand the questions, lots of biasing factors, not always obvious, lead subjects to over-report or under-report certain behaviors. Many surveys may be useless in that the behaviors they measure bear no relation to outcomes of interest. If wealthy Marin County, California, teenagers say they are twice as likely to have sex as teens elsewhere in the state yet have pregnancy, birth, and STD rates well below the state average, does that mean more sex by rich teens produces fewer sexual outcomes than less sex by poorer teens? (That's a great question, by the way, among many that interest groups do not pursue.) If Hispanic boys surveyed by the Centers for Disease Control report three times more sex by age 14 than Hispanic girls that age, yet California birth records show Hispanic girls have 18 times more babies by age 15 than are fathered by Hispanic boys their age, what have we learned? That boys exaggerate and girls demur? (Are not today's shameless girls supposed to be proud of their sexups?) That middle-school boys are fantastically more adept at contraception than older males? *What?*

A half-century of research led by social science's arch-methods-analysts Thomas Cook and Donald Campbell have identified weaknesses in the survey method that are devastating.[17] (Cook and Campbell even issued a tongue-in-cheek essay on how interests could manipulate apparently "scientific" surveys to produce any desired result.) These natural weaknesses of surveys are troubling enough. But when worded and administered by proprietary researchers expecting or seeking a particular result, surveys bombard respondents with powerful cues called "demand characteristics" that push them to provide answers that are pleasing to the researchers' hypothesis. These surveys balloon into outright fraud when "researchers" are paid to help an interest prove something.

The bulk of surveys today are not designed to pinpoint teen behaviors, but to produce the most alarming numbers possible. You do not get funding or grants in today's highly competitive fiscal climate by finding that teens do not really have burgeoning problems in the area you are asking for money to address. Afterward, it helps to have researchers who reliably "find" that your approach works to stem the teen crisis previously uncovered . . . as long as they also find sequel crises requiring more funding to fix.

After analyzing dozens of these (including for this book), I can safely say: interest-group surveys today are a racket. Many are so crudely biased as to be jokes. In a growing survey-fraud trifecta, biased wording is combined with biased method and alarmist media publicity to create the image of giant teen "crises." Those who produce, publicize, and apply warped surveys that wildly exaggerate teen problems should be called what they are: frauds, bullies, and profiteers.

WHEN NOT TO BELIEVE SURVEYS

Surveys are not always warped and wrong. So, how do we know which ones to credit and which to disdain? Analyzing survey validity requires, at the least, actually *obtaining* a copy of the survey questions, details on how the subject sample was drawn, the methods by which the survey was administered, the statistical techniques used to total the responses and account for missing data, and the way conclusions were derived from the findings. When published in journals, at least some of this information should be available, but publication itself is no guarantee of validity. Journals can be lousy at evaluating surveys; *Pediatrics* is only one among the worst examples. The American Academy of Pediatrics has staked out blaming the media for youth behaviors as one of its political wedge issues, rendering many media and culture-war studies published in the lobby's journal unusually dubious.

Even worse are the surveys administered in-house by interest groups, which typically issue alarming press releases hyping their results and praising themselves. Kaiser Family Foundation, RAND Corporation, Liz Claiborne Inc., Center on Addiction and Substance Abuse at Columbia University, the National Campaign to Prevent Teen and Unplanned Pregnancy, and other interests regularly issue in-house surveys of teens that are subjected to zero peer review. However difficult it is to evaluate their results independently from the scant information these groups typically provide, such survey findings inevitably support the interest group's agendas. I evaluate a few of these interest-driven surveys later. Make no mistake, this is reprehensible stuff. The research community needs to evolve sterner ethics to curb interest-group and hired-gun academic studies, particularly those afforded media accolades.

Then there are agency surveys such as the Centers for Disease Control's, which usually (though not always) observe higher standards but still require close reading to discern what they actually show—or do not show. For example, do you see some discrepancies in the proportions of school-age teenagers who, as reported by the 2009 Centers for Disease Control teen-risk report,[18] say they have had sex by age, gender, and race (Table 5.2)?

Note that black and Hispanic males report having had vastly more sex, especially at younger ages, than both white males and females of their races. Hispanic 14-year-old boys reported having had three times more sex than Hispanic 14-year-old girls. Now, it is technically possible to construct a scenario to justify these extreme puzzlers. Perhaps a small number of younger teen girls are really getting around. Or, perhaps black and Hispanic teen males have been having great sexual success with older women (¡Oye!). Or, perhaps far more black and Hispanic teens have homosexual relations than suspected.

Table 5.2   Percentages of U.S. Teens Age 15 to 19 Who Said They Had Sex by Ages 14, 15, and 17, by Race and Gender

	All	White	Black	Hispanic
Had sex by age 14				
Female	5.7%	5.3%	13.8%	4.9%
Male	8.0%	4.3%	24.2%	14.8%
Male:Female ratio	1.40	0.81	1.75	3.02
Had sex by age 15				
Female	13.1%	12.0%	22.2%	14.2%
Male	14.8%	9.9%	35.9%	23.3%
Male:Female ratio	1.13	0.83	1.62	1.64
Had sex by age 17				
Female	44.4%	40.4%	53.1%	47.7%
Male	40.0%	36.0%	65.2%	55.2%
Male:Female ratio	0.90	0.89	1.23	1.16

Source: Centers for Disease Control (2009).

Or, perhaps younger black and Hispanic girls are denying their dalliances, though black 14-year-old girls report having had *three times* more sex than white 14-year-old *boys*. Or, maybe white boys are pretending to chastity to be like the Jonas Brothers . . . right.

All this young-male sex is occurring amid some fairly solid outcome statistics showing that younger girls' rates of birth and STD are far higher for every race than among boys their age, indicating sex with considerably older males. For example, California figures indicate that while Hispanic girls under age 15 had 185 babies in 2002, Hispanic boys under age 15 fathered just 10.[19] National STD reports for 2008 find the infection rate for Hispanic girls age 10 to 14 (127 cases per 100,000 population) much higher than for Hispanic boys that age (14 per 100,000).[20] A similar young-female surplus in births and STD cases compared to young males exists for other races/ethnicities. So, we would have to conclude that if middle-school males really are having lots of sex with middle-school females, younger males are far more responsible in causing fewer pregnancies and diseases than older teen and adult males who have sex with middle-school age girls are.

We can lie and fantasize and indulge Rube Goldberg convolutions . . . or we can surrender to the most likely option: younger black and Hispanic males are exaggerating their sexual achievements . . . drastically. But, no. Instead of assessing how these large inconsistencies by race and gender affect the basic validity and usefulness of sex surveys, officials simply mash these confusingly disparate patterns into an amalgamation they call "teenage sex."

Just as surveys are slanted to disparage powerless groups, they also flatter popular prejudices and powerful interests. A big example was the popular *Sex in America* survey of the early 1990s, which at every stage was biased to show that American adults were moral and sexually responsible (*see sidebar*). Indeed, as its surveyors acknowledged, politicians led by then Senator Jesse Helms had threatened to slash the funding of researchers who found that American adults were promiscuous.

Even if an observer cannot get at the inner workings of a survey, there are ways to assess its validity. What kinds of visible, measurable behaviors would we *expect* to be seeing if, in fact, "one in four children is sexually solicited online" and masses of predators are stalking "your teens" in every community? If "teenage dating violence" truly menaces four in 10, or eight in 10, youths as young as 'tween years? If watching the mildly sexy television shows that have proliferated over the last 15 years effectively doubles the numbers of teen pregnancies? If epidemics of teenagers "sexting" and bullying each other via cell phones have erupted? If mindless, loveless, dangerous, narcissistic "hookup culture" has replaced the safer, sweet "teenage romances" of the past?

The answers are stark: we would expect to see exploding epidemics of teenagers being murdered, suffering rape and sexual attacks, getting pregnant,

SEX IN AMERICA: EXAMPLE OF A BIASED SURVEY

In 1994, America's news media trumpeted the most "definitive" survey of American adult sexuality, dubbed *Sex in America*.[21] The survey of 3,400 adults ages 18–59 provided wonderfully optimistic support for politicians' "family values" campaigns of the 1990s: it found adults were chaste, few had been promiscuous, very few were gay, nearly all were faithful to marriages, and few had had abortions and sexually-transmitted diseases. Unfortunately, some checking (which few in the media bothered with) showed the survey was a bit too optimistic. For example, the proportions of pregnancies ended by abortion (just 13 percent) that the subjects in the *Sex and America* survey reported predicted about 700,000 to 800,000 abortions every year. In fact, abortion providers reported an average of 1.5 million a year during that time, terminating 25% of all pregnancies. Similarly, *Sex in America* reported just one in six adults had any history of STDs, predicting about 250,000 cases per year, fewer than half the annual number of STD cases actually diagnosed (and confirmed diagnoses represent substantial underreporting of true STD rates). The survey also reported substantially fewer rapes by men and extramarital affairs than other surveys have.

How did these discrepancies occur? Checking the survey's method revealed that surveyors relied on personal interviews rather than anonymous paper surveys that can be filled out confidentially. Worse, a substantial number of subjects were asked potentially compromising questions *in front of other people*, most notably their spouses! These methods would encourage substantial underreporting of disapproved behaviors such as infidelity, STD, and rape, which the results reflected. *Sex in America's* authors were keenly aware of the dismissal of previous surveys—from Kinsey's 1952 report on female sexuality that was condemned by Congress to the 1987 National Institutes of Health survey that was derailed by Congress because it was expected to reveal substantial promiscuity among American adults. Clearly, unwanted findings on American adult morality are not wanted, even as alarms about rampant teenage promiscuity are welcomed.

---

being abducted and raped and killed by online predators in every community, reporting tremendous fears of their peers and devastating personal shame, and on and on. We would expect huge, erupting crises among younger and younger teens everywhere.

Yet, public health, crime, behavior, and other long-term statistics show nothing of the sort is happening. Kids are getting better and safer in virtually every way we can measure. Statistics, of course, are not everything, but when a variety of statistical sources that have reasonable completeness consistently contradict alarming survey findings, there are reasons to question the surveys. Unfortunately, more often, the malleable numbers surveys generate are used as excuses to ignore or downplay hard statistics, lending an unreal nature to public discussions of teenage issues.

"PROBLEM INFLATION" TRICKS

A common survey scam is to employ "problem inflators" that rope expanded age groups, harmless behaviors, rare behaviors, and speculative behaviors to grossly expand teen-problem numbers. We will see many, many, many of these. An example among hundreds is the junk survey by Kaiser Family Foundation and Joseph Califano, Jr.'s Center on Addiction and Substance Abuse (CASA) whose media-friendly design wildly exaggerated how many teens have sex after using drugs or drinking alcohol.

When this 2002 study accompanying a conference titled, *Dangerous Liaisons: Substance Abuse and Sexual Behavior*,[22] was released, the news media rang with trumpetings that 50 percent! 73 percent! even 89 percent!! of various classes of teens were indulging in drunken, drugged sex. "Millions of young people mix sex with alcohol or drugs," Califano's press release[23] screamed. "Study: Teen-agers often mix unsafe sex with drink, drugs," CNN proclaimed in typically slavish newsbray.

Neither CASA's press statements nor news reports mentioned what Kaiser's survey for CASA really found: *fewer than 5 percent of senior high school students reported ever having had unprotected sex after using drugs or alcohol, even one time.*[24] What a miserably disappointing result! So, Kaiser and CASA applied timeworn numbers-inflating tricks:

- The "age inflator." Teens, especially high schoolers, often yield low behavior risk numbers that really show how responsible most are. Bummer! So, Kaiser lumped 15 to 17 year-olds with adults ages 18 to 24 (an age group five times more likely to report having boozy sex than high schoolers) and trusted the press to call them "teenagers."
- The "behavior inflator." Because truly risky behaviors are quite rare among youths, harmless behaviors are included to puff up the numbers. In this case, Kaiser included non-risky sex, such as long-term and married couples'.
- The "one-time inflator." Real risk is defined by those who repeatedly or routinely engage in risky behavior. These numbers tend to be disappointingly small. So, Kaiser whooped numbers for one-time, never repeated behavior (even if it occurred years ago).
- The "guess-about-peers inflator." This is a classic. If one couple in a school of 200 students engages in a risky behavior, that is just 1 percent, but if 50 others found out about it, that makes it 25 percent! Ask youths vague questions about what some unspecified number in their entire generation *might* do, and still higher numbers are guaranteed. That is why Kaiser invited young people to speculate about whether "people my age" (whoever that is) mix drinking and sex "a lot" (whatever that means).
- The "risky subgroup inflator." Among all teens, risks typically are low, but among certain subgroups, such as sexually active teens who use alcohol and drugs, the percentage displaying the risk in question will be much higher. So, Kaiser high-lighted subgroup risk numbers and let the press run with them.

Presto! What should have been the real, maximum estimate of the risk fraction—the 5 percent (of 15 to 17 year-olds who admit ever having had unprotected sex after using alcohol or drugs)—was artificially ballooned to "as many as 89 percent" (of *sexually active* 15 to 24 year-olds who *speculated* that people "my age" *might* drink or use drugs and have sex "a lot"). That is a completely meaningless statistic. The only shocker is that 11 percent of young people thought *no one* their age could possibly have drunken sex.

As always, the press clarioned the heliumed numbers and thus joined Califano and Kaiser's noble efforts to convince both the public and youths themselves that wanton drunkenness, drugging, and sex are normal adolescent behaviors. Fortunately, the vast majority of young people ignored that toxic message.

Another shameful example involved a Centers for Disease Control "study" generating the widely publicized claim that "one in four teen girls has a sexually-transmitted disease."[25] A host of cloned media reports featured this report as "alarming," "shocking," "startling," and other boilerplate gaspings. "Startling government research on teenage girls and sexually transmitted diseases sends a blunt message to kids who think they're immune: It's liable to happen to you or someone you know," led the formulaically brainless March 11, 2008, *Associated Press* story.[26]

But did reporters actually read this study? Could anyone actually find it? My queries to CDC turned up nothing but a chart; no information on how the 838 girls were selected or screened, or what rates were among 18 to 19 year-olds versus the high schoolers the media berated. The scant information provided indicated that virtually all the STDs girls contracted were extremely common, low-level ones such as human papillomavirus (found in 18% of girls studied); all other STDs trailed far behind, affecting at most 2 percent to 4 percent of girls. Sadly, rates among 14- to 17-year-old girls would be very low. Worse, STD rates among African-American girls 2.5 times higher than whites and Latinas revealed the unwanted complication of poverty's contribution to disease. But, bless their hearts, all the Associated Press reporter and sources wanted to talk about was pop culture and sex-versus-abstinence education.

WHEN TO BELIEVE SURVEYS

It also should be noted that self-reporting surveys—done conscientiously by unbiased technicians, checked carefully for threats to validity, replicated in various settings, and matched for consistency with other reliable data— can be valuable research tools. When researchers make their surveys transparent by providing key details and taking effective steps to control for validity, we can have more confidence in them. One clear feature of good research is the authors' conscientious efforts to include questions, procedures, and conclusions likely to elicit information that might *contradict* their hypothesis. Unfortunately, carefully done surveys that include counter information rarely garner sensational political and media attention—often because their findings are much more calming about teenagers than interests want. So, we do not hear much about them. For example, surveys showing that very few teenagers suffer disastrously negative experiences with sex, detailed in Chapter 4, or that very few college girls really are depressed (see Chapter 8) get little notice.

The other way to credit good surveys is the same as used to discredit bad surveys: how well do self-reported attitudes and behaviors comport with *measurable real-life evidence*? If, for example, high school and college girls report to consistent, long-term surveys that they are happier, more optimistic, safer, readier for leadership, less "narcissistic," and more affectionate toward their friends today, what kinds of results would we expect to see in real life? For starters, we would expect other measures to show few, and fewer, murders, rapes, suicides, other violent deaths, assaults and violence (by both peers and "predators"), addictions, pregnancies, and so forth, and more girls graduating, going to college, achieving academically, and getting jobs. If more girls to say "I plan to go to college," we would not expect rising numbers of births by high school mothers and school dropouts.

Once again, we are not looking for an isolated number dredged up from here or there to sustain or dispute this or that survey finding, but consistency from a variety of sources. So, when our most reliable, non-interest-group surveys of young people such as Monitoring the Future[27] and The American Freshman[28] report generally optimistic trends in self-reported attitudes and behaviors among girls (and, to a lesser extent, boys), what do we find "on the ground"? We find, from a variety of measures, exactly the kinds of reductions in violence, early pregnancy, self-destructive outcomes, and dropout rates, and impressively more female achievement and fulfillment in real "body counts" that girls' optimistic self reports predict.

Bad research ethics, misuse of surveys, and problem-inflator scams produced a wealth of scary "findings" during the 1990s and 2000s that helped manufacture and maintain fear and outrage toward young people. These fed, and were fed by, the growing political climate in which politicians and interest groups across the political continuum sought to exploit young people for their own ends. Might as well start with fellatio.

THE ORAL SEX PANIC

As one interest put it in a 2000 report, teens are "experimenting with a wider range of behaviors at progressively younger ages," specifically oral sex. What evidence did this interest group offer? "Growing evidence, although still anecdotal and amassed largely by journalists."[29] In other words, *no evidence.* Was the interest spreading baseless fear of teen sex a right-wing lobby? No. It was the Alan Guttmacher Institute, which champions progressive, research-based sexuality policies. Why on earth was AGI fueling more fear, based on the worthless sensationalism of America's news media?

Any excuse to indulge lurid speculations about young-teen sex ignites a media stampede, and what better titillater than oral sex? "The Face of Teenage Sex Grows Younger," the *New York Times* announced in an April 2, 2000, front-pager.[30] The *Times* presented no evidence for that statement beyond crap quips by a Manhattan psychologist that oral sex "is like a goodnight kiss to them [middle schoolers]." The *Washington Post Magazine's* July 16, 2000, issue quivered with the "unsettling new fad" of oral sex indulged by "about half" of middle schoolers.[31] Evidence: zero. The *Post's* obsession with young-teen fellating in article after baseless article was disturbingly pedophilic. Talk-hostess supreme Oprah Winfrey, on her April 29, 2002, show on ABC, invited adult guests to deplore "the epidemic of oral sex in junior high." Evidence: zero. "The sexual revolution hits junior high," *USA Today* breathed in a March 15, 2002, front-pager.[32] Evidence: zero. "Increasingly, kids are turning to sexual behaviors that were once considered taboo," blared *U.S. News & World Report's* May 27, 2002, cover story: "They're Starting Earlier. The Growing Health Risks."[33] Let us take a quick glance at what passes for "facts" to such media writers and editors—in this case, *U.S. News* reporter Anna Mulrine:

> Kids from all walks of life are having sex at younger and younger ages—nearly one in 10 reports losing his or her virginity before the age of 13, a 15 percent increase since 1997, according to the Centers for Disease Control and Prevention. Some 16 percent of high school sophomores have had four or more sexual partners.

But *U.S. News's* own sources for this panic-mongering, the CDC's numbers for teens having sex by age, exposed the magazine reporter's and editors' abject lying (Table 5.3). Such junk-journalism relies on no one actually fact-checking the lurid tales.

What CDC really found is that the percentages of high schoolers reporting having had sex at least once, having had sex with four or more partners, and having had sex before age 13 all *declined* from the early 1990s to the late 1990s. Teens were having *less* sex with *fewer* partners and at *older* ages. Instead, *U.S. News* ignored this larger trend and fixated on the brief increase only from 1997 to 1999, rounded up 8.3 percent to "nearly one in 10," and then fabricated an "urgent" new crisis. Yet, when the next CDC survey showed a 20 percent *drop* in teens having sex before age 13 *to a level 35 percent below 1991's rate*, and drops in multiple partners and high school sex as well, big media went silent.

U.S. News and others also could have noted that the CDC survey found that far from affecting "kids from all walks of life," black youth were *four times*

Table 5.3   Percent of High School Students Reporting Having Had Sex at Least One Time

Year	All high school students	With 4+ partners	Before age 13
1991	54.1%	18.7%	10.2%
1993	53.0%	18.7%	9.2%
1995	53.1%	17.8%	8.9%
1997	48.4%	16.0%	7.2%
1999	49.9%	16.2%	8.3%
2001	45.6%	14.2%	6.6%
2003	46.7%	14.4%	7.4%
2005	46.8%	14.3%	6.2%
2007	47.8%	14.9%	7.1%

Source: Centers for Disease Control (2009).

more likely to report having had sex before age 13 and 2.3 times more likely to report having had four or more partners than were white youths. Maybe teen sex surveys are pretty damn silly, and braying huge alarms over small changes is sillier still.

Modern press stories on teenage sex are so mindlessly repetitive, lascivious in tone, and factless as to engender despair about whether today's media are capable of reasoned coverage of this issue. Of course, any reporter in any era (the earliest alarms I can find date back 150 years) can dig up excitable psychologists, counselors, and special-interest types to declare that younger teens "today" are engaging in ever riskier sex, then cobble articles that ignore what the best data show—which is that younger teens are having very little sex and are experiencing lesser consequences.

PREGNANT TEEN "SUPER-MODELS"

Shortly after Alaska Governor Sarah Palin was tabbed as the Republican candidate for vice president, a blog appeared in the online *Daily Kos* speculating that Trig, the candidate's Down Syndrome infant, actually was the baby of her 17 year-old daughter, Bristol. That steaming, made-up crap diminished the left-wing blogosphere—but it was rich crap. After all, Sarah Palin was a loud advocate of conservative "family values," publicly parading her family at public events as a shining example. It was all shortly debunked. Trig was Sarah's kid. Bristol was pregnant by her then-18-year-old fiancé, Levi Johnston. It was time for a new round of crap.

Everyone disgorged an opinion on Bristol. *Youth Today*'s exploitation was typical of the media formula.[34] It consisted of pitting a conventional liberal (Advocates for Youth) speculating that Bristol symbolized the need for more sex education versus a conventional conservative (Family Research Council) speculating that she was a typically wayward teen benefiting from mother Sarah's stern family values and warm family support. Neither, of course, knew Bristol personally. None of the opiners knew the circumstances of Bristol's pregnancy or what sort of mother she would make. None even bothered to investigate whether her school offered a sex education class (it did*) or what her family was really like. Bristol was simply a commodity, a useful foil to attack or defend Sarah Palin as pre-installed ideologies dictated.

Now, if Governor Palin's political critics wanted to make an issue of her family's reproductive decisions to counter her moral "values" rhetoric, why didn't they attack Sarah Palin directly? After all, Sarah became pregnant and chose to have a baby at age 43, when the risk factors for low birthweight (the best predictor of poor infant health) and other natal complications were much higher than for a 17-year-old.[35] Skyrocketing maternal and infant health complications related directly to skyrocketing childbearing by men and women age 35 and older led to some 12,000 seriously low birthweight babies in 2007, costing billions of dollars and severely straining medical resources. Why, then, didn't the moralists and critics vent their disapproval and anger at Sarah's ill-considered "personal choice" to become pregnant and to have a baby at her risky age—which would have directly addressed the all-important issue of candidate Palin's judgment—rather than railing against Bristol?

To pose this question is to answer it. *Criticizing a high-status mother raising a challenging child would be seen as unspeakably cruel.* However, cruelty toward teenage mothers is perfectly acceptable, such as Diane Sawyer's malicious beratings of teen moms holding babies during welfare reform and mean speculations about Bristol's motherhood now. It is cowardly, it is barbaric, and it is modern culture-media politics.

THE NON-TEEN-PREGNANCY NON-PACT

By 2008, the pregnant upscale white teen was drawing all the rage. *Time* reporter Kathleen Kingsbury got wind of a rumor and copped an international news story alleging a "spike" in teenage pregnancy in Gloucester, Massachusetts, blamed on a "pact" among 17 high school girls to raise their babies together.[36] *All* of the "facts" surrounding this mythical "pact" later turned out to be hallucinated.

---

*Wasilla High School, which Bristol and Levi attended, provided a "family life/human sexuality program" mandated by the Matanuska Susitna Borough School District that encouraged "students to be abstinent and to conceptualize sexual behavior in the ethical and moral context of marriage" while at the same time addressing "a full range of topics, including parenting and birth control."

Major media stampeded to ape *Time*'s June 18, 2008, careless journalism, solemnly reciting wild tales that pregnant Gloucester High School girls had forged a pact to deliberately get pregnant, were "high-fiving" each other in glee, had partners including a 24-year-old homeless man, and fronted a national trend toward rising teen pregnancy incited by popular culture, movies such as *Juno*, and whatever other notions commentators (most sporting zero knowledge of the situation) blurted.

When the real girls were finally interviewed, they expressed bafflement at the notion of a "pact."[37] The school clinic never heard of it. No one had. The principal quoted as the source for the malicious rumor denied using that term. Reporter Kingsbury insisted the principal had, but she never explained why she failed to conduct basic fact-checking before rushing to publish a load of compost.

The press also mindlessly recycled claims of a "spike" in Gloucester's teen pregnancies, which someone told them had averaged four or so in previous years but had jumped to 17 in 2008. These numbers also turned out to be questionable. Among mothers ages 19 and younger who were residents of Gloucester, nearly all of whom would have been attending the only major high school, the Massachusetts Department of Public Health[38] reported 19 births in 2006, 15 in 2007, and 15 in 2008 (all down from an average of 20 per year a decade ago). Clearly, Gloucester high schoolers experienced far more than four pregnancies in 2007, and there was no evidence of an increase in 2008, the year Gloucester's supposed "pregnancy pact" was supposed to have produced a "spike" in teenage mothers. In fact, there was no "spike." The *whole story* was a myth.

But none of the interests involved displayed concern as to whether the boiling pregnancy-pact furor *held any truth or not*. Spurred by press lies of spikes and pacts and *Time*'s thoroughly groundless speculation that the school's day care center facilitated girls' baby-making, conservative interests proposed getting rid of it. Apparently seeking to placate the numerous commentators, bloggers, and experts who so disturbingly *wished* the story had been true, the *Lifetime Movie Network* whipped up a dumb 2010 drama, *The Pregnancy Pact*, which hyped the worst fabrications as "inspired by a true story," which it most decidedly was not (see sidebar).

The Gloucester feeding frenzy recalled another famous 1980s hoax in which the San Marcos, California, school district credited an astonishing 85 percent decline in teen pregnancies to its abstinence-only "Teen-Aid" program. That "miracle" was too much even for the conservative *San Diego Union*,[39] which (unlike the 2008 Gloucester press herd) actually investigated where the numbers came from. Answer: the pre-program "147" figure was apparently just made up by school officials; the "25" post-program number was based loosely on later estimates by school counselors; and census figures

---

WHAT WOULD GROWNUPS DO?

Here's my idea for an honest *Lifetime* movie based on the Gloucester travesty, in the format of *Mean Girls*. A high school clinic in a wealthy town hypes a nonexistent "spike" in pregnancies at the high school to grab publicity and boost its funding. The principal, earnest to protect the school's sex education program from conservative blame for the nonexistent spike, invents a nonexistent "pact" among high school girls to get pregnant deliberately. A careless *Time* magazine reporter and editors get wind of the local tussle and splash an uncorroborated national story blaring the nonexistent "spike" and "pact." The usual herd of national reporters, pundits, experts, and talk-show types go wild without bothering to confirm the story's veracity. The hoax then unravels as baffled girls deny any "pact" exists, and the clinic and principal recant. My movie ends with the principal, *Time* reporter, clinic personnel, conservatives, pundits, and experts standing before a high school assembly apologizing profusely to students for exploiting made-up gossip about young people to push their own gains. *That* would evidence grownup maturity otherwise missing from the Gloucester debacle.

---

showed the birth rates among girls ages 14 to 17 in San Marcos actually increased over the period. The "miracle" was a "myth," investigations found— which has not stopped abstinence advocates from continuing to publicize it.

Over the last 15 years, I have analyzed hundreds of sensational, press-reported teen legends, many detailed in these pages and in articles for Fairness and Accuracy in Media's *Extra!* magazine.[40] In nearly every case, investigation yielded the same dismal results: these stories were not just false, but often crazily so. The next chapters will investigate today's multiple panics over teens.

Chapter Six

GENERATION MEAN

If "they're bad," that means "we're good." Consider some typical statements contrasting yesterday's good teenagers (that is, us) versus today's bad teenagers ("them") issued by Ph.D.s, professionals, and assorted commentators whose books have sold millions of copies and garnered loads of media praise:

- "Sexual intercourse, once considered a pleasure reserved for adults, has become commonplace among kids and has led to dramatic increases in the rates of out-of-wedlock childbirth, welfare dependency, fatherlessness, and abortion," reflecting "the profound transformation over the last thirty years in the way children look and act."—Kay Hymowitz, senior fellow, Manhattan Institute, 1999[1]
- "I have known sixteen year-olds who would have agonized over whether or not to kiss on the first date thirty years ago today nonchalantly report on their multiple sex partners."—James Garbarino, psychology professor, Loyola University Chicago, 2007[2]
- "While it is true that some young people in past generations have engaged in sex at an early age, have become pregnant, contracted venereal disease, and so on, they were always a small proportion of the population. What is new today are the numbers, which indicate that pressures to grow up fast are social and general. . . . The proportion of young people who are abusing drugs, are sexually active, and are becoming pregnant is so great that we must look to the society as a whole for a full explanation. . . ."—David Elkind, Tufts University child studies professor, former *Parents* magazine columnist, popular author, 2006[3]
- Kids today are suffering and perpetrating more "pathological sexual behavior" due to the "new, sexualized childhood" driven by media images.—Psychologist Diane E. Levin and Media Education Foundation producer Jean Kilbourne, 2009[4]

- Children are "engaging in sexual activities that were once taboo," with the result that "rates of teen pregnancy are rising in the United States and elsewhere."—M. Gigi Durham, journalism professor, University of Iowa, 2008[5]
- Teenagers "are taking greater risks" with sex, "with consequences that include sexually transmitted diseases, unwanted pregnancy, and pathological relationships, among others."—Lynn Ponton, psychologist, 2002[6]

These authors are making nasty charges that an entire generation has declined into debauchery. The theme repeated throughout these books and similar commentaries is that the past was a paradise of innocent teenhood and the present a sinkhole of promiscuity, sexual pathology, early pregnancy, and disease.

Such authors relentlessly proclaim the moral and intellectual superiority of themselves and their older generations. Note popular author Meredith Maran's self-serving rationalization of her own 1960s generation's indulgence in drugs, sex, and sexualized language as "revolutionary:"

> We weren't just getting high, as our kids seem to be doing now. . . . We were fighting for racial and gender equality, ending a war, changing the world. We weren't just mouthing off to our parents. We were building a new society from the ashes of the old. Whatever the particularities of our paths, we children of the sixties grew up questioning orthodoxy, fighting for democracy, opposing hierarchy.[7]

. . . and Mary Pipher's immodest claim that she and her friends just did not do or think terrible things when she was growing up: . . .

> Why are girls having more trouble now than my friends and I had when we were adolescents? Many of us hated our adolescent years, yet for the most part we weren't suicidal and we didn't develop eating disorders, cut ourselves, or run away from home.[8]

Factually, these boastings are easy to demolish. Maran fails to mention that her generation spawned epidemics of overdoses, violent and property crime, violent deaths, and venereal disease worse than anything going on among today's youth. That is hardly revolutionary. The cold statistics show Pipher's adolescence in mid-1960s Nebraska featured much higher rates of births and self-destructive deaths among teen girls than now; runaway statistics from that era are quite high; and cutting and eating disorders were not tabulated back then as they are now. One can look at the glaring numbers documenting Baby-Boomer scourges of drug abuse, crime, imprisonment, and family breakup and wonder in mystification that these Boomer experts, especially the family psychologists, could fail to notice them.[9]

Or, consider San Diego State University psychologist Jean Twenge, whose *Generation Me* (2007) was treated as gospel by the press.[10] Twenge argues that unlike past generations whose behaviors were tempered by "strict social rules," today's "Generation Me" displays a "profound shift in American character" led by a supposed "rise in narcissism" among the young that means "more kids these days are behaving badly" and displaying a "decline in manners and politeness" and a "disrespect for authority." Why? "Narcissists are more likely to be hostile, feel anxious, compromise their health, and fight with friends and family . . . they don't feel close to other people," Twenge adds. "They lash out aggressively when they are insulted or rejected" and suffer from dangerous "externality," which is "correlated with the impulsive actions that tend to get young people in trouble, like shoplifting, fighting, or having unprotected sex" as well as "powerlessness" and "a society of dropouts."

As we will see, Twenge is abysmally wrong on virtually every count, another example of today's "Make It Up" culture. In fact, today's young display dramatically lower rates of crime, violence, pregnancy, and dropping out than their elders did. By what ego inflations, then, do these authors and commentators glorify *their* memories extolling their superior attitudes and behaviors (even if recounted truthfully) as the universal index by which entire generations can be compared?

Call me old-fashioned, but praising one's own virtue and wisdom—which I wish I could do without laughing—provides strong reason to *doubt* an author's credibility. It took me a long time to understand why authors' and commentators' braggadocio proved impressive to reviewers and reporters. The best explanation I can give is that in today's privatized social-issue discussion, self-praise and self-promotion are akin to commercial advertising, communicating an assured image of superiority and aggressive style that wins competitive advantage.

Whatever the puffed up psychologies behind them, teen-fearing works represent among the worst anti-scholarship I have seen, infested with virulent prejudices, scant and warped evidence, and disturbing irrationality. While many authors complain of today's culture of permissiveness, the permissiveness most in evidence is their own sloppy research standards, in which anecdotes and quips are paramount, a worst case becomes a generality, and mass denigrations are applied to 30 million teenagers in ways that would be branded hate speech if applied to adult groups.

True, some cultural excesses these authors present (in lurid detail, for our edification) are offensive, violent, sexist, or whatever condemnation fits. Keen analyses of direct and subtle popular culture symbols and images are valuable contributions to scholarship, literacy, and public discussion. Deconstruct away. However, authors invariably go beyond expressing personal indignation at media excesses to assume that *because they are so offended at them*, popular culture *must be* corrupting today's teenagers into ever-rising dissolution. Unfortunately, the standard response by reviewers, news reporters, and academics to teen-fearing books such as *The Lolita Effect, So Sexy So Soon,*

Unhooked, Ready or Not, Generation Me, The Hurried Child, The Sex Lives of Teenagers, and *Reviving Ophelia,* commentaries by journalists such as Carol Saillant and Caitlan Flanagan, and other standard youth-bashings has been to praise the authors for courageous challenges to modern peer/popular/corporate culture. I rarely see any effort to examine the fundamental question of whether these authors' statements are *true.*

My response to these books and commentaries has been the opposite: I closely examined their statements presented as fact, including checking sources, studies, and statistics (when offered, which was rarely). I uncovered an astonishing array of complete falsehood. The dominant discussions of teenage sexuality and youth issues from far Right to far Left, from journalist to Ph.D., from sex-education advocate to abstinence devotee, reflect what I term "Make It Up" culture. Some is ironic without being funny. For example, authors who deplore the "meanness" of teen girls who call each other "sluts" see no contradiction in their own brandings of today's generation of girls as randomly promiscuous—that is, sluts.

Where do teen-fearing authors get their information? Mainly from themselves. Psychologists such as Elkind, Ponton, Pipher, and Garbarino, who dominate teen-pathology books typically focus on their selected clients in clinical treatment. "My clients are not that different from the girls who are not seen in therapy," declares Pipher, providing no documentation. Authors select cases to feature that support their views. "Everything in this book comes from what girls have told me over the last ten years I've been teaching," Rosalind Wiseman says. Courtney Martin's *Perfect Girls, Starving Daughters* (2007) makes sweeping pronouncements about the misery and pathology of her 20-age generation based on her own manifest unhappiness and interviews with "friends, friends' friends, and friends' friends' friends."[11]

A second major source of information for popular authors consists of assembling a clipping file and online links to news reports to buttress their claims that this or that teenage misbehavior must be widespread. This tactic reflects a fundamental misunderstanding of how the news media work. "News" does not consist of the *common* realities of the world, but the *rare exceptions.* When, for example, a news show features a teenager who overdosed on prescription drugs or was abducted by an online predator, that means such cases are *extremely rare.* Conversely, common events, such as the 500 substantiated cases of violent and sexual abuses parents inflict on their children every day rarely appear in the news due to their commonality, unless they include some celebrity or sensation-grabber. Public confusion over this media paradox is exacerbated when reporters aggrandize their stories by amplifying rare events to make them appear common—the "tip of the iceberg," "a wake-up call," "a community in denial," or other standard reporter clichés. The press's rush to make a gang rape involving a handful of men and boys outside a Richmond, California, high school dance appear a common problem perpetrated by the young all over the country represents a fundamental violation of journalistic ethics. If youthful gang rape were common, the media would no longer find it newsworthy. When interests and news reporters feature rare cases to generalize about powerless groups such as youth, readers and viewers are wise to assume the *opposite* is the case.

This chapter offers detailed analyses of typical treatises about modern youth. That so many crazy themes continue to get published and taken seriously, including by academic and institutional scholars who surely know better, indicates a major breakdown in the information used to frame and address teenage issues, including sex.

MORE TEEN SEX, LESS PREGNANCY, DISEASE, AND DRAMA

Are more teens having sex, getting pregnant, getting diseases, and suffering debilitating emotional consequences from sexual experimentation? We begin with an interesting conundrum. Teens today do report having more sex at younger ages than their parents or grandparents did (or admitted to), but today's teens appear to suffer far fewer consequences from sex than did past generations.

A trend often cited as confirming cultural degeneration is reported in the National Survey of Family Growth (NSFG), whose latest survey finds around 25 percent of 15 year-old girls say they have had sex at least once, compared to fewer than 5 percent in 1970.[12] Among all girls age 15 to 19, the proportion affirming their own nonvirginity rose from 29 percent in 1970 to nearly half today. A small part of this increase might be due to the falling age of puberty.

Alternatively, all that may be occurring is that today's teenagers are more likely *to report on surveys* that they have had sex. If you do not automatically take surveys at face value, you would find some puzzlers in this trend interesting. For example, in 1970 more than twice as many 15-year-old boys than girls that age told the NSFG they had had sex, a proportion which fell to 1.7-to-1 by 1988, 1.1-to-1 in 1995, and dead even today. There are several contradictory and implausible explanations for such a trend, but the most reasonable is that boys were exaggerating and girls, at least on earlier surveys, were minimizing their experiences. To borrow from Tom Wolfe, girls' shamelessness now matches boys'.

But Pipher, Elkind, the Media Education Foundation, and other shockees immediately blamed "toxic" modern culture of salacious images luring ever-corruptible young teens to defy their wise parents to sink into unheard-of debaucheries. More plausible correlates, such as the enormous growth in divorce, extramarital sex, and unwed birth rates among adults over the last 40 years have been too uncomfortable for the pop commentariat to engage.

Yet, taking the NSFG at face value, *virtually all of the growth in sex among young teens occurred during the 1970s and early 1980s*. That is, it was sparked by the *mothers* of today's teen girls long before the advent of the post-1990 "toxic culture" blamed for sexing up modern teens. Whatever junior-high sexual revolution there was happened from 25 to 40 years ago, in an era politically dominated by the Reagan presidency and culturally dominated by videogames such as Pong and the cartoonish Super Mario Brothers and mostly-innocuous television programs led by *Happy Days* and *The Cosby Show*.

Indeed, after peaking in the late 1980s and early 1990s at around 30 percent, teen sex then declined during the 1990s and 2000s. By 2007, 25 percent of girls said they had sex before age 16. For all girls, the most recent (2009) Centers for Disease Control report[13] points out that "the percentage of high school students who ever had sexual intercourse (i.e., sexual experience) decreased from 54.1 percent in 1991 to 47.8 percent in 2007." That is, *as nearly all of the objectionable cultural trends proliferated over the last two decades, the proportion of teens having sex decreased.*

The most important trend, if the NSFG figures are accurate, is that the rate of pregnancy among sexually active younger-teen girls has fallen by over 80 percent since the 1970s. That is, as the rate of *sexual activity* among girls age 15 and younger supposedly multiplied several-fold, the rate of *pregnancies* among girls that age fell by half. That trend would make the young-teen contraceptive revolution even more astounding than the so-called sexual revolution.

One fascinating development drawn from combining the best measures available, as discussed in the following chapters, is that girls' higher level of acknowledged sexual activity accompanied dramatically *increased* academic, job, and leadership status of young women and dramatic *decreases* in self-destructive behaviors. These developments all seem to be part of the larger girl revolution detailed in Chapter 7.

If more teens today have sex at younger ages, what would we expect to result? The consequences experts claim are connected to younger-teen sexual activity include more pregnancies, sexually transmitted diseases (STDs), exposure to sexual violence such as rape, and emotional trauma. What do real outcomes show? *Just the opposite.*

Table 6.1 shows the trends since 1930, around the time when the national birth registration system first became reasonably complete.[14] Teen birth rates (the only outcome consistently reported) are at their lowest levels today since the first national statistics compiled 90 years ago, while pregnancy rates are at their lowest level since first reliably reported in 1973. Regardless of what teens say they do, clearly measurable outcomes from teenage sex stand at all-time lows, and the youngest teens show the biggest declines. A good case could be made that Boomer and older Generation-Xer teens had trouble with sexual activity, but younger Xers and Millennial teens have dramatically fewer outcomes.

In any case, we might as well toss sex surveys aside and deal with the outcome measures. After all, it is the outcomes that are important, not the yes/no marks teens make on pieces of paper.

Table 6.1   Aren't Teens Getting Pregnant and Having Babies and Abortions at Younger Ages Today? NO!

| | Pregnancies per 1,000 teenage females by age group | | | | | |
| | Pregnancies | | Births | | Fetal loss/abortion | |
Year	10–14	15–19	10–14	15–19	10–14	15–19
1930			0.6	57.4		
1940			0.6	53.0		
1950	*	*	0.9	80.6	*	*
1955	*	*	0.9	89.9	*	*
1960	*	*	0.8	89.1	*	*
1965	*	*	0.8	70.4	*	*
1970	*	*	1.2	68.0	*	*
1973	2.9	96.1	1.3	59.3	1.6	36.8
1976	3.2	101.4	1.3	53.5	1.9	47.9
1980	3.2	110.0	1.1	53.0	2.1	57.0
1985	3.6	106.9	1.2	51.3	2.4	55.6
1990	3.5	116.3	1.4	59.9	2.1	56.4
1995	3.0	101.1	1.3	56.8	1.7	44.3
2000	2.1	84.5	0.8	47.7	1.3	36.8
2005	1.6	70.6	0.7	40.5	0.9	30.1
2006 (latest, all)	1.5	71.5	0.6	41.9	0.8	29.6
2008 (latest birth)	*	*	0.6	41.7	*	*
Change, 2006 v. 1973	−49%	−26%	− 55%	−30%	−47%	−20%

*Indicates no data are available for that year. Miscarriage rates were higher in earlier years, and illegal abortions were estimated by public health authorities at 750,000 to 2 million per year prior to legalization in 1972.

Note: The Alan Guttmacher Institute provides estimates of total pregnancies by age for 1973 through 2006. The NCHS provides estimates for 1976 through 2005. Both are shown in the table.

Sources: National Center for Health Statistics (2009); Guttmacher Institute (2010), U.S. Teenage Pregnancies, Births and Abortions: National and State Trends and Trends by Race and Ethnicity. At: http://www.guttmacher.org. Births for 2008 are from just-released update: B. E. Hamilton, J. A. Martin, and S. J. Ventura (2010). Births: Preliminary Data for 2008. National Vital Statistics Reports, 58:16 (April 2010).

TEEN STD AND AIDS CASES ALSO FELL

A similar trend occurred for sexually transmitted disease, though STD trends have to be viewed with caution. The only STDs consistently tabulated over the last half century are gonorrhea and primary/secondary syphilis.[15] Cases of chlamydia, herpes, and human pappilloma virus (HPV) were not screened until recently; we simply do not know their prevalence in past generations. Asymptomatic STD cases in females in particular were poorly

Table 6.2   U.S. Teenage Gonorrhea and Syphilis Diagnoses Per 100,000 Population, 1960–2008

	Male 10–14	Female 10–14	Male 15–19	Female 15–19
1960–1964	10.0	20.7	484.6	317.0
1965–1969	14.3	22.8	708.0	407.0
1970–1974	21.8	51.0	1,062.4	1,002.2
1975–1979	22.8	75.7	1,021.2	1,448.6
1980–1984	24.1	75.4	963.0	1,420.2
1985–1989	31.4	98.5	949.8	1,275.8
1990–1994	23.3	90.3	749.8	982.9
1995–1999	9.3	59.3	357.9	724.3
2000–2004	7.1	45.0	287.0	662.9
2005–2008	6.0	33.7	277.0	636.8

Source: Centers for Disease Control (2009).

diagnosed prior to the 1970s. By the 1990s, routine screenings for HIV, chlamydia, and HPV also contributed to diagnoses of other STDs, all leading to bigger numbers, particularly for females. Higher teen female rates also reflect the more common liaisons with males age 20 and older, a pattern experts have been very reluctant to acknowledge.

Although gonorrhea and syphilis remain very much a problem today, rates have dropped dramatically among both sexes and young ages from their 1980s peaks for age 10 to 14 and 1970s peaks for age 15 to 19 (Table 6.2). Further,

Table 6.3   Sexually Transmitted Infection Rates by Age and Race, 2008

	Chlamydia, gonorrhea, and syphilis cases/100,000 population		
Rate 2005	**White**	**Black**	**Hispanic**
10–14	26.3	370.5	69.4
15–19	957.2	8,871.5	2,081.2
20–24	1,205.0	9,174.9	2,510.4
25–29	532.3	4,231.1	1,151.1
30–34	227.2	2,028.0	551.9
35–39	109.1	984.1	310.2
40–44	60.4	549.3	168.3
45–54	26.8	276.2	91.2
55–64	8.2	93.6	24.9
65+	2.1	25.3	8.7
Total	206.8	2,161.6	581.9

Source: Centers for Disease Control (2009).

Table 6.4   HIV Infections Diagnosed by Age

Age group	Changes, 1993–2007, in:			New cases diagnosed in:	
	Net change	Population	Diagnoses	2007*	1993
0–12**	–	–	–	199	794
13–19	–28%	1.206	0.869	1,703	1,959
20–24	–49%	1.104	0.568	4,907	8,643
25–29	–59%	1.034	0.421	5,771	13,716
30–34	–53%	0.857	0.403	5,089	12,615
35–39	–29%	0.967	0.690	6,088	8,822
40–44	+19%	1.140	1.356	6,554	4,833
45–49	+67%	1.426	2.382	5,172	2,171
50–54	+109%	1.634	3.414	3,489	1,022
55–59	+135%	1.702	3.996	1,938	485
60–64	+141%	1.401	3.376	942	279
65+	+140%	1.150	2.759	803	291
Total	–34%	1.158	0.767	42,655	55,630
Percent of cases diagnosed in:					
Age 13–29	–34%			29.0%	43.7%
age 30–39	–32%			26.2%	38.5%
Age 40+	+172%			44.3%	16.3%

*New HIV/AIDS syndrome expanded definitions for diagnosis beginning in 2001. Rates are not calculated since criteria were expanded and diagnoses are from 34 reporting states. The net change is the percentage change in the ratio of the change in diagnoses to the change in population, 1993–2007.
**Cases diagnosed before age 12 nearly all are pediatric, not sexually transmitted, and are not included in the comparison.
Source: Centers for Disease Control and Prevention (2009).

the higher rate of STD among 15- to 24-year-olds is due to very high rates among African Americans, not the younger population in general (Table 6.3). Revealing yet again the problems of poverty, the STD rate among black 30-year-olds is higher than among white 15- to 24-year-olds.

HIV/AIDS diagnoses reveal a similar decline among young people.[16] Allowing for expanded diagnostic criteria and the fact that HIV/AIDS is diagnosed six months to 10 years after the disease is initially contracted, the most inclusive approach is to look at trends among those aged 13 to 29, who in 1993 accounted for 44 percent of new diagnoses; those aged 40 and older accounted for just 16 percent. By 2007, the share among those aged 13 to 29 had fallen to 28 percent of all new cases, while the share among those aged 40 and older comprised 43 percent (Table 6.4). That this dramatic trend, obvious in the CDC's own figures, has received no notice should demolish confidence in both official and popular claims about the direction of this deadly epidemic.

THE INCONVENIENT DECLINE IN RAPE

Nor have teenage relationships become more "pathological," at least in the terms we can measure. In particular, rape and sexual violence have fallen to all-time lows, our most comprehensive measure of crime, the Bureau of Justice Statistics' National Crime Victimization Survey (NCVS), reports (Table 6.5).[17]

Commensurate with these declines in sexual attacks reported by young women, the NCVS found victims of all ages reporting vastly fewer rape and sexual assailants who were (or appeared to be) under the age of 21 than in the past. In the early and mid-1990s, NCVS figures projected over 300,000 rapes and sexual assaults (including completed, attempted, and threatened violence by both single and multiple offenders) involving assailants aged 12 to 20 every year. By the mid and late 2000s, that total had fallen to fewer than 150,000, even as the young-male population grew by 2 million.

Since 1995, NCVS has also compiled a special measure of intimate partner violence involving couples in relationships. This index also shows large declines among young couples over the last decade, as detailed in Chapter 9.

The NCVS is a self-reporting survey, however, so how do we know it is reliable? The survey of tens of thousands of Americans chosen to be representative of the population generally is considered to be the best measure of crime because it captures offenses that are not reported to police. The NCVS found women reporting a higher percentage of rape and other sexual victimizations to police

Table 6.5   Rape Victimization Recently Fell Dramatically Among Young Women

| Annual average | Sexual violence per 1,000 females age 12–24 | | |
	Rape	Other sex assaults	Total
1973–1974	3.4	*	*
1975–1979	3.6	*	*
1980–1984	3.4	*	*
1985–1989	2.9	*	*
1990–1994	3.0	6.5	9.5
1995–1999	2.9	3.8	6.7
2000–2004	1.9	2.9	4.8
2005–2007	1.9	2.1	4.0
Change, 2007 vs. 1993	−37%	−68%	−58%

*The NCVS was expanded substantially beginning in 1993. Questions about sex crimes other than rape, including thwarted and threatened sexual assaults, are not included on pre-1993 surveys.
Source: Bureau of Justice Statistics (2010).

today than in the past, in line with awareness campaigns, police and hospital improvements in rape investigation, and laws that expand the definition of rape to include spousal, disabled, same-sex, and intoxicated victims. Indeed, the survey itself expanded in 1993 to include more sex offenses. So, the drop in rape does not reflect less reporting.

Further, the declines in rape and sex offenses found in the NCVS closely parallel other measures. The FBI reports major declines in the numbers and rates of young men arrested for rape, especially since the early 1990s. Uniform Crime Reports,[18] adjusted for population coverage, shows that rape and other sex offense arrests of young men under age 25 peaked in 1990 at around 71,500 and then plummeted, reaching a record low of 41,700 in 2008. Violent offending by young men has fallen to its lowest rate since at least the early 1960s, when crime reports were less complete and arrested juveniles were more likely to be charged with vaguer "status" offenses. In California, crime reports[19] show fewer youths were arrested for rape in 2008 (236) than in the first year statistics were reported, 1957 (331), even though the number of teens had tripled.

Claims that rape must be increasing due to rising young-male savagery fed by gang, popular media, and college fraternity cultures appear dubious. In 1980, 1,059 white (non-Hispanic) males under age 30 were arrested in California for rape; in 2005, 269 were arrested for the same crime, a per-capital decline of 70 percent. Meanwhile, rape arrest rates of young black and Latino males dropped by an amazing 76 percent. Nor is rape "getting younger." In fact, the youngest teens show the biggest improvements. The first crime reports detailing ages in the 1970s showed 150 to 200 Californians aged 10 to 14 arrested for rape every year. In 2008, in a population of 1 million larger, just 51 were arrested. Rather, it is older generations that are lagging. Before 1980, teens aged 10 to 17 were more than twice as likely to be arrested for rape than older adults. Today, teens have lower rape arrest rates than adults up to age 50. California's unusually detailed crime statistics parallel trends found nationally.

Still more measures agree that young women are safer today than ever. Self reports such as Monitoring the Future[20] find girls reporting fewer assaults, robberies, and other violent victimizations and more saying they feel safer than their counterparts did in past decades. In 1990, for example, 66 percent of high school senior girls reported feeling satisfied with their personal safety (5% felt truly unsafe), which rose to 68 percent (with the proportion feeling unsafe falling to 4%) by 2008—the lowest rate of anxiety over personal safety since the survey began in 1975.

Public health statistics also support the consensus that girls are safer from violence today.[21] Murders of girls have plummeted in recent decades. From 1990 to 2006, the population-adjusted rates of homicides against girls and young women fell by an astounding 40 percent for those aged 20 to 24, 42 percent for those aged 15 to 19, and 52 percent for those aged 10 to 14. New, 2007 figures from California show another big drop in murders of girls and young women,[22] with the rate now at its lowest level in at least 40 years. (I say "at least" because police investigations were much less efficient in past decades.)

Likewise, the U.S. Department of Education[23] reports a dramatic decline in school dropout by both sexes (females are improving a bit faster) and all races, though Hispanic levels remain high. School achievement by standard measures, which dipped during the Baby Boom student era of the 1970s, rose sharply both for standardized tests such as the SAT and ACT and for criterion-referenced tests such as reading and math scales. Compared to students of the past, today's students are much more likely to take rigorous math and science courses, to enroll in college, and to graduate. In 1970, just 26 percent of 18-to-24-year-olds were enrolled in higher education; in 2008, 38 percent were, and college students today are much more likely to pursue higher degrees such as masters, Ph.D., and professional accreditation. Young women show especially dramatic gains, as documented in Chapter 7.

As for measures of well being, Monitoring the Future's annual survey of thousands of high school seniors finds general increases over the last 30 years in the percentages reporting that they are happy, having fun, satisfied with possessions and life, optimistic about the future, and eager to assume leadership roles. *The American Freshman* annual surveys of hundreds of thousands of incoming college students finds big declines in drinking, smoking, and depression (despite a rash of thoroughly false claims of new "campus crises") in recent decades.[24] Crime and public health measures reveal similar trends, with large declines in serious crime, suicidal deaths, firearms mortality, and most other violent deaths among young people to record low levels today.

When measures from a variety of fields—crime reports, victimization surveys, personal surveys, education statistics, public health statistics—agree so consistently, it is safe to say we are talking about *real trends*. Yet, weirdly, culture warriors and privatized profiteers remain hell-bent to convince young men that they are rapists and failures and young women that they are crazy sluts endangered by unheard-of perils.

Clearly, the favorable picture of young people today that emerges across a consensus of standard references is exactly the opposite of the dismal depiction of the young that we get from popular media and books. Why are so many authorities so crudely and so unconscionably misrepresenting teens' trends? Why is there no outcry against their lies from agencies and legitimate researchers?

POPULAR BOOKS ON TEEN SEX

San Francisco psychologist Lynn Ponton's *The Sex Lives of Teenagers: Revealing the Secret World of Adolescent Boys and Girls* (2000) made a big splash, mainly due to her unfortunate fascination with tabloid-style trash (i.e., a teen who masturbates with a vacuum cleaner) and the sensationalized first and last chapters that undermine her better points. Ponton wants more Americans to "view adolescent sexuality as a potentially positive experience, rather than sanctioning it as one fraught with danger."[25] Her strategy, sadly mismatched to that worthy goal, is to scare adults with panicky anecdotes of teenage danger.

Contrary to the book cover's promise, *The Sex Lives of Teenagers* does not reveal "the secret world of adolescent boys and girls." It simply recounts some lurid stories from her more extreme clients that she misrepresents as signs of the times. Teenagers, she says, "are taking greater risks" with sex, "with conse-quences that include sexually transmitted diseases, unwanted pregnancy, and pathological relationships, among others." She claims that "HIV infections are falling in the United States, but they are not falling for young people" and that "half of the forty thousand people being infected with HIV in the United States are twenty-four years old or younger." As we have seen, this simply is not the case. Teens today display substantially lower rates of pregnancy, birth, abortion, HIV, and other STDs we can measure over time, which are fairly solid mea-sures of sexual risk-taking. Far from being younger and younger, teens who get pregnant today tend to be older (18 or 19) than in the past.

The reason for Ponton's strange deceptions soon becomes evident. She seems to believe that if the public and policymakers can be convinced that teens are taking more dangerous risks, they will implement her brand of benign sexuality education and liberal programs. Instead, as we have seen, the predictable reactions to negative depictions of teenage sex have been anger, repression, and the same abstinence-only regimes Ponton rues. Progressives who think that creating more fear of young people will advance their liberal ideals must have been under a rock for the last 30 years. The best way to pro-mote sex-education, as opposed to abstinence-education, is to depict young people's sexual trends accurately.

Ponton could have made a stunningly factual case that despite apparently engaging in more sex, teens today are taking far fewer risks and suffering dimin-ishing pregnancy and disease outcomes and therefore merit more confidence and affirmation. Instead, by airing dire myths of rising teenage sexual risk-taking and consequences, Ponton sabotages her own appeal that Americans accept teenage sexuality.

The Hurried Child: Growing Up Too Fast Too Soon (2006, 2001, 1988, 1981), by David Elkind, professor of child development at Tufts University and long-time *Parents'* magazine columnist, may be the best-read work on youth issues. In my view, Elkind has been a major generator of demeaning myths about adolescents for decades. His 1970s notions (mostly gleaned from reading some diaries) that adolescents, unlike adults, suffer delusions of "imaginary audience" and "personal fable" were bad enough. His major work, now in its fourth edition, arguing that the innate incompetence of youths combined with destructive pop-culture images have created a crisis of "growing up too fast" is even worse. Unfortunately, it is often cited as a classic.

Elkind's books present a dizzying array of flatly wrong numbers, uncorrected even in later editions, to buttress his claim that childhood today is "under assault." On the subject of teen sex, his claims that teenage pregnancy and STDs have risen to "general . . . great" [meaning high] levels today versus only "small . . . numbers" in the past have already been rebutted.[26] A few more samples of craziness from *The Hurried Child*:

- "In 1995, the rate of childbearing among women between the ages of 15 to 19 was 90 births per 1,000 women."
- The decline in teenage birth rates from 1995 to 2000 "is more an index of the increased availability of abortion than it is of a decline in teenage pregnancies."
- The teenage "share seems to be increasing" for sexually transmitted diseases and AIDS cases.

Perusing readily available, standard reports reveals Elkind's tendency to fiction:

- The CDC reports the birth rate was 57 per 1,000 women ages 15 to 19 in 1995 (not 90), far below the peak at 97 per 1,000 in 1957. Since 1995, the birth rate among women age 15 to 19 has fallen still further, to 42 per 1,000 by 2008.
- Abortion has dropped as well. From 1995 to 2000, the CDC reports, the birth rate fell 15 percent and the abortion rate fell 16 percent among teens. By 2006, teen pregnancy rates had fallen to their lowest levels since first reported in 1973.
- The CDC's surveillances show rates of STD infection in teenagers have been dropping since 1975 and now stand at the same level as in 1955, when reports were much less complete. Teens are the only age group to show declines in new HIV and new AIDS cases from the early 1990s through the latest, 2008, CDC surveillance.[27]

These are only a few of Elkind's easily-documented errors across a variety of teen issues. When errors this egregious persist through edition after edition (I have pointed out Elkind's gross inaccuracies for years), it is fair to say the author and publishers do not regard factuality as important. And no wonder. Accuracy would disconfirm Elkind's thesis of adolescence gone terribly wrong due to young people's incompetence and pop-culture influences.

Manhattan Institute scholar and *Youth Today* columnist Kay Hymowitz, author of *Ready or Not: Why Treating Children as Small Adults Endangers Their Future—and Ours* (1999), is another practitioner of Make It Up ethics. Her conservative nostalgia myth that the pre-1960s represented a golden era of "procultural" values and the present a dystopia of "anticultural" youthful immorality is even sillier than Elkind's.[28] Hymowitz lionizes the 1950s and earlier eras as times of healthy "republican values" in which "kids" did not have sex. All that is needed to demolish this fanciful thinking is to check easily available vital statistics reports, which show that more than 1.5 million girls under age 18 gave birth during the decade of the 1950s. The birth rate among girls under age 15 was 50 percent higher then than now. Teens most certainly did have sex back when *Father Knows Best*, Doris Day, and Pat Boone ruled the airwaves.

Is more "kids" having sex responsible for the "dramatic increases in the rates of out-of-wedlock childbirth, welfare dependency, fatherlessness, and abortion," as Hymowitz charges? No. Not even nearly. Hymowitz does not tell us how she defines "kids" or over what period "increases" are calculated. So, let us adopt the standard definitions: under 18 years old, and since 1960. Before that, teens were raised in the 1940s and 1950s eras that Hymowitz lionized. Nothing she claims turns out to be occurring on this planet. For example, from 1960 to 2007, the number of births by unmarried couples rose from 224,300 to 1,714,600 (that is, by nearly 1.5 million):

- Of this increase, 90,000, or 6 percent, involved "kids" (mothers under age 18, mostly with fathers over age 18).
- Babies produced by two "kids" under age 18 (as opposed to a "kid" with an adult partner) accounted for less than 3 percent of the total increase.
- Mothers under age 20 (again, most fathers were over age 20) accounted for less than one-fifth of the increase; babies conceived by two teens, less than 10 percent.[29]

The increase in unwed childbearing has, overwhelmingly, been an adult phenomenon kicked off in a big way by *elders raised in the pre-1960 era*, not by modern teens. Repeating these calculations for abortion (difficult, since statistics are not available before 1973), fatherlessness (the census-measured proportions of families in which one parent is not present), and welfare costs shows sex by "kids" accounts for only minuscule fractions. What kind of grownup blames "kids" so that adults can evade responsibility for their behaviors?

Hymowitz's partisan dishonesty is revealed by her abrupt reversal in a 2004 article, in which she admitted statistics show "kids are improving."[30] Her article is peppered with the usual specious anecdotes claiming to show that suddenly Americans are embracing "old-fashioned virtues like caution, self-restraint, commitment, and personal responsibility," and that "family values are hot!" Why the about-face? Because, unlike in 1999 when she clarioned teenage apocalypse, conservative Republicans she liked ran the country in 2004, led by George W. Bush, a president she declared young people supported more than anyone. (Another fiction. Exit polls in both 2000 and 2004 showed young voters resoundingly rejected Bush.)

It is true that 2000s teens were showing signs of reacting against Boomer irresponsibilities—specifically, the deteriorating behaviors of the older generations raised during the "republican" past eras Hymowitz lauds—but most of these trends had been building over decades. In any case, Hymowitz, displaying singular instability, quickly returned to her youth-trashing ways—after all, a Democrat now occupies the White House. Her more recent writings show no more respect for factuality and scholarship than in the past.

THE NEW MEDIA REVOLUTION

Media in both traditional and radical new forms and teens' access to media have exploded in the last two decades.[31] For examples:

- In 1990, just 54 million households had cable TV (59% of all households); in 2008, 100 million (89% of all households).[32]
- In 1990, only scattered artists produced gangster rap, then popularized by the growth of NWA's album, *Straight*. The 1992 release of Dr Dre's *The Chronic* and Ice T's *Home Invasion*, and growth of Death Row records spurred sales into the millions. By the mid-2000s, gangster sales topped 200 million units annually, in addition to online downloads.[33]
- In 1990, Internet usage totaled just one terabyte per month, nearly all within businesses. Today, Nielsen/Net Ratings and Pew's Internet Project report, 75 percent of Americans have Internet access at home, and 89 percent to 96 percent of youths aged 12 to 17 have online access, with roughly half of all teens going online every day.[34]
- In 1990, interactive, first-person videogames of the type now rated M (Mature) or AO (Adults Only) were nonexistent. The first violent games, Mortal Kombat (1992) and its graphic Sega version (1994), were followed by Quake, Doom, Pioneer, and increasingly violent themes.[35] Sales of M-rated games escalated to 5 million units in 2008, one in six games sold, the Entertainment Software Association Reports. A 2007 study (accuracy unverified) by Massachusetts General Hospital's Center on Health and Media of 1,200 teens aged 12 to 14 found that "two-thirds of boys and more than one in four girls regularly played violent M-rated videogames 'a lot in the past six months.'"[36]

Teens now have access to a global information structure, and little can be done to regulate it. This development of youths choosing their own information sources from a worldwide menu is scary to many liberals and conservatives alike. For a major liberal/left example, The Media Education Foundation (MEF) bills itself as a leading producer of educational videos in cultural and media criticism.[37] I have used MEF videos in my classes as examples of the incisive dissection of cultural imagery, marketing techniques, and subtle (and unsubtle) messages about gender, race, and political issues.

Unfortunately, MEF's criticism carries its own reactionary message. In video after video, MEF tells us, America of the past was a safer culture in which children were raised by parents and communities that cooperated to shield the young from damaging influences; today, children are bombarded with corporate ads and entertainment that sell products via violence, sex, and sexism that is warping the values and behaviors of the young. With regard to the behaviors and attitudes of modern youth, MEF is as relentlessly negative and fearful as conservatives.

A constant MEF theme, repeated in videos such as *Game Over: Violence in Video Games* (2000), *Deadly Persuasion* (2002), *Wrestling with Manhood* (2002), and *Spin the Bottle: Sex, Lies, and Alcohol* (2004), is the insistence that girls and women are in vastly greater danger from physical and sexual violence today. MEF links sexist images in alcohol advertising to "widespread and increasing violence against women" perpetrated mainly by "young men." MEF decries sexism but also is deeply disparaging toward modern young women, whom its videos relentlessly misrepresent as more disturbed, depressed, promiscuous, alcohol-abusing, and media-driven. In the MEF video *Reviving Ophelia* (1998), psychologist Mary Pipher declares that "the culture has changed a lot," becoming more "toxic" and fueling "very dangerous trends" among girls. "It's totally simple what girls think," Pipher condescends. (How would MEF react if a beer ad said that?) *Dreamworlds 3* (2007), MEF director Sut Jhally announces, "offers a unique and powerful tool for understanding both the continuing influence of music videos and how pop culture more generally filters the identities of young men and women through a dangerously narrow set of myths about sexuality and gender."

That is, MEF goes beyond media criticism to dispense the standard, negative stereotypes and fear-mongering toward today's more diverse youth of the very type it claims to expose. None of these are accurate. As I have repeatedly shown, MEF's dire image of girls is thoroughly contradicted by a consensus of compelling references showing that violence against girls and women, especially rape and sexual assault, has plummeted in the last decade to all-time lows—and that young men show the biggest declines of any group in all types of violence.

MEF is particularly fearful of young people and New Media. It advertises *Generation M: Misogyny in Media and Culture* (2008), based on a Kaiser Family Foundation study, as chronicling "the dangerous real-life consequences of misogyny in all its forms" tied to

> the destructive dynamics of misogyny across a broad and disturbing range of media phenomena: including the hyper-sexualization of commercial products aimed at girls, the explosion of violence in video games aimed at boys, the near-hysterical sexist rants of hip-hop artists and talk radio shock jocks, and the harsh, patronizing caricatures of femininity and feminism that reverberate throughout the mainstream of American popular culture.

That young people might *not* be flocking to ape the worst aspects of popular culture and, in reality, are displaying good adaptive skills in selectively consuming and participating in the vast array of media they grew up with is not reflected in MEF videos. MEF's nostalgic mythmaking and primitive insinu-ations of youthful monkey-see monkey-do imitations of destructive New Media images evidences its failure to evolve by matching analysis and criti-cism of media culture to real trends among modern youth. MEF is just another reactionary force in the culture war.

HEALTHY ADAPTATIONS TO NEW MEDIA

Rather than rationally analyzing how young people consume New Media in the contexts of their larger lives, culture warriors imagine the most objectionable images must be driving adolescents to act in the worst ways. However, Kaiser Family Foundation's study of 2,000 American youth, *Generation M: Media in the Lives of 8 to 18-Year-Olds*,[38] though suffused with an undertone of anxiety, nonetheless suggests young people are successfully integrating modern media into their lives without descending into wastage and mayhem. Kaiser begins by noting the ubiquitous use of modern media by young people:

> Over the past five years, there have been numerous incremental changes that, added together, have substantially expanded the presence of media in young people's lives. Today, there are more young people with cable or satellite TV in their home (up from 74% to 82%), with subscriptions to premium TV channels (from 45% to 55%), with three or more VCRs or DVD players (from 26% to 53%), and with multiple video game consoles (from 49% to 56%) in their homes. And more of these media have migrated to young people's bedrooms . . . The sheer amount of time young people spend using media—an average of nearly 6 1/2 hours a day—makes it plain that the potential of media to impact virtually every aspect of young people's lives cannot be ignored.

So, where is the damage? Even the usually fretful Kaiser fails to find much:

> Contrary to most expectations, it does not appear that spending time with media takes away from the time children spend in other pursuits; in fact, it seems that those young people who spend the most time using media are also those whose lives are the most full with family, friends, sports, and other interests . . . Indeed, com-pared to teens who consume media the least, teens who consume the most media spend 78 more minutes per day with parents, 21 more minutes in physical activities, 66 more minutes on hobbies, four less minutes doing homework, and 10 more minutes doing chores.

More than three-fourths of teens say their parents have no rules about what they can do on the computer; more than five in six have no rules about what music, television, and videogames they can access. And why would they need them? According to the Kaiser study, four in five teens are doing fine: "Most young people indicate that they have lots of friends, get good grades, aren't unhappy or in trouble often, and get along pretty well with their parents."

Of course, Kaiser acknowledges, the fraction of teens with bad relation-ships with family and school may use media more to compensate. "Many chil-dren played the games to manage their feelings, including anger and stress. Children who played violent games were more likely to play to get their anger out," commented one research team after studying video gaming among teenagers:

> Violent game play is so common, and youth crime has actually declined, so most kids who play these games occasionally are probably doing fine. We hope that this study is a first step toward reframing the debate from 'violent games are terrible and destroying society' to 'what types of game content might be harmful to what types of kids, in what situations'. We need to take a fresh look at what types of rules or policies make sense.[39]

The bottom line remains that as teens as a generation used more media over the last 15 to 20 years, their behaviors and attitudes dramatically improved. Indeed, given the insistence by Diane Levin and Jean Kilbourne that "popular culture is still the leading source of sex education in the nation,"[40] the sharply downward trends in teen pregnancy and STDs are very difficult for culture-war authors to admit (see Chapter 8). When surveyed, young people wisely rank the economy, education, war, environment, health care, and a dozen other real problems as far more important than ads and media images (which teens rarely mention at all). It is time that media critics adapted to complex new realities as well as young people have.

Culture-war interests also have ignored the striking reality that while young people are doing better as New Media proliferated, another group is not—their parents. Key risks have shifted from teen and young adult ages to middle-aged years in the last three decades. Pregnancy, birth, and abortion/fetal loss trends again reveal very large declines among teens but increases among ages 40 and older, when maternal and infant health is a much greater risk.

Parent ages also show an enormous increase in drug abuse, serious assault, and imprisonment. In 1990, youths aged 10 to 19 and adults aged 40 to 59 had equal rates of being locked up. By 2008, middle-ager's doubled imprison-ment rates rendered them twice as likely to be behind bars compared to teens. While young people have shown declines in violent death and suicide, their parents have shown increases, in most cases to levels higher than even older teens experience. In particular, the teen gun death rate was higher than the middle-aged rate in 1990; now, while both have dropped, middle-agers are now more at risk of gunshot killing than teenagers are. "Kids and guns" has been supplanted by a new epidemic of "middle-agers and guns." Interestingly, the only major crime to show a similar, and large, decline among both young and middle ages is rape and other sex offenses. This would seem to contradict fears that today's media provoke more sexual violence.

Why does a book on teen sex and pregnancy veer into trends in middle-aged crime, violence, drug abuse, and pregnancy? First, these developments are exactly the opposite of what culture-war authors like Levin and Kilbourne, who pose a "conflict between family culture and commercial culture," would predict. Second, these trends are vital to scrutinize because they are markers of the difficulty young people face in coping with an increasingly troubled parent generation. Traditionally, one of the most powerful predictors of youthful behavior outcomes is the corresponding behavior outcomes of their parents and the adults of their communities and demographics. That trends in some key youth risks are diverging sharply and positively from those of adults is big news. If institutions and experts really were serious about using the best information to analyze social issues, they would have leapt on these unusual trends as a gold mine of insight.

PABULUM FOR GROWNUPS

For all their dark cultural invocations and alarms about youth today, culture-war authors dispense feel-good books for adults. There is very little discussion in these books about the real causes of dangers to youth such as poverty, family abuses, and increasingly disarrayed parents. To the extent that these kinds of simple-answer pop-escapisms are embraced by Americans, our singular inability to design effective measures to combat the highest levels of social and health problems of any comparably affluent Western country will continue.

Media literacy can be advanced without fabricating misinformation and slandering the young as dissolute savages. Unfortunately, many advocates take the low road. In today's Make-It-Up culture that is dominating popular books and commentary on youth, teen troubles are reducible merely to incompetent kids consuming bad pop-culture messages sold by evil intruders into idealized American family life. Until authors, academics, interest groups, and the press extend ethical standards—particularly those that protect adult groups against wanton vilification and hate speech—to their commentaries about young people, popular claims should be met with extreme skepticism. The next chapters examine how teen-sex panics relate to the resurrection of traditional racism and sexism.

Chapter Seven

SAME OLD RACISM

When we hear the oft-repeated statement, "teen pregnancy . . . rates in the United States are still the highest among fully industrialized nations" (National Campaign to Prevent Teen and Unplanned Pregnancy),[1] what does it really mean? I suggest the belief that "teen pregnancy" constitutes an "epidemic social problem" is inextricably tied to the following fact: In affluent, modern nations, "teen pregnancy" rates simply reflect *the racial diversity of a nation's population.* Stripped of euphemism, the new concern over "teen pregnancy" is the official and institutional code for the old fear that dark-skinned people (and poorer whites who act like *them*) are having too many babies.

Those Western nations with the highest rates of teen pregnancy are those with the highest proportions of populations originating in Africa, Latin America, and indigenous cultures. It is difficult to determine racial and ethnic populations in most countries uniformly, but in the United States roughly 30 percent of the total population (including 40% of the population under age 20) is of African, Hispanic, or Native origin, as is around 25 percent of New Zealand's, 10 percent of Canada's, 8 percent of the United Kingdom's and Australia's, 3 percent of Germany's and France's, 2 percent of the Netherland's, and 1 percent of Japan's.

This relationship also applies in the United States. The higher the proportion of African, Hispanic, and Native Americans in a state or local population, the higher its teen pregnancy rate. The states with the highest rates—Nevada, Arizona, and Mississippi—have among the highest proportions of these populations; the states with the lowest rates—New Hampshire, Vermont, and, North Dakota—are the whitest.[2] To add one further complication: minority populations of Northeast Asian origin (Japanese, Chinese, Korean) generally have lower teen pregnancy rates.

If this chapter looks like it is headed in a disturbing direction, read on. The problem is not the rational behavior of poorer minorities, but that privatized social policy interests have invented the "teen pregnancy" euphemism to avoid confronting difficult and unpopular questions. Let us unravel these uncomfortable matters.

IS TEEN PREGNANCY JUST ABOUT RACE?

If you look only at whites of European origin, the United States barely has a teen pregnancy problem. Nor, to a lesser extent, do the United Kingdom, Canada, or Australia, where teen pregnancy also has surfaced as an issue. Anglo nations appear to have high teen pregnancy rates because they— particularly the United States—have vastly higher proportions of African, Latin, and/or indigenous populations than do non-Anglo Western nations such as Germany and Japan.

The numbers speak for themselves. Pregnancy rates among U.S. black and Hispanic teens are two to three times higher than among teen women in the United Kingdom and other English-speaking nations (Table 7.1).[3] However, pregnancy rates among U.S. white, non-Hispanic teenagers actually are lower than those in the United Kingdom, Canada, Australia, and New Zealand and

Table 7.1   **Pregnancy Rates Per 1,000 Females Age 15–19**

	Birth/abortion totals	Live births	Abortions
US Black	110.4	63.1	47.3
US Hispanic	109.7	82.6	27.1
US all races	85.8	55.6	30.2
New Zealand	55.9	33.4	22.5
United Kingdom	51.3	30.0	21.3
Canada	45.4	22.3	23.1
Australia	45.0	20.1	23.9
US White	38.1	26.7	11.4
Norway	31.9	13.6	18.3
Sweden	25.4	7.7	17.7
France	22.6	9.4	13.2
Germany	18.3	13.0	5.3
Netherlands	11.6	7.7	3.9
Japan	11.0	3.9	7.1

Sources: Ventura, Abma, Mosher, & Henshaw (2009); UNICEF (2001).

approach those in Norway. These UNICEF figures omit the small number of miscarriages and note that abortion may be underreported in some countries.[4]

A truthful comparison would thus focus on why pregnancy rates are so high among black, Native, and Hispanic teens. The distinctive factor, as noted in Chapter 1, is their very high rates of poverty compared to teens in other Western nations, where minority teens also have high birth rates. High birth rates in the United Kingdom, Canada, Australia, and New Zealand largely can be explained by their higher proportions of minorities as well. Comparing only whites with whites (or Japanese), U.S. teen pregnancy rates would be within the Western mainstream, lower than the rates of other English-speaking nations, comparable to Scandinavia's, and higher than those of continental Europe and Japan. This becomes clearer when the nation's birth rate in general is considered. For example, 7 percent of births among U.S. whites are by teenagers, only slightly more than in Norway (5%) and Germany (6%) and below Australia (8%), Canada (13%), the United Kingdom (14%), and New Zealand (14%)—and 14 percent among U.S. Hispanics, and 17 percent among U.S. blacks.

Even the fact that the rate among U.S. white teens remains considerably higher than for continental European and Japanese teens relates to the higher rates of poverty among U.S. white youth than among youth in those countries. For example, the internationally comparable poverty rate among U.S. white youth is about three times higher than for Dutch youth. Within the United States, rates of pregnancy among white teens are some 15 times higher in Mississippi, and five times higher in Minnesota, than in the District of Colombia, closely paralleling poverty levels. So, a more correct phrasing is that *teen birth rates track not racial composition, but poverty levels.*

So, one can argue the U.S. teen pregnancy rate is not unusual; what is unusual is our demographic and economic structure. If the United Kingdom or Sweden had the same demographics as the United States, then the United Kingdom and Sweden would have teen pregnancy rates much closer to that of the United States. This reality challenges ideologues on the Left who blame the U.S.'s sexual irresponsibilities on destructive Puritanism and those on the Right who blame sexual permissiveness and promiscuity.

DISTORTION BY DESIGN

Chapter 2 suggested that the rising alarm over the "epidemic of teen pregnancy" coincided with the realization that most teen mothers were not white, and even more were poor. In that regard, the National Campaign to Prevent Teen Pregnancy (now retitled to add Unplanned pregnancy, but only among young people) epitomizes all that is wrong with America's teen-sex and teen-pregnancy discussion. Its first major report in 1997—the absurdly titled

Whatever Happened to Childhood?, which revealed in one phrase the National Campaign's politics-dictated cluelessness—voiced the standard lament that U.S. teen pregnancy rates are higher than Europe's. For a fleeting moment, it seemed as if the National Campaign might actually talk about some important issues:

> We ... need to recognize that, especially for those at highest risk, reducing teen pregnancy often requires that better, more attractive options be on hand. In a community characterized by poor schools, insufficient adult attention and guidance, limited jobs, and few recreational opportunities, early pregnancy and childbearing can sometimes seem the most appealing life course available. Babies, after all, can bring purpose and joy to life, even in the most stressful circumstances, and such early family formation is sometimes a more reasonable choice than it seems. We need to give teens ample reasons not to become pregnant or cause a pregnancy by pointing them toward a better future. ... [5]

The National Campaign then proposed exactly *nothing* to improve the poor schools, limited jobs, and bleak futures it admitted often make teen parenthood a reasonable choice. Even these limited social concerns later disappeared from National Campaign's Web page and public statements.

Worse still, the 1997 report signaled the National Campaign's mission to *interfere* with efforts to address economic and racial disadvantage: "Much concern has been voiced about this nation's lagging rate of economic growth and widening income disparities," the report declared. But the real problem was that "too little attention has been paid" to ensuring "that as many children as possible begin life with parents who are ready to nurture and care for them." Translation: do not put resources into reducing poverty and economic inequality. Instead, give more money to the National Campaign and its clients to conduct negative eugenics crusades.

This claim—which comes dangerously close to saying only rich people should have babies—has matters backwards. Very little official concern was then (or is now) being expressed about structural issues such as three decades of widening income gaps between rich and poor. But a huge amount of Clinton-era publicity argued that the poor are poor because they lack "personal responsibility," exemplified by teen parenthood. All remediations recommended by the National Campaign to reduce poverty that I can find focus on changing the attitudes and behavior of poorer teenagers through programs and "messages," not changing the attitudes and behaviors of policymakers, institutions, and businesses to reform the economic structure.

Today, the National Campaign barely mentions key issues such as poverty and racial disparity. Even after admitting in "Teen Pregnancy, Poverty, and Income Disparity" that "poverty is a cause as well as a consequence of early childbearing," the National Campaign's "Policymaker" page indulges the coded racism that minority teens are the problem: "Recent data suggest that the significant progress the nation has made in reducing teen sexual activity, improving contraceptive use among sexually active teens, and reducing the teen birth rate has stagnated and/or reversed—for minorities in particular."[6] The National Campaign's remedy was The Communities of Color Teen Pregnancy Prevention Act of 2007, which proposed no reforms to reduce economic disadvantage and improve schools and job opportunities, but simply more sex/abstinence education, school-based projects, program interventions, "multimedia" campaigns, and similar measures to benefit its constituent interests. The National Campaign's talking points concern only "personal responsibility regarding sex," "responsible policies that will increase the use of contraception," and "*more education* to teens, parents, and young adults" regarding how to prevent teen pregnancy. The debate was more sophisticated than this in 1912.

It is not difficult to decode "teen pregnancy" as "minority-group pregnancy," the social problem the National Campaign is really talking about. Indeed, more affluent, overwhelmingly white and Asian teens already have low pregnancy rates, and nearly all who have babies do so at age 18 or 19, not in high school years. Among teens under age 15, the pregnancy rate among blacks (4.4 per 1,000 girls age 10 to 14) is seven times higher, and among Hispanics (2.5) four times higher, than among whites (0.6). This recoding becomes even clearer in the newest National Campaign report at this writing, *The Fog Zone*, which—in classic social entrepreneurship expanding its market—accuses 18-to-29-year-olds of "misperceptions, magical thinking, and ambivalence" that "put young adults at risk for unplanned pregnancy."[7] Look inside the report, and you find to whom the National Campaign is attributing delusional mentalities: African Americans and Hispanics.

Move along to the numbers and rates of unintended pregnancy broken down by age, race, and income. Note, in the lefthand column of Table 7.2, that there were over 3 million unintended pregnancies among women of all ages in the United States in 2001 (the most recent report I could find),[8] nearly half of all pregnancies. Teens accounted for just one-fifth of unintended pregnancies in the United States. The number of pregnancies among women under age 20 (647,000) was only a little higher than for age 25 to 29 (611,000) and fewer than for age 30+ (811,000). In terms of rates per 1,000 women, the rate for age 15 to19 was lower than for women age 20 to 24 and higher than for women 25 and older. Further, the rates of unintended pregnancy among black women of all ages (101 per 1,000 females) and for women living in households with incomes below poverty level (87) are higher than, and the unintended rate for Hispanic women of all ages (78) is nearly as high as, the unintended pregnancy rate for teens of all races age 15 to 19 (82).

Table 7.2 Unintended Pregnancies by Age, Race, and Income of Women in 2001

Characteristics of woman	Number of pregnancies		Pregnancy rate*		Unintended rate*		Percent unintended
	Total	Unintended	Total	Unintended	birth	abortion	
All women	6,404,000	3,074,000	107	51	24	20	48%
Age							
<15	29,000	23,000	5	4	2	1	79%
15–19	811,000	624,000	107	82	33	38	77%
15–17	271,000	217,000	76	61	24	27	80%
18–19	540,000	400,000	155	115	48	54	74%
20–24	1,681,000	958,000	184	105	52	43	57%
25–29	1,566,000	611,000	170	66	32	25	39%
30–34	1,364,000	436,000	120	38	18	15	32%
35–39	766,000	291,000	56	21	10	8	38%
40+	186,000	84,000	15	7	3	1	45%
Race/ethnicity							
White	3,552,000	1,492,000	88	37	16	0	42%
Black	1,182,000	816,000	146	101	51	15	69%
Hispanic	1,278,000	613,000	160	78	36	38	48%
Income as a percent of poverty threshold							
<100%	1,513,000	923,000	142	87	37	40	61%
100–199%	1,625,000	861,000	122	65	31	27	53%
200%+	3,266,000	1,274,000	94	37	19	12	39%

*Pregnancy rates are per 1,000 women by age, race, and income level in 2001.

Source: Adapted from Finer & Henshaw (2006).

Once again, the troubling question arises: is teens' higher-than-average rate of unintended pregnancy compared to adult women's largely a function of their young age or of the fact that teens are more likely to live in poverty than are older adults? I cannot find statistics broken down by age and race/income, but the few that exist suggest that a considerably higher rate and proportion of black teens' pregnancies are unintended compared to pregnancies among white and Hispanic teens. It is reasonable to surmise that a white teenaged woman may be less likely to experience an unintended pregnancy than black or low-income *adult* women.

The rate of unintended pregnancy among U.S. women of all ages (51 per 1,000 women age 15 to 44) is considerably higher than other developed areas such as Western Europe (31 per 1,000), East Asia (30 per 1,000), and Canada (39 per 1,000), though the rates for U.S. white women and more affluent women (both 37 per 1,000) are comparable.[9] All of these are considerably lower than the unintended pregnancy rate in the developing and poorer countries of Asia, Africa, and Latin America (78 per 1,000). This pattern reiterates that poorer conditions are associated with difficulties in planning and timing pregnancies—and perhaps a more positive response to unplanned ones—for women in general, not just teenagers.

THE MIDDLE-AGE PREGNANCY EPIDEMIC

That teen pregnancies and outcomes relate much more to teens' low socioeconomic status than their age becomes clearer still when additional realities are confronted. For example, one of the best all-around predictors of infant health is weight at birth, which generates serious (often critical) immediate complications and life-long difficulties. A 2001 national study found that compared to babies born with normal weight, the 8 percent of infants born with low birth weight were kept in hospital care seven times longer and generated 25 times more in hospital costs—about $5.8 billion in total costs, or $15,000 per baby, in 2001. Very low birthweight babies, those under 1,500 grams, were 100 times costlier to care for than normal-weight babies.[10]

And here is where the blinding obsession with teen pregnancy has allowed other major problems to grow unattended. While the National Campaign and its constituents have assured us that preventing teen births would greatly improve maternal and infant health, just the opposite trend has transpired (Table 7.3). Over the last 10 to 15 years, as birth rates among teens plummeted, maternal and infant health actually *deteriorated* dramatically.[11]

From 1995 to 2006, the number of low birthweight babies born to American women leaped by 23 percent to 352,000, and the percentage of babies with low

Table 7.3   Percent of Babies Born with Low Birthweight (under 2,500 grams) by Race and Age of Mother, 2003–2006

Age of mother	All	White	Black	Hispanic
Under 15	13.2%	11.5%	16.6%	10.7%
15–19	9.9%	8.9%	14.4%	8.0%
20–24	8.2%	7.2%	13.4%	6.5%
25–29	7.3%	6.5%	13.0%	6.1%
30–34	7.5%	6.7%	13.7%	6.7%
35–39	8.7%	7.8%	15.6%	8.1%
40–44	10.8%	9.7%	17.7%	10.0%
45–49	19.8%	19.8%	21.5%	16.4%
50 and older	34.4%	35.6%	30.6%	27.3%
Total	8.1%	7.2%	13.8%	6.9%

Source: CDC WONDER (2009).

birth weight rose from 7.3 percent to 8.3 percent. The problem now is the *increasing* age of mothers (Table 7.4). The decline in low birthweight babies born to teen mothers (down 4,000) was more than offset by increases of 19,000 among mothers age 40 and older and 12,000 among mothers age 35 to 39. Most worrisome, very low birthweight numbers (babies weighing under 1,500 grams) generating critical health problems and very high costs also have risen sharply due to large increases among older mothers. We have a rising crisis costing many billions of dollars every year and, more importantly, in quality of children's lives, and health authorities have been very slow to respond to it.

Table 7.4   Births and Births per 1,000 Females by Age of Mother, 2007 Versus 1990

Age of mother	Numerical change, 2007 vs. 1995	Rate change, 2007 vs. 1995	Rate, 1990	Rate, 2007
Under 15	− 5,400	− 57%	1.4	0.6
15–19	− 76,800	− 29%	59.9	42.5
20–24	+ 10,900	− 9%	116.5	106.4
25–29	− 68,604	− 3%	121.2	117.5
30–34	+ 96,100	+ 24%	80.8	99.9
35–39	+ 182,300	+ 50%	31.7	47.5
40+	+ 63,800	+ 70%	5.6	9.5
Total	+ 158,900	− 2%	70.9	69.5

Source: CDC WONDER (2009).

One response, by the logic of today's eugenics movement, is for officials to establish an "ideal age" for having babies—say, 19 to 32—to prevent social and health costs and campaign against having babies when younger or older than the ideal range. But even that misses the point. While teens' low-birthweight propensity is due largely to the fact that teens are poorer than older adults and thus unable to afford better care, the low-birthweight risks among over-35 mothers appear physiological in origin. Why, then, are we stigmatizing teen parents for infant health problems that could be ameliorated by changes in economic policy while ignoring those same problems among over-35 parents that relate more generically to their aging?

This question relates directly to the fact that those who control policy and media presentations identify with older childbearers, regard their problems more sympathetically, and are willing to spend resources on them that they resent spending on younger parents. That sympathetic identification, I argue, is *tribal*. It is strongly rooted in the fact that over-35 childbearers are more likely to be white (62%) and more affluent, while under-20 mothers are more likely to be darker (61% are of color) and poorer. The larger, unspoken principle seems to be that privileged groups have a right to impose social costs on society without stigma; underprivileged groups do not.

But let's go even further. Table 7.3 shows that African Americans at *every maternal age* are much more likely to suffer low birthweight infants, as well as a host of other mother and child complications, than even the *youngest white teenagers*. In other words, "black childbearing" is considerably riskier than teenage childbearing.

And here we have arrived at the minefield inherent in present policy. The National Campaign's argument that preventing teens from having babies is important because, statistically, teens are at higher risk than older mothers would apply even more aptly to preventing births by African Americans. Today's natality debate is dominated by nineteenth-century dogmas spackled over with twentieth-century codewords.

Or, we could view (correctly, I believe) that all or most of the higher risks of African American childbearing are consequences of systemic faults such as high rates of poverty, poor health care, and service deficiencies that are the responsibility of government to address. Why, then, doesn't National Campaign hold government responsible for confronting the high rates of poverty, poor health care, and service deficiencies teenagers—particularly minority teenagers—suffer instead of ascribing consequences simply to poorer teens' bad choices? Agencies and their constituent interests will earn the moral right to pontificate on the poor choices of parents (that is, personal irresponsibility) only *after* government has met its own obligation to ensure that parents of all income levels have access to high-quality natality and children's services.

WHEEL SPINNING

The ongoing failing of privatized social policy is that root problems underlying crises go unaddressed. As we have seen, as one crisis drops, another arises to supplant it, and then the first crisis returns. Even as the National Campaign pats its own back, without justification, for reducing teen births, the crisis of poor natality outcomes among African Americans of all ages persists and that of mostly-white older mothers skyrockets. Until we confront the root cause of poor family, maternal, infant, and child outcomes, the United States will continue to lead developed nations in poor outcomes. As long as we continue to blame unpopular populations and crow over "success" in reducing this or that problem "they" cause, we will see the problem erupt among some other population more virulently than before.

Eruptions in drug abuse, crime, HIV, and poor infant health among middle-aged populations that *were not supposed to have such problems* suggests we have not paid enough attention to root causes. A big reason Americans fail to address real issues, in addition to the sacrifices required to do so, is the constant distraction by phony ones. As detailed in Chapter 9, preoccupation with emotional, culture-war crusades has drowned out serious, scientific analysis. For example, consider the increasingly virulent claim that modern black youth are not victims of poverty and discrimination so much as the corrupting music, dress, and lifestyles they supposedly favor.

IS THE PROBLEM JUST BLACK TEEN CULTURE?

Because the vast majority of popular books and media commentaries on youth today deplore affluent white teens (the ones who directly bother affluent, white commentators) does not mean similarly distorted demonizations of black youth should be ignored. As seen in numerous tables throughout this book, African Americans *of all ages* have much higher levels of unplanned pregnancy, abortion, miscarriage, sexually transmitted infections, HIV, violent death, crime, violence, and imprisonment than do other races. The biggest correlate of their higher risks is widespread, concentrated poverty.

It is getting hard to distinguish the racist attacks by white supremacists from the disparagements many black luminaries hurl at black youth. Indeed, had some liberal commentator rephrased white, former "shock jock" Don Imus's "nappy-headed ho's" slur against the Rutgers University girls' basketball team in proper PC-speak (i.e., "young African-American women afflicted with promiscuity and pseudo-native hairstyles promoted by corporate media")—that is, nappy-headed ho's—he would have been hailed as a courageous culture critic.

President Barack Obama, as a candidate, vilified an "entire generation of young men" whose "violence" is "sickening the soul of this nation."[12] Liberal columnist Bob Herbert, excoriated young blacks as "insane," "predators," "running wild" and perpetrating "self-destructive sexual behavior and drug use."[13] Conservative pundit Shelby Steele declared black teen pregnancy rates did not relate to poverty, but to the lack of the moral standards among black teenage girls abetted by the provision of *too many* public services.[14] Liberal commentator Juan Williams lamented the passing of the "values of the strong black community that nurtured children" versus today's "failure to take personal responsibility," "criminally bad parenting," "growth of black crime," and "crisis of school dropouts and teen pregnancy" stemming from the "self-defeating habits of many young black people."[15] Comedian Bill Cosby bellowed in a largely unintelligible rant during the 2004 NAACP awards dinner that the typical "young girl" among black "lower economic and lower middle economic people" has "got her dress all the way up to the crack and got all kinds of needles and things going through her body."[16] This is the same Cosby who had a nasty extra-marital affair after being named "Father of the Year," who refused for years to take a paternity test for the child he apparently fathered out of wedlock, who was accused by two young women of sexual assault, and who publicly disparaged the misbehaviors of one of his daughters but refuses to discuss his own deplorable behaviors.[17] Cosby's personal conduct seems to provide the credentials to be hailed from Fox News on the right to MSNBC on the left as a sage on the failings of the young.

Even famed 1960s black author Claude Brown, quoted by black columnist Clarence Page in 2002 shortly before Brown's death, said he was "dismayed with the . . . hip-hop generation." His generation had it bad, he said, but this new one, in an era of drive-by shootings and crack cocaine seemed "worse off, even more tragically devoid of hope."[18] This seems hard to believe. Brown's *Manchild in the Promised Land*,[19] published in 1965, recounted his own 1940s and 1950s Harlem preteen sexual experiences, school expulsions, and whisky drinking; getting shot during a robbery at 13, youthful heroin and cocaine abuse, kids tossing another kid off a roof to his death, and his years spent in juvenile jails, amid endless delinquencies. Very, very few young blacks today acted as badly as Brown did growing up a half century ago (even though few will write about their youths as vividly as Brown did) or as badly as Bill Cosby did as an adult.

The most representative commentary I could find on black teens and sex is *Rap and the Eroticizing of Black Youth* (2007) by Savannah State College teacher and counselor Michael Porter.[20] Like most teen-sex commentaries, Porter's heads straight for the superficial: he blames rap music and media. While "in its early days rap music led to black consciousness," his cover summary states:

> the current preoccupations of rap—especially the erotic themes expressed and their dramatization in music videos—have led to an unthinking youthful acceptance of

profanity, vulgarity, sexual abuse, and violence. The book advocates for a return to
rap's origins, for young people to become more selective and critical of today's
music, and for parents to take a more active role in monitoring their children's
listening habits.[21]

In the post-1990 period, "most Rappers are negative Rappers," Porter
declares, displacing a prior era of 1970s and 1980s hiphop that was more positive in theme. "Most Rappers, through their music, videos, and lifestyle,
encourage Black youth to have sex . . . to kill other Blacks . . . to smoke mari-
juana and to drink malt liquor and liquor." We get it. Porter is offended at
negative rap, honestly so, and has every right to take it to task.

In the area relevant to this book, Porter insists that, "Rap music videos and
Rap songs leads (sic) to increased sexual activity among black children."
Given the "negative Rap influence in the lives of Black girls," Porter asks,

> Can we expect a decrease in HIV/AIDS in Black communities? No. Can we expect
> a decrease in sexual offenses against females with this occurring in Black commun-
> ities? No. Can we expect a decrease in teen pregnancies and abortions with this
> occurring in Black communities? No. . .I predict that by 2010, the number of young
> (12 and older) sex offenders will substantially increase in the United States.

I think he meant, "12 and younger." Porter even accuses rappers and media,
led by Black Entertainment Television, of inciting black youth "to engage in
sexual activity . . . with animals (usually family pets)." Porter lists himself as a
counselor for adolescent sex offenders; perhaps he is unable to separate his
most disturbed clients from the ways the vast majority of black youth act.

If a white commentator vilified black people as "unthinking," accepting of
"sexual abuse and violence," and bestial, wouldn't we call that bigotry? That
older African Americans, who surely remember the way such terms instigated
fear and violence against blacks in the lynching days, use and tolerate them so
easily to denigrate black youth today is very disturbing.

But is what Porter says true? In the era of "negative rap," have black youth
become more violent, rapist, drug-dealing, and promiscuous? Here, the case is
open and shut. *The behaviors and attitudes of younger blacks have improved more
dramatically over the last decade* than ever before, than for any other age group,
and certainly more than for black elders. Table 7.5 brackets changes in rates of
key behavior outcomes during the "positive rap," or hiphop, era, generally
dating from the mid-1970s to 1990, with changes in the same behaviors
during the "negative," or gangster, rap era that began around 1990.

Black youths' arrest rates for violent and sex offenses rose during the 1980s
to their highest levels ever, then plummeted during the 1990s and early 2000s
to their lowest levels since the mid-1960s. The most dramatic declines for
every offense occurred from the early 1990s to the early 2000s, ironically the

Table 7.5   "Positive Rap" Accompanied Worsening Behaviors among Black Youths; Gangster Rap Era, Major Improvements, Especially in Murder and Rape

Black youth ages 10–17 changes over period in:	Positive rap era, 1975–1990	"Gangster" rap era, 1990–2000s
Violent crime rate	Up 56%	Down 40%
Murder arrest rate	Up 135%	Down 73%
Rape arrest rate	Up 56%	Down 69%
Sex offense rate	Up 36%	Down 33%
Drug offense rate	Up 191%	Down 13%
Homicide death rate	Up 129%	Down 52%
Pregnancy rate <18	Up 19%	Down 49%

Source: FBI (2009). National Center for Injury Prevention and Control (2009).

very period Porter claims black youth have been increasingly poisoned by negative cultural images.[22] While Porter charges that rap is fomenting earlier and more promiscuous sex, leading to more AIDS and pregnancy among black youth, just the reverse is true: pregnancy rates among black teens dropped dramatically, by 57 percent, from 1990 to 2005, the CDC reports.

Other measures agree. Even given the National Crime Victimization Survey's[23] major expansion in 1993 to include a larger array of sexual offenses and attempted offenses (even threats), it is evident that the rate of sexual violence declined rapidly during the last dozen years to levels that are the lowest since the survey first began in 1973 (see Table 7.6). In fact, sexual offenses, HIV/AIDS, and pregnancies and abortions have all *declined dramatically* among African-American teens over the last decade. Porter, like other

Table 7.6   Black Women's Violent Victimizations Have Dropped Dramatically Since the Early 1990s

Victimizations of black women age 12–24	Raw numbers		Rates/100,000 population		
	1993	2006	1993	2006	change
All violence	473,970	205,790	13,955.7	5,065.0	−64%
Rape/sexual assault	46,050	27,990	1,355.8	688.9	−49%
Assault	369,130	156,350	10,868.8	3,848.2	−65%
Homicide*	638	326	18.9	8.0	−58%
Black females, violent victimizations by age					
Age 12–15	138,660	66,710	12,937.6	5,059.3	−61%
Age 16–19	156,110	69,220	15,480.7	5,507.5	−64%
Age 20–24	179,200	69,860	13,616.3	4,696.3	−66%

*Sources: Bureau of Justice Statistics (2006); National Center for Injury Prevention and Control (2009).

authors, seems unable to distinguish between fictional cultural images the most objectionable of which they have selected (from a huge array of imagery, positive and negative) on the one hand, and the real world of how young people think and act on the other.

The unspoken context of bashing black youth is the growing social-class chasm along generation lines, starker than for any other race.[24] Today, a black middle-ager enjoys a median family income nearly triple that of a black 18- to 24 year-old householder and double that of a black 25- to 34-year-old. Splits in interests between increasingly well-off Baby Boom blacks and increasingly poorer ones have led to exactly the kinds of attacks on younger blacks that University of Pennsylvania humanities professor Michael Eric Dyson correctly identifies as generational in nature.[25]

Yet, strangely, middle-aged African Americans show massive increases in drug abuse (measured in overdose deaths), serious crime, violence arrest, and imprisonment over the last three decades. Drug abuse death rates exploded *20-fold* among African Americans age 35 to 64 over the last four decades but *fell* by 50 percent among blacks age 15 to 24.[26] From 1990 through 2008, violence, felony,[27] and imprisonment[28] rates soared among blacks age 35 and older but fell sharply among blacks under age 20. In 1993, blacks under age 25 accounted for 22 percent of new HIV cases among blacks, compared to 16 percent among blacks ages 40 and older. In 2004, just 16 percent of new black HIV cases were under age 25, while a staggering 43 percent involved blacks 40 and older.[29] These trends certainly do not indicate some rap-driven teenage promiscuity, violence, and HIV epidemic. As the least powerful group in society, however, black teenagers are the easiest to scapegoat.

In short, as for whites, it is *older* African Americans who show increased crime, violence, and imprisonment in recent decades while younger ages show improvements. As with whites, the worst damage and most bigoted images are being foisted on black youth not by cultural icons, but by their own privileged, increasingly ill-behaved elders. And, as with other races, the most successful generation of black girls ever is the target of the craziest new panics, as the next chapter will explore.

Chapter Eight

SAME OLD SEXISM

Wrapped up in the New Racism of teen pregnancy discussion is the New Sexism. Neo-sexism is based on fears of a "New Girl." The New Girl is depicted as randomly hypersexual, aggressive, and violent at young ages. She bullies and gets bullied by peers, sexes up too young, swills booze and drugs, gets pregnant and disease at epidemic levels, and is brutally criminal like the boys. No girl like this ever existed before. Except . . . the image of the New Girl suspiciously resembles the old image of the Black Girl.

Today's New Girl is more disturbing, though, since she mediates her resurrected underclass pathologies with new middle-class contradictions. She is both too tough and too fragile, too thin and too fat, too medicated and too anxious, over-achieving while failing miserably. She swallows advertiser-dictated identities and materialism and wallows in suicidal depression from comparing her imperfect body to svelte media images. So the modern femmette fatale legend goes.

You would think with such a load of dismal preoccupations filling her plastic little skull, the New Girl would have no room for anything else. Yet, compared to young women of the past, she is also vastly more academically successful, eagerly assuming more leadership roles, and invading formerly male territories like orcas chewing through a flounder shoal. That last development, I argue, is exactly why we are hearing a raft of girl-fearing malarkey.

Girls are taking over. Young women comprise 6 in 10 college undergraduates and masters' degree candidates, half of new grads in business, law, medicine, and physics, half of all Ph.D.s and bar exam candidates, and 45 percent of math (yes math!) degree holders.[1] Young women now seem poised to move into the last male bastions of corporate, religious, and political leadership in coming decades. Half of girls today say that is exactly what they intend to do, aspiring to be leaders at more than double the proportion their mothers reported 30 years ago. Women under age 25 now earn more than males the same age.[2]

Conservatives must feel the ill winds blowing. Had only young women ages 12 to 24 voted in 2008, Barack Obama would have won the presidency by an electoral margin of three to one, carrying all but a few white-religious fiefdoms like Oklahoma, West Virginia, Utah, and Idaho.[3] Young women, in complete contradiction to their elders' views, overwhelmingly endorse such liberal social reforms as gay marriage and communitarian initiatives. Never, even in the 1960s, has the generation gap been so wide.

By self reports, the New American Girl is more likely to have sex at a younger age—or, at least, to unashamedly say she does—and more likely to talk frankly and publicly. At the same time, compared to her mother and grandmother, she is much less likely to get pregnant, drop out of school, commit suicide or die from self destructive behaviors, get raped, murdered, or beaten up, commit a serious crime, drink, smoke, use prescription drugs, or be depressed. She is vastly more visible in public, more likely to graduate from high school, feels better about herself, is having more fun, feels more connected to her friends, likes the challenge of school and career, works to finance her education, seeks financial independence, and is optimistic about the future. First World girls now connect to a worldwide culture directly from their bedroom Internet screens and a fast-expanding array of mobile technologies. What is most encouraging: American young women's rapid improvements and successes occurred as they evolved into global diversity. In 1950, one in six females under age 20 was nonwhite; today, 43 percent.

Scary, scary stuff. The girl revolution seems out of control. Young women outcompeting males at every turn is not the Natural Order of things. There *must be* a "dark side" to these unsettling changes manifest in the darker-complected New Girl who is so disturbingly . . . out there. America's institutional bullies and culture warriors, wielding weird tones of sympathy and hostility and the potent weapon of Make It Up, are assembling to take her down.

SLUTS, VIXENS, AND FATALES

Fear of the New Girl is eternal. Peter the Hermit berated "the young people of today" in 1247 A.D., but he really meant girls, who "are forward, immodest and unwomanly in speech, behavior and dress." Not much new has been said in the last eight centuries, other than updating epithets.

During World War II, for example, major magazines like *Life*, *Reader's Digest*, and *Ladies Home Journal* blazed with new alarms that hundreds of teenage "pickups" as young as 12 were making "the sex delinquency of young girls" a new urban plague. In "Are These Our Children?" (*Look*, September 21, 1942) and "Boston's Bad Girls" (*Pic*, August 17, 1943), reporters clarioned that "Everytown, USA" was being terrorized: "Arrests for drunkenness of girls are up 40 percent . . . prostitution, 64 percent . . . truancy cases are up 400 percent . . . sex offenses involving teen-age girls, up 200 percent . . . the average age of offenders is fifteen. . . . " "V-girls" as young as 12 or 13, according to *Ladies' Home Journal*, in the new teenage "canteen culture" helped the war effort by giving departing soldiers that sendoff thrill.[4]

Likewise, in the popular *Reviving Ophelia* (1998), psychologist Mary Pipher pronounced girls a miasma of "eating disorders, school phobias, self-inflicted injuries . . . great unhappiness . . . anxiety . . . a total focus on looks . . . moody, demanding, and distant . . . elusive . . . easily offended . . . slow to trust . . . sullen and secretive . . . depressed . . . overwhelmed . . . symptomatic . . . anorexic . . . alcoholic . . . in a dangerous place . . . traumatized . . . fragile . . . saplings in a hurricane."[5] And we are not even halfway into the first chapter! The first 15 pages of Rosalind Wiseman's *Queen Bees and Wannabes* (2002) likewise labeled girls "confused," "insecure," "lashing out," "totally obnoxious," "moody," "cruel," "sneaky," "lying," "mean," "exclusive," and "catty."[6] Or, wrapping up everything in a single phrase, Courtney Martin tells us: "We are more diseased and more addicted than any generation of young women that has come before . . . a bubbling, acid pit of guilt and shame and jealousy and restlessness and anxiety."[7]

When authors and commentators express their fear and anger toward girls, why do we automatically presume the problem lies with girls? Maybe, as Northwestern University psychiatrist and long-term researcher-emeritus on adolescence Daniel Offer suggested, we older folks are just jealous. "I have always believed that part of the underlying dislike Americans have towards their young is due to the tremendous fear they have of getting old," Offer wrote.[8] Eight million cosmetic procedures among Americans aged 35 to 64 every year would seem to back that up. What accounts for all this name-calling?

Have Pipher, Wiseman, et al. really suffered such depressing associations with girls that they view the entire younger female generation as one of sadness and tragedy? They seem unable to differentiate between normal girls and the small numbers they see with psychological problems—ones whose stories deserve to be told and their miseries addressed, to be sure, but who hardly are poster children for all 25 million American girls age 10 to 24. The healthy diversity of girls shows up nowhere in these books. When Pipher says, "it's totally simple what girls think,"[9] I could not disagree more. Girls think in all kinds of ways.

If these authors are entitled to generalize from personal experiences, so am I. The girls I worked with over 15 years in home, community, and wilderness programs were individuals, so different from each other that I could not imagine lumping them into an archetype. I would say 80 percent to 90 percent of the girls I encountered in family and wilderness programs, including the ones from abusive backgrounds, were generally healthy, happy, resilient, fun to be around, and eager to talk about problems. At the risk of sounding sappy (or weird), teenage girls, far from being shrinking and distant, seemed to hug more than anyone else—and not just their boyfriends, but boy friends, each other, grownups, children, babies, dogs, gerbils, stuffed animals, embarrassed basketball coaches, even ugly old men. I have actually seen girls hug trees. Very few hold back on the emoting, even though—unlike the psychologists who, their books tell us, always said and did the right thing—I cannot say I saved any kids, though working around them usually kept me out of trouble.

Yet, Pipher and other authors are endlessly miserable around girls and find almost nothing good about them save the select few they claimed to have rescued. Let me venture the opposite speculation: What did these authors do to turn girls into such shrinking abrazophobes? Perhaps, as psychologists, they might want to consider their own bad attitudes. The truly messed-up girls they seem to find typical represented only a fraction in my experience. Certainly, I and co-workers heard about and saw school hierarchies, risky behaviors, depression, and mean peers. But that was not *all* I saw, nor were such problems confined to young women. Cruelties, hierarchy enforcements, harassments, and violence also were inflicted by parents, teachers, principals, cops, and psychologists. Massive increases in middle-aged crime, drug abuse, imprisonment, and HIV shown in previous chapters afflict the parent generation. Girls who suffered nearby adults who were suicidal, drug and alcohol abusers, violent, sexually abusive, felonious, imprisoned, disappearing, divorced, and just plain messed up were the ones with the worst problems themselves—as major studies repeatedly found.[10] The *Rape in America* report found that among girls and women who had been raped, serious drinking problems were 12 times higher, drug abuse 25 times higher, and suicide attempts 13 times higher compared to those who had not been raped.

To answer Cheryl Dellasegga and Charisse Nixon's (*Girl Wars: 12 Strategies that Will End Female Bullying*, 2003) big question—"Why are today's girls so willing to be this cruel to one another?"[11]—just look in the mirror. Just as some girls emotionally abuse their subordinates, some authors stereotype girls as cruel, violent, shallow, hateful, and randomly promiscuous, evils they depict as unheard-of among themselves and adult peers.* If the individual insults teenage alphas inflict on outcasts are mean and bullying, aren't mass insults inflicted by

---

*The exception that proves the rule, Dellasega's *Mean Girls Grown Up: Adult Women Who Are Still Queen Bees, Middle Bees, and Afraid-to-Bees* (2007) didn't sell nearly as well, and *Publisher's Weekly*'s reviewer complained about her "simplistic categorizing of women."

adult authors and commentators on an entire generation of young women ultra-mean mega-bullying?

But no matter what one's personal experiences and recollections might be, the fact remains: no author, commentator, or expert—not them, not me, a 59-year-old man with an unfortunate last name—knows even a fraction of a fraction of a fraction of America's huge, diverse young female population that qualifies us to make general pronouncements about "girls today." Nor do our sanitized memories of yesterday's teenagers, biased by benign views of ourselves, permit generational comparisons. Again and again, the documentation of authors like Pipher boils down to "what I saw in my practice" or "we feel it in our bones."[12]

If statements are to be made about girls *in general*, then *general measures sufficient to sustain them* must be marshaled. Large-scale, long-term surveys of thousands of girls—in which girls are allowed to speak for themselves rather than secondhand through the selected, filtered, always-gloomy voices of the girl-fearing commentariat—are available. They comport well with vital, education, crime, public health, and other statistical measures showing girls in general are safer, less troubled, and more accomplished today.

WHAT GIRLS SAY ABOUT THEMSELVES

What do general measures about the New Girl show? As we have seen, she is better in every way along major indexes of well being such as victimization, crime, death, suicide, murder, unwanted pregnancy, abortion, and other key measures than young women of the past or older women today. Her attitudes have evolved as well, according to the best, most consistent, long-term surveys: the University of Michigan, Institute for Social Research's *Monitoring the Future* (MTF) (which has polled half a million high school seniors from 1975 to 2008),[13] and UCLA, Higher Education Research Institute's *The American Freshman* (which has surveyed 20 million first-year college students averaging 18 and 19 years old from 1966 through 2009).[14]

Are girls and young women today sicker? Hardly. Thirty-four years of MTF reports span a generation, and the improvements in young women's attitudes across a variety of dimensions are clear (Table 8.1). Substantially more high school senior girls say they are satisfied with themselves, their education, and their lives; substantially fewer feel friendless, left out, and "no good at all." Girls today are less fashion conscious and less willing to accept inequality and dramatically more interested in becoming leaders, improving society, and financial independence. Youths have been criticized for this last goal by sanctimonious elders who apparently have not checked out the staggering college loan debts today's students have to pay off thanks to their elders' selfish demand for lower taxes rather than well-funded colleges. Other measures such as happiness, getting along with parents, and

Table 8.1   Percentages of High School Senior Females Responding to Monitoring the Future:

	Senior Class of:				
	1975/76	1980	1990	2000	2008
Happiness					
I'm "very happy"	21%	18%	18%	23%	22%
Satisfied with life as a whole	63%	66%	65%	64%	72%
Having fun	64%	67%	68%	65%	63%
Enjoys fast pace and changes of today's world	45%	42%	58%	56%	48%
Daily participation in active sports/exercising	36%	38%	34%	35%	33%
Satisfaction with (percent agreeing). . .					
Yourself?	66%	71%	69%	71%	74%
Your friends?	85%	85%	87%	83%	85%
Your parents?	65%	69%	65%	68%	67%
Your material possessions?	75%	75%	71%	73%	74%
Your personal safety?	68%	67%	66%	69%	68%
Your education?	56%	64%	64%	64%	69%
Your job?	56%	54%	60%	56%	55%
Values (percent agreeing)					
Important to be a leader in my community	19%	20%	33%	40%	46%
Important to make a contribution to society	55%	52%	62%	65%	72%
Important to have latest music, etc. fashions	77%	78%	70%	59%	51%
Important to have latest-style clothes	42%	47%	57%	42%	37%
Wants to have lots of money	35%	41%	63%	57%	62%
Women should have equal job opportunity	82%	88%	96%	97%	96%
Wants to correct social/economic inequality	37%	35%	44%	39%	46%
Depression/pessimism					
Dissatisfied with self	12%	10%	13%	10%	12%
Sometimes thinks "I am no good at all"	28%	27%	28%	25%	21%
I'm "not too happy"	13%	17%	12%	14%	14%
Feels I am "not a person of worth"	5%	5%	6%	7%	7%
Often feels "left out of things"	33%	34%	36%	34%	31%
Feels there's usually no one I can talk to	6%	5%	6%	6%	6%
Wishes "I had more good friends"	50%	46%	50%	52%	42%
Not having fun	19%	13%	16%	20%	19%
Thinks "times ahead of me will be tougher"	47%	54%	45%	42%	48%
Don't participate in sports/exercise (<1/month)	22%	20%	25%	22%	27%
Feels "people like me don't have a chance"	6%	5%	5%	5%	6%

Source: Institute for Social Research (1975–2008).

satisfaction with friends have not changed much, refuting notions that girls today are miserable, alienated, and peer-tortured.

Contrary to the drumbeat of pessimism over their attitudes and mental health, Girls generally are happier and more fulfilled today. Contradicting

Table 8.2   Percentages of High School Senior Females Telling Monitoring the Future They. . .

	Senior class of:				
	1975	1980	1990	2000	2008
Smoked cigarettes daily	29%	23%	19%	20%	11%
Smoked daily before 9th grade	13%	18%	10%	10%	6%
Drank alcohol (more than two drinks in lifetime)	82%	84%	79%	71%	63%
Drank alcohol before 9th grade	21%	26%	29%	25%	24%
Binge drinking (5+ drinks in a row, past 2 weeks)	26%	30%	24%	24%	22%
Binge drinking more than 1 time	16%	20%	14%	14%	13%
Used amphetamines at least once	23%	28%	18%	16%	11%
Used amphetamines before 9th grade	1.5%	1.1%	1.6%	1.2%	0.6%
Used marijuana/LSD/other psychedelics*	46%	56%	37%	54%	40%
Used sedatives/barbiturates/tranquilizers*	18%	15%	7%	9%	9%
Used heroin/other narcotics*	10%	10%	8%	10%	12%
Used cocaine/crack*	7%	13%	7%	8%	5%
Used drug as prescribed by physician, at least once					
Amphetamines/stimulants	15%	11%	6%	6%	6%
Barbiturates/sedatives	13%	8%	3%	2%	6%*
Tranquilizers	17%	15%	9%	9%	8%
Narcotics	17%	19%	23%	15%	17%

*Uses the highest percentage for each drug. 2008 survey included sedatives with barbiturates.
Source: Institute for Social Research (1975–2008).

pharmaceutical industry claims repeated uncritically by press reports (whose herd stories brand youth today as "Generation Rx") and authors such as Jean Twenge,[15] the decline in girls' rates of suicides and self-destructive behaviors is not due to more prescribed antidepressants or stimulants; in fact, their use of drugs of all types, cigarettes, and alcohol are sharply lower today than by their mothers in the mid 1970s (Table 8.2).

A similar pattern is evident for the half of all young women today who go to college (Table 8.3). The American Freshman's survey of 200,000 first-year women averaging 18 to 19 years old finds dramatically more aiming for higher degrees, leadership, and financial independence and using loans and work to pay for school. Fewer drink, smoke, and accept at-home roles. Nor, despite false press and lobbying campaigns by interests such as mental health and college employee unions, are college women more depressed today. In fact, the number reporting they felt depressed in the past year has dropped dramatically (Table 8.4). More report feeling stressed by all they have to do, which might be expected given the rising numbers seeking higher degrees and who have to work at jobs to pay off higher education loans.

Table 8.3   Percentages of College First-Year Women Who Say They (Are)...

	Freshman class of:		
	1970	1990	2006
Aiming to obtain high degree (PhD, EdD, MD, JD, etc)	12%	32%	32%
Financing education through loans (first asked 1978)	27%	42%	64%
Planning to work off campus to pay for education	23%	21%	31%
Drank beer in the last year	43%	51%	37%
Smoked cigarettes in the last year	11%	8%	5%
Think married women should stay home	33%	18%	16%
Agree it's important to be community leader	12%	34%	35%
Agree it's important to be well off financially	25%	68%	72%

Source: Higher Education Research Institute (1970–2006).

Of course, these are all self-reporting surveys, meaning they are subject to the usual flaws (see Chapter 5). However, we can have a bit more confidence in the Monitoring and Freshman surveys, since the trends they report match real-life declines in girls' self-destructive behaviors such as suicide, drug overdose, and dropout.

WHAT POPULAR AUTHORS SAY ABOUT GIRLS

Contrast the generally more optimistic views of young women today with the relentlessly gloomy impressions that modern authors and commentators disgorge about them. Pessimistic views toward girls seem tied to the fact that more girls are outward today and willing to say they have had sex.

Pipher, for example, is so deeply fearful of girls' sexual activity ("the issues I struggled with as a college student—when I should have sex, should I drink, smoke or hang out with bad company—now must be considered in early adolescence") that she imagines nonexistent crises must be resulting ("the

Table 8.4   Percent of College First-year Women Saying They Feel...

Classes	Depressed	Overwhelmed by all I have to do
1985–89	11.4%	25.8
1990–94	11.0%	30.9
1995–99	10.4%	37.7
2000–04	9.3%	35.9
2005–06	8.7%	36.8
Change	−24%	+43%

Source: Higher Education Research Institute (1966–2009).

incidence of rape is increasing over time").[16] Extending from Pipher's gloom over girls' supposed precocities are a crop of books that openly blame girls' supposedly sexuality for practically every dysfunction worldwide short of climate change. The most prominent at this writing are University of Iowa communications professor M. Gigi Durham's *The Lolita Effect: The Media Sexualization of Young Girls and What We Can Do About It* (2008)[17] and educator Diane E. Levin and the Media Education Foundation's Jean Kilbourne's *So Sexy So Soon: The New Sexualized Childhood and What Parents Can Do to Protect Their Kids* (2008).[18] More of the same appear with dismal regularity.

Durham, Levin, Kilbourne, and other liberal culture warriors present arguments very similar to those of conservatives. Instead of honestly discussing young people's real trends and challenges, these authors barrage readers with selected clinical cases, anecdotes, quips, news clippings, and a few surveys (most grossly miscited) to argue that the popular-culture and advertising images these authors find gut-wrenchingly offensive simply *must be* spawning a younger generation of rapists and sluts. Durham is particularly extreme. She blames the "Lolita effect" (the influence of "the media" to create younger "hypersexualized girls") for rising, global epidemics of teenage pregnancy, sexually transmitted disease, HIV, abandonment of children into prostitution, sex tourism, maternal and infant deaths, African intertribal rape, and Islamic honor killings. Durham's argument that religious and tribal rapes and killings are really rooted in new-media-warped young girls acting out Lolita fantasies is not just idiotic on its face; it is outrageously offensive victim-blaming.

I have advocated for many years for more attention to the crucial, difficult issue of the sexual abuse of children and teens, and readers may excuse my anger at Durham, Levin, and Kilbourne's crowd-pleasing trivialization of this brutal reality as merely the product of sexy, media-seduced kids. Indeed, these authors invite readers to put their pop-culture bogey ahead of real abuses. For example, Levin and Kilbourne express near-panic over an incident in which a kindergarten boy told a girl he wanted to "have sex" with her. (None of the handwringing adults were present for this remark; how could they know what it meant?) Levin and Kilbourne, after mentioning the commonly held belief that "such comments from young children can be an indication of sexual abuse" histories, then drop that possibility to urge instead (absent any evidence) that "it's probably safe to assume that the popular culture could very well have played a significant role."

I find myself wishing these and other culture-war authors could get this upset about the 30,000 children under age 12 who are *substantiated* victims of sexual abuse by their parents or caretakers *every year*. Perhaps the little boy in the previous paragraph had been among those. Books like *Lolita Effect* and *So Sexy So Soon* distract us with fictional media images from the disturbingly real abuses of children within families.

Nor, if we are into anecdotes, is this new. As previous chapters noted, the proliferation of urban prostitutes in the 1800s,[19] 1940s and 1950s sex and violence scandals involving grade-schoolers and middle-schoolers,[20] Manson Family inspiration by Beatles' songs and Biblical passages for orgies and killing, and other fearsome cases in past eras existed long before TV or mass Internet porn appeared. Durham, Levin, and Kilbourne ignore a wealth of solid references showing rape, violent crime, and dating violence have plunged sharply among teens.

Instead, they invoke liberal puritanism directed at the symbol of corrupted, suburban white teenaged girls, in which *any hint* of sexuality is fearsome. Begin with the covers of their books, featuring white teen girls, one applying lipstick, the other wearing jeans cutoffs. What do these images illustrate? The new terrors of lipstick and bare knees? While the authors issue rhetorical odes to healthy sexuality (Levy and Kilbourne list elements of normal child sexuality, while Durham calls herself "a pro-sex feminist" who believes "sex is a normal and healthy part of life, even children's lives"), they then deplore each and every instance of anyone under age 20 actually engaging in even the mildest sexual expressions, or even thinking or talking about sex.

For Durham, the mere presence of sex in popular culture is *always negative*, corrupting every aspect of young people's lives. "Toddlers see R-rated films; preschoolers watch MTV; grade-school children tune in to Victoria's Secret fashion shows; everyone gets in on the Internet," she laments:

> Children are being exposed to sexual messages at increasingly early ages, and the sexual content of children's media is on the rise: a study of prime-time TV showed that references to sex are common in the programs children and adolescents watch the most. A Kaiser Foundation study reported that in the last two decades sexual references have increased both in number and in explicitness.

The effect, she says, is to "limit, undermine, and restrict girls' sexual progress," push children into "engaging in sexual activities that were once taboo," and make "sexual violence . . . hot."

One example (among many) of Durham's pursed-lipped disapproval of even the most innocuous interactions even among older teenagers is her attack on the 2000s television series, *The O.C.* She indicts its "frequent scenes of girls in their underwear or other states of undress" who are "designated as objects of desire for the boys in the cast." She cites the show's teenaged "hot-tub threesomes" as a case of "casual 'hookups' unencumbered by prophylactics or forethought—or even foreplay."

It is hard to imagine a more sex-obsessed misrepresentation than Durham's. *The O.C.*'s alleged "hot-tub threesomes" scene (there is only one) consists of a 45-second segment in Season 3, Episode 16.[21] In it, three swimsuited high school seniors—ultra-nerd Seth, Seth's long-term girlfriend

Summer, and Summer's best friend, Marissa (the girlfriend of Seth's adopted brother, Ryan)—engage in mild banter in which Summer and Marissa express a mocking desire for each other and gentle teasing toward Seth. That is it. There's *no sex of any kind.* That Durham would see this comical nothingness as "Lolita" "threesomes" of "casual hookup" sex is truly disturbing.[†]

Durham tells us elsewhere that she strongly supports "girls' right to be sexual, to develop sexually, or to explore sexuality safely and satisfyingly." Presumably, a satisfying sex life includes being desirous and desirable. In *The O.C.*, boys also were depicted in underwear and as objects of girls' desires. Sexual relationships between the show's alpha couples, Summer-Seth and Marissa-Ryan, slow in developing after a lengthy chastity, were consensual, safely conducted, and (after the usual misfires) mutually satisfying. The show depicted rape in harshly condemning terms and promiscuous sex (which occurred much more often among the series' grownups) as disappointing to disastrous.

Durham spends many pages condemning the "exhibitionist antics of Paris Hilton and the Pussycat Dolls," "thong underwear for ten-year-olds adorned with seductive slogans like 'Wink, Wink' and 'Eye Candy,' " " 'Little Miss Naughty' underwear that offers push-up bras and lacy briefs (for) pre-teens," "Playboy t-shirts" for "three-year-olds . . . " "Peek-a-Boo Pole Dancing Kits," "Pimp Juice" ads, and the like. Had *Lolita Effect* been a catalogue of Durham's offense at objectionable images, that would have been fine. The problem— and it is egregious—is that Durham then goes on to imagine all kinds of resulting teenage depravities. This is where *Lolita Effect*, like other culture-war pamphleteering, veers from potentially valuable cultural criticism to destructive escapism and trivialization of very real sexual discrimination and violence toward girls worldwide.

Durham's descent into self-indulgent fog begins with the condescending assumption that teenagers (driven by some mysterious urge to self-destruct)

[†]Durham's puritanism was recapitulated by conservative culture warriors in a November 3, 2009, letter by the Parents' Television Council threatening local TV stations that planned to air "the November 9th episode of the teen-targeted drama 'Gossip Girl' [that] will feature major characters in a sexual threesome" with retaliation for being "complicit in establishing a precedent and expectation that teenagers should engage in behaviors heretofore associated primarily with adult films." The far-right-wing PTC gave no reason why teens would rush into three-ways after viewing the scene, which consisted of few seconds of mild kissing among three older teens and no explicit sex. Of much more concern was the show's implied attraction between a married congressional candidate and one of his nubile young staff workers. Why didn't PTC berate the show's potential for inciting impressionable congressmen to adult-film debaucheries? Ironically, the November 9, 2009, *Two and a Half Men*, a CBS sitcom airing at the same time, did show a three-way bed-scene involving two drunken 40-age brothers and a drunk woman they picked up at a bar. The brothers were the uncle and the father, respectively, of a teenage boy. The grandstanding PTC failed to cite the show as illustrating that parents' and adults' real sexual behaviors are the biggest influence on teens.

and their parents (following some mysterious imperative to destroy their kids) will stampede like lemmings toward the worst, most degrading images today's diverse modern media offer. That is, if hordes of adolescents like Britany Spears's music, they must be champing to emulate Spears' addictions and destructive excesses. "Perhaps because of media representations of carefree and impetuous sex," Durham guesses, "both girls and boys are engaging in sexual activities at younger ages—with serious consequences." She nowhere documents these demeaning assumptions. That *she is offended* is proof enough.

Durham argues that "the Peek-a-Boo Pole Dancing Kit . . . the sexy French Maid Halloween costumes sold in toddler sizes . . . the Playboy bunny motifs on children's accessories," and similar "cultural artifacts" are "not only engaging children in an adult performance of sexuality, they are sending a powerful message to adults: that sex, or more specifically sex work, is an acceptable part of childhood." If Durham really is arguing that media images are inciting adult men (the ones who cause the large majority of pregnancies and diseases among younger girls that Durham laments), then the title of her book should have been *The Humbert Effect.*

Durham then advances a roster of global crises "evident in every country in the world" she blames on this new crop of "sexy little girls" molded by sexualized modern pop culture: "domestic violence, rape, and sexual assault, sexual exploitation and sex trafficking and/or female genital mutilation . . . in the developing world;" "children as young as eleven . . . working as prostitutes" in Lithuania; "girls" being "kidnapped, raped, and prostituted" in South Africa; "young girls (some as young as twelve) being murdered by their families in so-called honor killings or forced into suicide" in Turkey; attacks on girls engaging in "un-Islamic behavior" in Iraq; that "seventy thousand girls in the developing countries die every year from complications of childbirth and pregnancy;" adults "selling children (including their own) for sex" in France; girls abused, prostituted, locked in basements, and gang-raped from India to New York; etc. Make no mistake: Durham is blaming the "Lolita Effect"—that is, "sexy little girls" seduced by their own cultural consumption—*as the root cause of these horrors.* Incredible! How does destructive irrationality like Durham's get published, let alone win praise?

Because so many, including progressives, seem to take such craziness seriously, let us consider some serious global sex realities. It should be common knowledge, especially among feminist scholars, that modern-media sexualized little girls dressing, flirting, and enticing boys and men are hardly the cause of violence and oppressions against women, particularly those that have been going on for millennia. Finally, three pages before the book's end, Durham spends a couple of sentences on some non-media triflings that just might be more important: ancient domestic violence traditions, widespread poverty, repressive anti-female customs, brutal tribalism, sexist religious and political discriminations, substandard education, and sexual exploitation and violence toward girls that began long, long before MySpace and thong underwear appeared. Durham offers no recommendations to address these real crises afflicting girls.

There is so much misinformation in *The Lolita Effect* that a new book would be needed to catalog it. "Two recent U.S. surveys indicate that one in five young adolescents (younger than fourteen) has had sex and that many more are engaging in oral sex," Durham continues. That is not what the surveys she cites show at all. The first, the Henry Kaiser Family Foundation's (2003), found 21 percent of adolescents younger than 15 had felt "a lot" (7 percent) or "some" (14 percent) "pressure to do something sexual;" how many *had* sex, oral or otherwise, was not reported.[22] The other survey, by the National Campaign to Prevent Teen Pregnancy (2003), did not mention teens under age 14 but did report mid-1990s surveys finding one in five adolescents under *age 15* said they were "sexually experienced" (see Chapter 5).[23,24] Black males were by far the most likely to report having had early sex, which is not exactly Durham's image of "Lolitas."

"Because children are engaging in sexual activity at earlier ages, rates of teen pregnancy are rising in the United States and elsewhere," Durham declares. No, they are not. The most recent pregnancy tabulations, as we have seen, show much lower levels among teens now than in any year since the first tabulations in 1973, including 15 straight years of decline from 1990 through 2005.[25] *Birth* (not pregnancy) rates among older teens rose slightly in 2006 and 2007 (and are still lower than in any year since at least 1940) but have *continued to fall among younger teens*[26]—the "Lolitas" of Durham's concern—to the lowest level ever reliably recorded. A check of the United Nation's Demographic Yearbook[27] reveals teenage birth rates have fallen sharply all over the world in recent years. Countries that report abortion and infant mortality statistics also show declines.

Media and popular culture influences are much more varied than Durham acknowledges from picking the worst of the worst, but they do have influences worth dissecting. Incisive analysis and criticism of sexist, degrading media images and products are valuable contributions. Going off the rails is not. Presenting little girls themselves seduced by their own inexplicable masochism to ape the most degrading media as the cause of "The Lolita Effect," and this "effect" as the biggest cause of global violence and oppression toward young women, is a monumental disservice to girls who suffer *real* problems at the hands of the powerful political, economic, and religious hierarchies who should be held firmly accountable.

THE NEW "SEXUALIZED CHILDHOOD"

Education professor Diane Levin and media critic Jean Kilbourne (2008),[28] like Durham, also declare that offensive cultural and media symbols must be driving kids today to "pathological sexual behavior." Like Durham, they never bother to show kids actually are acting that way. "Sexualized childhood" is "new," they insist, the fallout from the popular media's frightening new culturescape:

- "Young people today spend an average of nearly six and a half hours a day using media."
- "Media violence has not only increased in quantity in recent years—it has also become more graphic, sexual, and sadistic."
- "The average American teenager views nearly fourteen thousand sexual references in the media every year."
- "Two-thirds of young people ages eight to eighteen have TVs in their bedrooms" and "two thirds live in homes with cable TV."
- "Seventy percent of all TV programs contain sexual content."
- "Forty percent of the [popular music] lyrics studied contained sexual content."
- "In 2003, girls between the ages of thirteen and seventeen spent $152 million on thongs."‡
- "Twelve percent of all [Internet] Web sites are pornography sites, and 25 percent of all search engine requests are for pornography."
- "Many M-rated (Mature) videogames are specifically marketed and deliberately sold to youths younger than seventeen."

Why are these media snips *So Sexy So Soon* lists important? Not, assuming media has some important impact on behavior, to explore why more explicit media culture accompanied *lower* rates of murder, rape, unwanted pregnancy, and other bad stuff among teens. Rather than looking at realities, Levin and Kilbourne present their horrified reactions to some anecdotes presented under apocalyptic headings like "childhood lost" and "sexual development derailed," which they blame *entirely* on the images they select from modern advertising, videogames, music, TV, films, and celebrities.

Levin and Kilbourne are curiously indifferent to real problems. "Child sexual abuse is beyond the scope of this book," they default after a brief paragraph. This is not quite true. What the authors mean is that they have little interest in talking about the hundreds of thousands of real, documented abuses inflicted by grownups, mainly parents, on children and teens every year that are firmly linked to young people's violence, suicide, drug abuse, early sex, depression, and other serious ills.[29] Rather, Levin and Kilbourne want to limit discussion to *hypothetical* abuses they speculatively blame on "boys" incited by "media with highly sexualized imagery." Just like the 1970s, conservatives who blamed sex education for made-up tales of boys

---

‡I have not priced thongs, but it looks (from 40 seconds' online research) that your self-respecting wearer would pay at least $15 for one. Expenditures of $152 million in 2003 work out to 0.9 thongs per girl age 13–17 per year. Teen-thong alarms from *Time* to *The Nation* notwithstanding, I think the Republic will survive.

raping teachers. "The popular culture not only objectifies women and trivial-izes sex, it also often links sex with violence—with dreadful consequences," Levin and Kilbourne declare in their eagerness to blame young people's zeal to consume harmful media for *all* sexual violence against girls. "Media vio-lence has not only increased in quantity in recent years—it has also become more graphic, sexual and sadistic. Quite a few young men have learned to associate sex with domination and violence. . . . "

Naturally, Levin and Kilbourne wax nostalgic for the imaginary, clean-culture past of Elvis and the Rolling Stones—before the porn-infested Internet appeared, before Pimp Juice and Abercrombie & Fitch, before violent video-games like Grand Theft Auto were joysticked, before Ludacris and Eminem rapped and Britney gyrated, before *American Pie* and more "graphic and extreme" movies were screened, before thongs shrunk, before television programs filled with "sex talk and scenes" and "extremely graphic violence." They fail to mention that just about everything they deplore, from murder, violence, and rape to pregnancy and disease was *more prevalent* among teens in those halcyon days of yore than today.

Like Durham and other culture-war authors, Levin and Kilbourne are not shy about misleading readers. "Forty-one percent of the teenage girls (age fourteen to seventeen) in one study had had unwanted sex at some point," they write. However, they failed to note the study they cite for this number was of a small number of destitute clients at an inner-city health clinic.[30] "Girls are twice as likely as boys to experience a major depressive episode by the age of fifteen, placing them at increased risk of suicide," they write. "Between 2003 and 2004, the suicide rate for girls ages ten to fourteen jumped 76 percent." Again, they failed to note that suicide increased among all ages and both sexes in 2004,[31] that suicide and self-destructive death rates have been plummeting among girls age 10 to 14 for decades, that younger girls have by far the lowest suicide and self-destructive death rates of any age, and that their tiny suicide numbers are easily influenced by small ups or downs. In 2004, there were 98 suicides among girls ages 10 to 14; among their mothers age 45 to 49, 994; among their fathers that age, 2,749. In 2005 and 2006, suicides dropped dramatically among girls age 10 to 14—a point no one cited. Did media suddenly get better?

Levin and Kilbourne then make a curious admission that wrecks the prem-ise of their entire book: "Almost no research has been done on the impact of sexualized popular culture on younger children," and "there hasn't been much research on teenagers, either." For all their anecdotes, horror, and insistence, these authors cannot show from solid research that the media sex they deplore actually makes teenagers or preteens act sexier. No wonder that when it comes to the behaviors they claim to be concerned about, they ignore real, consistent statistics that consistently and crushingly refute claims of a violently sexualized younger generation; that teens today, saturated with explicit media, behave far better than teens of tamer media eras of the past; that if media critically influence youth behavior, it must be for the better.

THE VIOLENT NEW GIRL

Others say girls are worse today because teenagers are just innately bad people seduced by worsening modern influences. Barbara Kantrowitz of *Newsweek*, who has gotten away with years of baseless youth-bashing, opines: "But even the authors say Girl World in 2002 isn't all that different from the same planet in 1972, when today's mothers were buying *their* first training bras. For both girls and boys, early adolescence is a bubbling cauldron of hormone-laden emotion that can explode, at any moment, into full-blown hostilities."[32] *OMG! Bubbling cauldrons! Exploding* early-teen hostilities! What a shock to learn from FBI reports that the violence rate among girls age 13 to 14 is about the same as . . . 50 year-olds'. Why, a whopping 12 or so of those bubbling little cauldrons are arrested for murder every year, the same number as for 65 year-olds![33]

"There's been a disturbing increase in violence by girls," Kantrowitz recites. "Girls now account for 27 percent of all arrests (compared with 22 percent a decade ago)." Like other popular-media reporters and editors, she apparently does not do original research or fact checking. By the best evidence, much-quoted authors who claim to have researched girls' violence trends are largely making it up. For examples, Loyola University psychologist James Garbarino proclaimed a "recent, dramatic increase in violence by troubled girls" (*See Jane Hit*, 2006),[34] and Harvard School of Public Health professors Deborah Prothrow-Stith and Howard Spivak warned of "increased rates of girls' arrests for violent crime, including homicide" (*Sugar and Spice and No Longer Nice*, 2005).[35] As usual, the authors' spend hundreds of pages blaming popular culture—especially the "violence" by Lara Croft Tomb Raider, Hermione in the Harry Potter movies, and the Powerpuff Girls (*seriously!*)—without offering an iota of credible evidence.

Larger, long-term research into multiple measures of violence show no increases among girls over the last generation. Increases in the *percentage* of arrests involving girls results from a major *decline* in arrests among boys, not a rise among girls.[36] In fact, for major felonies, including homicide and robbery, girls' arrest rates are *lower* today than at any time in at least three decades. The only offense for which arrests increased among girls was assault, chiefly misdemeanor assault—which rose for all age groups and both sexes due to greater policing of domestic violence over the last three decades.

Strangely, even this limited increase in girls' assault arrests occurred from 15 to 30 years ago and has now abated. From 1995 to 2008—the period when

Lara, Hermione, Blossom, Bubbles, and Buttercup ran amuck—FBI reports adjusted for population changes show serious violent crimes, including aggravated assault, plunged among girls under age 18 from 22,600 to 16,800. When teenage population increases are factored in, that is a rate decline of 32 percent. Yet again, *the real problem is among the parent, not the youth, generation.* Among women aged 40 to 49, violence arrests leaped from 12,400 in 1995 to 17,200 in 2008—a rate increase of 19 percent.[37] Today's more racially diverse girls are the scapegoats by which privatized interests and culture-war commentators evade discussion of troubling trends among their own, older generations.[38]

COSMETIC LIES ABOUT GIRLS

Even if America's New Girl is healthier, saner, safer, happier, and dramatically more accomplished by nearly every major index, do subtler psychological trends show she's sicker today? Let us get to the sexuality-centered issue of modern worries about girls' attitudes: body image. In Courtney Martin's unhappy world, crushing anxiety about inadequate bodies is what the large majority of girls and young women *"wake up in the morning to . . . walk around all day resisting . . . go to bed sad and hopeless about"* (emphasis hers).[39] This sort of anxiety supports traditionalists' views that females are too fragile to assume larger roles in society and should be confined safely to the kitchen.

But surely, experts and *People* magazine covers proclaim, girls' body-image miseries are reflected in an epidemic of cosmetic surgery? The New Girl is supposedly so body-obsessed that, in the words of journalist Alissa Quart in *Branded: The Buying and Selling of Teenagers* (2003), "teenagers now alter their bodies extremely and proudly." She quotes a teen (yes, *one*) declaring that the new "teen breast augmentation fetish" among her peers (but not herself) is "totally common."[40] Then, Quart gives us a number: about 6,000 teens under age 19 had breast augmentations *or* liposuctions in the most recent year she cites. That is a whopping 0.0003 of 20 million teen girls. That is what she means by "totally common."

"Teens and 'tweens are perhaps open to altering or branding their bodies than adults," Quart continues. Utterly false. The American Society for Aesthetic Plastic Surgery's statistics show (Table 8.5) that girls under age 19 obtain fewer than 2 percent of all cosmetic procedures, a declining number, and even these mostly involve minor procedures.[41] What little anxiety exists seems mainly about ears, not boobs.

Today, 77 percent of medically unnecessary cosmetic surgeries are on adults 35 and older, and 9 in 10 of these involve women. The obsession with a few teens who get plastic surgery is a cover-up, once again, for the vastly greater obsession with appearance among their Baby Boom elders.

Table 8.5   Teens Aren't the Ones Getting Surgical Makeovers

	Cosmetic procedures, 2001		Cosmetic procedures, 2007		
Age group	Number	Percent	Number	Percent	Top procedures
Under 19	298,000	4%	205,000	2%	Ear, hair removal
19–34	1,870,000	22%	2,400,000	21%	Breast augmentation
35–50	3,740,000	44%	5,400,000	47%	Liposuction
51–64	2,100,000	25%	2,900,000	25%	Eyelid surgery
65+	425,000	5%	700,000	6%	Eyelid surgery
Total	8,500,000		11,605,000		

Source: Plastic Surgery Research Info. (2009).

WHY DEBUNKING LIES ABOUT GIRLS IS IMPORTANT

Today's epidemic of made-up myths about teenage sex and pregnancy are wrapped up in the manufactured image of the New Girl. For those authors touting their scholarly and professional credentials—which is nearly all of them—the persistent refusal to engage realities that dispute their emotional theses reflects a disturbing anxiety that turns up again and again in girl-fearing commentary.

Behind authors' and commentators' irrational attacks on girls lies their deep discomfort with worldly, successful young women. Just as nineteenth-century anti-suffragettes couched their fears of and for women voting in contradictory declarations of sympathy for the fragile female psyche and anger at females' unladylike assertiveness, modern authors begin their books by expressing intense fear that young women's increasing education, careers, and unprotected outside-the-home life *must be* producing rising depression, addiction, physical risk, and sexual denouement.

That is, it's the same old sexism. Pipher juxtaposes girls' supposedly new endangerment and misery with the purported fragility and vulnerability of girls venturing out of their once "protected place in space and time" into today's "toxic culture."[42] Prothrow-Stith and Spivak blame girls' supposed increase in violence on the fact that boys' and girls' "socialization differences are lessening, as illustrated by girls' participation in sports, enhanced academic opportunities, and expanded job possibilities" and equalized media treatments.[43] "It used to be competitive aspects were not emphasized for young women, but now we're in a totally different world where they are actually encouraged to be aggressive," laments a minister approvingly quoted by Dellasegga and Nixon.[44] "Girls becoming more assertive" has produced "the good news of liberation and the bad news of increased aggression [that] is the New American Girl," warns

Garbarino.[45] "Underneath the Pollyanna story of our high achievement is an ugly underbelly" of rising mental illness, addiction, and self-destructiveness, writes Martin.[46] The implications behind girl-fearing authors' made-up pathologies are clear: girls should go back to hiding behind Mommies' skirts.

The encouraging real-world attitudes and advancements of girls do not seem to matter; these authors and commentators clearly *need* girls to be getting worse. While the offended could just as effectively make their point by declaring, "modern ads and cultural images negatively affect *me*," spreading fear of girls is a more comfortable way for commentators to express offense at modern popular culture and advertising images they see as promoting violence, unhealthy sexualization, thinness, addiction, and consumerism.

Interestingly, girls themselves do not rank these culture-war nemeses as terribly troubling. When asked what they see as their most important problems, most girls cite issues such as education, economic concerns, family breakdown, war and violence around the world, poverty, global warming, anti-immigrant sentiment, government failures, drug abuse, environmental issues, racism, and discrimination[47]—that is, *real* problems. Virtually none cite MySpace, Internet threats, advertising images, fashion ads, beer commercials, MTV videos, Powerpuff Girls, or other fictional menaces that authors insist are driving girls to misery and mayhem.

Why, then, don't we see more feminist and progressive authors vigorously defending young women's modern achievements against conservatives' antipathy toward racial diversity, charges that venturing too far into the male world corrupts female morals and sensibilities, and demands for more supervision of young females? Why aren't those favoring progressive politics delighted at attitude trends among young women?[48] The eagerness of twenty-first century authors and commentators of both sexes, white and black, across the political spectrum to demonize girls with groundless panics *specifically linked to girls' rising success and externality* suggests how deeply threatening the traditional, gut-level fear of and for "girls out in the world" remains.

The harsh, analytical lens has been trained on girls long enough. It is time to refocus it on those who fear and condemn them. Strange enough that in the rich, dynamic diversity of modern American girls, girl-fearing authors and commentators who see only desolation, brutality, and helplessness win accolades. Stranger still that they cast every standard of modern research and ethics aside in a monomaniacal stampede to deny girls' optimistic generational voices, active agencies, and tangible gains and to propose more female sequestration and supervision. Quailing fear toward the New Girl is not a girl problem. It reflects the maladaptation of many adults to beneficial changes in society. Girls are more independent, outward, and successful today because they have to be, ought to be. Their sexual assertiveness is part of that change . . . not the cause of it.

Chapter Nine

PANICS DU JOUR

"We have lost all those battles," James Dobson, resigning as director of Focus on the Family, assessed conservatives' scorecard in the "culture war."[1] Dobson is right: the Right lost. Americans eagerly consume a much sexier, wide-open public culture than conservatives, traditionalists, and even many liberals want. I suspect the reason is more humbling than prurient: sex is just so damn funny. Endless sex jokes seem to write themselves. Lots of Americans, though, are not chuckling. Following Dobson's charge that "America is awash in evil," Focus on the Family posted a strikingly unpatriotic song ruing that God does *not* bless America.

In 2010, sex is explicitly everywhere. Nearly every television program, even on "family" channels, features sexy words and situations broaching new boundaries that never besmirched the 1950s screen. True, sex was not completely banished from pre-1960's television and movies. I was recently surprised to find references to sex—and cynical ones at that—in rewatching some episodes of Sally Field's television version of *Gidget*. Sex is no big deal, Fields, depicting a 15-year-old, nonchalantly declares to abashed father; it's just for making babies. Her uptight psychology-student brother-in-law suggests Gidget's zaniness stems from sexual repression.

Pretty bold for 1965. Many of us guessed that *Gunsmoke*'s Miss Kitty (please) ran a cathouse above the Long Branch Saloon where Matt Dillon, Doc, and perhaps even Chester (no one seemed to have spouses) partook. Television shows and cartoons of the 1950s and 1960s were rife with mystery.

Where did Olive Oyl's rugrat Sweat Pea come from? Huey, Dewey, & Louie? If you had a genie like Barbara Eden at your command, what would your first wish be? What's with all those bachelor dads? It left much room for untoward speculation.

Adults of those times certainly blamed cultural manifestations for youth scandal. In 1965, seven members of my high school tennis team abducted a 15-year-old runaway girl from a drive-in restaurant, took her to an oilfield, gang-raped her, and left her alive but severely injured under a bridge. Although general sentiment at my high school held that the rapists deserved horsewhipping and even more appropriate punishments, many Oklahoma City adults insisted this brutal crime was the signature of modern youth raised amid sex-saturated Natalie Wood, *La Dolce Vita*, Elvis's hips, Chuck Berry's ding-a-ling, and Mick's let's-spend-the–night-together. (Just a decade earlier, the same city's upscale youth had been indicted in legislative and congressional hearings for heroin- and pill-fueled sex orgies involving kids as young as 10, abortion scandals, and a teen-murdered policeman, but convenient memories are short.)

A covey of ministers blamed drive-in restaurants—Sonic, Dairy Queen, A&W Root Beer, the lot—for the rape and demanded that they be shut down. Still others cited the Supreme Court's 1963 decision banning school-sponsored prayer, though my high school's administrators still required daily Bible readings over the scratchy intercom. Another cabal blamed modern dancing, in which couples mashing together must be having impure thoughts, even as the Twist was gaining popularity and teens danced farther apart than ever. In a nutshell, the culprit was—and always is—modernity.

All that seems perfectly innocent now that public culture has gotten much, much worse. Prime time television shows (as of this late 2009 writing) boast baldly sex-riddled plots, and some like *Two and a Half Men* and *How I Met Your Mother* seem dedicated to stuffing as much sex into a half hour as possible. Teenage sexing is routine in TV scripts, with a wide range of outcomes: romantic, comical, disastrous, or nothing at all. In the biggest revolution, gays went from screen invisibility before 1970 to token and subdued in the 1980s to ubiquitous and flaming on *Ugly Betty, Chelsea Lately* (2009 Teen Choice award winner for best late-night talk show), and dozens of other programs. Onscreen teens have gay friends who banter about their sex lives with the brazenness of straights. A gay youngster's coming-out, once a shattering family crisis (note PBS's 1970s proto-reality TV show on the Loud family) is the new normality, even the ideal. (A Kardashian sister muses that every upscale family needs a gay member.) Openly gay Rachel Maddow has her own prime-time talk show on MSNBC; Ross Mathews, who all but burns down the set, has a celebrity talk program on NBC; new celebrity outings bounce along by the week, it seems.

Dobson's conservatives not only lost the culture war, they suffered a four-quarter beatdown. While the Right maintains some political success against abortion and gay marriage, it has lost the media battle in a route. A lot of liberals agree with the Right: there is too much sex, and of the wrong kind, in public culture. Many feel we have moved far past the slogan of one lobby: enough is enough.

For decades, culture warriors have indulged fantasies of walling off "innocent children" (up to age 20 or even older) from the adult sexual world. It is a laughable crusade. Birth registration, STD, and marriage statistics for nearly a century have shown that adult-teen sex is the rule. Now, the polite pretenses of the past are finally yielding to reality: twenty-first century children and teenagers cannot be shielded from the riot of sexual imageries and information in public culture. For all the fulminations about "the children," no system of ratings, ID checks, or even criminal laws has dented youthful consumption of R-rated movies and sexually explicit songs, books, and videogames. The Internet is a buffet of sexuality in every flavor. No matter how filtered and nannied, any child can find hardcore porn online at home within a click or two of seeking it. Whether youth consume the worst or not depends on their own inclinations, not adult controls.

The fact that *nothing* can be done to prevent young people much past kindergarten from independently accessing any information they wish appears to have unhinged a large chunk of Americans, organized into a strikingly similar Culture-War Right and Culture-War Left. There are some differences. Conservatives tend to attack pornography and permissiveness while liberals attack corporate advertising and profit from degrading messages. But both sides buy into the Nostalgia Myth: that society has degenerated from yesterday's idealized, sternly moral past in which parents, laws, institutions, and business cooperated to protect children and teens from premature exposure to salacious cultural manifestations. Both accept the traditional puritan belief that children are "innocent," corrupted when ill-motivated grownups reveal the reality of sex. Both reject scientific method and present themselves as holy crusaders, which apparently justifies making things up as necessary to win.

Today, there is just about no sexual expression by young people, especially girls, of which either conservatives or liberals approve. PG-13 emails, bathing-suit pictures, cell phone texts, conversations, and even mild displays of affection by teenagers are coming under intensified condemnation as dangerous "sexting" and "hooking up." One prominent organization receiving fawning news and political attention defines middle-school interactions as simple as sitting next to a person of the opposite sex in classes or thinking of one another as "dating" and therefore troubling. I have to look twice to see whether a fearsome anti-teen-sex rant is from the liberal *Alternet,*

Mother Jones, or *Huffington Post* or a right-wing outlet like Heritage Foundation or Parents Television Council.

The liberal and conservative positions on teenage sex are now defined strictly by whether one favors sexuality or abstinence education. Both sides require an endless barrage of teenage crises to blame on the other. And so, an endless barrage of teen crises is guaranteed. This chapter looks at the most prominent panics du jour—hooking up, Internet predators, teen dating violence, sexting, and the old standby, sex on television—with knowledge that by the time this is read, new ones will have been invented.

HOOKING UP

The notion that random, impersonal sex now dominates high school and college relationships offers fodder for moralists, whether corporate commodification of youth or moral breakdown fostered by liberal permissiveness are blamed. A rash of books, *Unhooked: How Young Women Pursue Sex, Delay Love, and Lose at Both* (2007) by Laura Sessions Stepp; *Hooking Up, Hanging Out, and Hoping for Mr. Right: College Women on Dating and Mating Today* (2001) by the Institute for American Values; and *Hooking Up: Sex, Dating, and Relationships on Campus* (2008) by Kathleen Bogle, span the left-right gamut, as do a Titanic-load of identical Sunday magazine articles and media reports. For examples, see Benoit Denizet-Lewis's "Friends, Friends with Benefits, and the Benefits of the Local Mall" (*New York Times Magazine*, May 30, 2004); Sharlene Azam's undocumentary, "Oral Sex Is the New Goodnight Kiss;" the Christian guide, *Teaching True Love to a Sex-at-13-Generation*; Deborah Roffman's "Dangerous Games: A Sex Video Broke the Rules, but for Kids, the Rules Have Changed" (*Washington Post*, April 15, 2001); Lisa Belkin's "The Making of an Eight-Year-Old Woman" (*New York Times Magazine*, December 24, 2001); on and on. Most are too mind-numbingly baseless to scrutinize. I will examine just a few of the most popular, representative works.

Washington Post reporter Stepp's *Unhooked* [2] received widespread attention even though, as in her similarly ungrounded stories for the *Post*, she presents no real evidence for her premise that random, loveless sex has become the "primary currency of social interaction" between the sexes in high school and college. Her tales, anecdotes, and quips about young people—mostly from nine young women she selected to profile *precisely because they would validate her thesis*—followed by her shocked reactions provide little to buttress her claim of mass generational "hooking up."

"Hooking up" sounds bad, but what is it? "It can mean anything from an innocent kiss to sexual intercourse." So, 1950s Doris Day movies are rife with hooking up? "It isn't exactly anything," Stepp admits. Oh, yes it is. "Hooking up" functions as a derogatory-*sounding* contrivance youth-bashers deploy to disparage even the most harmless relationships as slutty.

Stepp's tabloid style begins on the first page with anecdotes of gossip about oral sex at a middle school and a college "date auction," followed by her insistence that nothing like this ever could have occurred in the chaste decades before 1990. "Casual sex . . . was the exception in college even during the '60s, '70s, and early '80s, when most of these kids' parents were dating," she declares.

Evidence for these statements? Not a shred. Here's Stepp's *idea* of evidence: she hears *one* modern teen express surprise at "holding hands." Proof: no teens today hold hands. Therefore: teenage romance is dead. That is the book's pattern. A girl tells Stepp (or tells someone who tells Stepp) that she once engaged in or heard of someone engaging in ___. Bam: all young women ___. *Unhooked* amounts to pages of sexy anecdotes and dire quotes that could be assembled about any group. None of the "hookup"-asserting authors bother to show that a young couple having sex in 1960 or 1975 acted out of pure romantic love and commitment while a similar couple in 2009 was indulging interchangeable physicality. None of them cite the best measures available—for obvious reasons.

For example, Monitoring the Future[3] seems to document an opposite trend. In 1976, 74 percent of high school seniors said they eventually planned to get married, and 85 percent wanted a mate for "most of (their lives)"; by 2008, those numbers had risen to 80 percent and 86 percent, respectively (Table 9.1). In both years, an identical five in six said they were very likely or fairly likely to stay married to the same person for life. Delusional, perhaps, but hardly hookup mentality. True, the 2008 Monitoring the Future survey found 53 percent saying they "go out with a date" two to three times a month or more often, versus 66 percent in 1975. So, fewer teens date frequently (imagine the horrified reaction if more did!), and, reflecting the later age of marriage, a slightly smaller percentage say they are currently engaged or married. But the proportion who plan to marry is actually a bit higher than 30 years ago.

To the most relevant question asked in *American Freshman*: "If two people really like each other, it's all right for them to have sex even if they've known each other only for a very short time," 44 percent of entering freshmen, including 29 percent of women, said "yes" in 1974 (the first year the question was asked), compared to 45 percent, including 34 percent of women, in 2005. The peak year was 1987, when 51 percent answered "yes." In another relevant question, Monitoring the Future found an identical 27 percent of high school seniors agreeing that "having a close intimate relationship with only one partner is too restrictive for the average person" both in 2008 and in 1975.

This stability among youth is all the more remarkable given the increases in family breakup among their parents—the ones lauded by Stepp and others for

Table 9.1   The Best (and Only Long-Term) Surveys Show No Evidence of "Hookup" Culture

Monitoring the Future (high school seniors), yes response:	*2008*	*1975/76*
Just one intimate partner is too restrictive for most people	27%	27%
Wants one mate for "most of life"	86%	85%
Goes on dates 2 to 3 times/month or more	53%	66%
Currently married or engaged	6%	10%
Plans to get married in future	80%	74%
American freshman (first-year younger college students):	2000s	1970s
OK to have sex with partners you just met	45%	44%
Men entitled to sex if woman "led him on"	20%	89%
Currently married	0.4%	1.6%
Their parents' trends (decennial census), age 35–64	2000	1970
Women age 35–64 married and living with a husband	69%	84%
Divorced/separated	19%	8%
Never married	10%	6%
Men age 35–64 married and living with a wife	69%	86%
Divorced/separated	15%	7%
Never married	12%	7%

Note: This table compares responses to the earliest instance of the question (1975–1976 for Monitoring the Future, (1968–1974 for American Freshman), to the most recent (2008 for Monitoring the Future; 2001–2006 for American Freshman).

Sources: Monitoring the Future (2009), op. cit; Higher Education Research Institute (2009), op. cit.

their affinity for lifelong love and kisses. From 1970 to 2000, the Census showed the proportion of non-widowed women aged 35 to 54 who were divorced doubled, and the proportion who did not live with husbands rose from around one in six to one in three.[4]

The biggest change among young people went in a positive direction: In 1968, just 20 percent of entering college freshmen thought that "just because a man thinks that a woman has 'led him on' does not entitle him to have sex with her," compared to 89 percent in the most recent year this question was asked, 2000. The enormous leap in the proportion of students of both sexes who rejected male entitlement to sex—what we now unequivocally brand as rape—is a stunning blow to "hookup" authors' claim that today's youthful sex is more dangerous. So, naturally, they never mention it.

Stepp does cite a 2002 Centers for Disease Control survey finding that one in two 15-to-19-year-olds say they have engaged in oral sex. We are not told why this is important. When examined, that report states that less than one-quarter of 15-to-17-year-olds ever had oral sex, versus around two-thirds of 18-to-19-year-olds. "Earlier surveys of such scope don't exist, so there's no way to know how this compares to older generations," Stepp admits. However, ignorance does not stop Stepp from asserting, "Adults in their forties and older believe that it occurs more frequently now than when they were young." Nowhere does she tell us how she knows what adults think or how they would know what tens of millions of teens are doing now versus back then.

Stepp also combines zero scholarship with rotten scholarship to blame "hooking up" for the "epidemic of depression on campus," rising women's binge drinking, rape, and the "stubbornly high" rate of sexually transmitted disease. Aside from presenting zilch evidence, she cites all of these trends incorrectly. Monitoring the Future does not show students, male or female, more depressed today than a generation ago, The most recent *American Freshman* survey reports "stress and depression on the decline" to its *lowest level* since the survey first asked the question two decades ago. Survey press releases have clearly pointed this trend out, and interest groups have repeatedly misrepresented it. If "hooking up" pivotally affects students as Stepp insists, it must be making them happier.

"Young women's alcohol consumption has risen over the past ten years to where it almost matches that of men," Stepp writes, citing Monitoring the Future (2003). What Monitoring the Future actually shows is that women show *no increase* in any of the four measures of drinking (annual, monthly, daily, or binge), either in the last decade or since 1980. Nor do women show any increase in drinking relative to men since 1980. Women's drinking matches men's only for having had a drink in the past year (in 2003, 82% of both male and female college students had at least one drink in the previous year, versus 90% for both sexes in 1980). For daily drinking and binge drinking, women's rates remain well below those of men. *The American Freshman* likewise finds rates of drinking by first-year college women today are much lower than among their parents in the 1970s. The impression Stepp creates that more binge drinking by women and more "hooking up" are parallel trends is wrong on all counts, even by the source she cites.

Further, Monitoring the Future finds that while 40 percent of high school seniors (16% of boys and 43% of girls) said they drank alcohol on dates in 1976, only 28 percent did so in 2005 (25% of boys and 31% of girls). Girls' higher rates may reflect the age-old tendency of girls to date older men, but in any case the connection between drinking and dating has declined.

Stepp further alleges (citing no evidence) that "hooking up" promotes more rape. But if that's the case, why has rape been plummeting—most rapidly among young women aged 18 to 24—over the last three decades as "hooking up" supposedly replaced traditional dating? Stepp's evidence for alleging more ambiguous "gray rape" today consists of a couple of anecdotes that are amply contradicted by more comprehensive information (see Chapters 6 and 8). Indeed, the 2002 National Institute of Justice study she cites, *Campus Sexual Assault*, notes that "in recent years, rape reform law has moved toward expanding the definition of rape to include various forms of sexual abuse and degrees of severity," from completed rape to threats.[5] Recent research reported by the National Institute of Justice (2006), the 2005 National Violence against Women Survey, and the 2006 National Crime Victimization Survey find women today, particularly younger women, are more likely than women of the past to correctly define victimizations as rape and to report them to police than in past decades.[6,7]

"STD rates remain stubbornly high" among 15-to-24-year-olds, Stepp notes, adding that "more young women than men now contract STDs." It is amazing how many authors who claim dramatically worse behavior changes among modern youth have never bothered to look at the prevalence of those same behaviors in the past. For those STDs the Centers for Disease Control consistently measures, rates are considerably lower than in the early 1970s, and young-female rates have been higher than males' for decades. Thus, while Stepp's *Unhooked* provides personal accounts of a promiscuous lifestyle that does exist and always has among certain sectors of the population, her thesis that "hooking up" represents some new, dangerous trend is groundless.

LaSalle University sociologist Kathleen Bogle's, *Hooking Up: Sex, Dating, and Relationships on Campus*, explores college dating largely through interviews with 76 selected students.[8] The book begins on a frivolous note with the quip from journalist Tom Wolfe cited in the Introduction to set up her point that "clearly, times have changed." Indeed they have; pregnancy, rape, and other sexual violence, early marriage in or just after high school, and consistently measured STDs have *declined* among teens in recent decades, especially at the youngest ages. However, Bogle does not refer to these changes or how they might relate to modern young people's patterns of interaction. Rather, after warning against the presumption that traditional one-on-one dating represents a superior form of relationship, Bogle then lapses into vague unease over modern "hooking up."

Bogle's evidence for a new epidemic of hooking up (or even what the term means) fueled by drinking, fraternities, and some unnamed cultural dissipation is thin. There is some evidence for back and forth trends in romancings, with *any* youth behavior imagined as different from their parents' bringing grownup anxiety. In 1965, for example, popular advice columnist Ann Landers lamented the 1950s trend toward one-on-one dating and "going steady" as promoting exclusion and excessive sexual intimacy; back in the 1920s and 1930s, Landers reminisced, teens went on safer group dates and only later chose romantic partners.[9] Now that teens and college students socialize in groups and group dates have (allegedly) returned to vogue, "traditional dating" is fondly recalled as the romantic ideal.

Virtually all of Bogle's evidence for a new "hookup culture" on college campuses is more than 20 years out of date. The one exception is an unpublished

Institute for American Values study that found "40 percent of women said they had experienced a hook up."[10] Wild sounding stuff, until you read that "hookup . . . can mean anything from kissing to having sex." One could argue from this definition that Tom Sawyer and Becky Thatcher, or Mommy and Santa Claus, "hooked up." Indeed, as Bogle points out, "necking and petting" (which involve kissing and considerably more) were common among young people who were informally acquainted as long ago as the 1920s. Nothing new.

The report by the conservative Institute actually found that 70 percent of the college women surveyed in 2001 said they had gone on dates, including 50 percent who had gone on six or more dates, with college men. That sounds like dating is still alive and well on campus. The biggest finding was that 60 percent of young college women today had not so much as kissed a college man, even once, who they were not formally dating. Where *is* all this campus risk-taking we are hearing about? Unfortunately, the Institute's authors then romped far beyond their statistical findings to imagine a crisis their own selected interviewees never suggested:

> There are few widely recognized social norms on college campuses that help guide and support young women in thinking about sex, love, commitment, and marriage . . . As a result, the culture of courtship, a set of social norms and expectations that once helped young people find the pathway to marriage, has largely become a hook up culture with almost no shared norms or expectations. Hooking up, hanging out, and fast-moving ("joined at the hip") commitments are logical, though we believe seriously flawed, responses to this disappearance of a culture of courtship. The options available to college women are obviously strongly influenced by choices that other young men and women make, but each young woman today tends to see her choices as wholly private and individual. For example, while most college women expect to marry for life and 88 percent would not personally consider having a child outside of marriage, 87 percent agree that "I should not judge anyone's sexual conduct except my own." Consequently, when women are hurt or disappointed by the hook up culture, they typically blame themselves.
>
> The lack of adult involvement, guidance, and even knowledge regarding how young people are dating and mating today is unprecedented and problematic. Parents, college administrators, and other social leaders have largely stepped away from the task of guiding young people into intimate relationships and marriage. Few older adults are aware of what hooking up or dating means for college students today, and the institutional arrangements of space on many campuses, such as coed dorms, clearly help to facilitate the hook up culture.

These appallingly backwards assertions go beyond even those one would expect from a right-wing institute seeking more "male initiative" and old fashioned "courtship." The Institute for American Values actually deplores the fact that today's women take responsibility for their sexual choices rather than blaming others! The Institute argues for the lauded 1950s "culture of courtship" that, the report fails to note, was followed by 50 percent to 60 percent divorce and family breakup rates to guide today's young women who are assuming refreshing responsibility for their own lives. That liberals, including feminists, would cite this confused, backwards nonsense and its assertions that so profoundly disaffirm women shows the link between culture warriors of the Left and Right. "Hooking up" as a mass characterization of young people's interactions is just name calling. It allows a flawed grownup culture to praise itself by disparaging the young, made all the easier since no real evidence is required.

IS THERE AN EPIDEMIC OF "TEEN DATING VIOLENCE"?

"Hooking up" may be a chimera of modern culture war's Make It Up ethic, but there is no question that violence between romantic partners—spouses, housemates, daters, teen and adult alike—is a critical issue. California alone documents some 200,000 reports of domestic violence to law enforcement every year, and few doubt the crime is severely underreported.[11] That is why the most compelling, valid science must be applied to delineating the scope of the problem to design effective countermeasures. The hijacking of this vital issue by teen-fearing interests pursuing their private agendas, and their sensation-seeking politician and news media sycophants, represents a despicable hindrance.

In contrast to serious violence analysis and prevention efforts, "teenage dating violence" ("TDV") has become a political and marketing logo designed for news media consumption. It is prejudicial because it connects an entire demographic to a negative behavior (imagine the term, "Jewish dating violence"). It is inaccurate because, like "teen pregnancy" and "youth violence," it misrepresents the phenomenon as confined to teenagers even though their behaviors are inextricably intertwined with those of adults. In this case, adult partners are responsible for a significant share of what we mislabel TDV (in fact, many interests define "TDV" as including adults over age 20), and histories of childhood abuses by adults are precursors of later dating violence. The Bureau of Justice Statistics' non-prejudicial term, "Intimate Partner Violence" (IPV), applies to all ages and is used here as the referent term.

In a classic example of privatized social policy, American secondary schools recently have come under intense pressure from corporations and politicians, aided by near-hysterical news media blitzes, to implement "teenage dating abuse" programs profiting the same corporations and politicians whipping up fear of it. A resolution by the National Association of Attorneys General urged "school districts to incorporate dating violence education into health education curriculums in middle and or high school." Declared Rhode Island Attorney General Patrick Lynch, the resolution's chief sponsor: "A curriculum such as

Liz Claiborne Inc.'s Love Is Not Abuse is an effective way to begin the process of education, prevent abuse and help to save lives."[12] Liz Claiborne? The fashion mogul? The one marketing its program to schools, legislators, and always-pliant news reporters, and its logoed clothing and jewelry to teens, fueled by promotional claims that "teen dating violence" is "increasing" to "staggering" levels?

The commercial and political nature of "teen dating violence" becomes evident in the targeting of a powerless demographic for negative portrayal based on made-up standards that would make any group look bad. Commonly cited numbers reported in the press and by program advocates, summarized by the American Bar Association's Teen Dating Violence Initiative, indeed appear alarming. "Approximately 1 in 5 female high school students reports being physically and/or sexually abused by a dating partner . . . Females aged 16 to 24 are more vulnerable to intimate partner violence than any other age group—at a rate almost triple the national average."[13]

Alarming, yes . . . if any of this malarkey were true. However, the most alarming numbers being cited reflect limited 1990s data that do not belong in a professional lobby's 2007 report. Curiously, the Bar Association study leaves out the most authoritative report, the Bureau of Justice Statistics' (BJS) *Intimate Partner Violence*. Perhaps that is because the BJS study found that 2.1 percent of students ages 12 to 19 (including 0.9% of youths age 12 to 15 and 3.4% of those age 16 to 19) experienced any form of physical violence that would meet the definition of a serious or minor violent crime from an intimate partner (a spouse, ex-spouse, boyfriend/girlfriend, ex-boyfriend/girlfriend, same-sex partner) at any time in the previous year.[14] This report relied on the National Crime Victimization Survey, America's largest, most consistent, and only long-term measure, with annual samples of at least 70,000 Americans since 1993—one that does not include the "problem inflators" embellishing other surveys.

Recent, comparative surveys do not find teens uniquely at risk. *Intimate Partner Violence* reports that from 2001 to 2005, teens aged 16 to 19 had lower rates of intimate-partner violence (3.4%) than adults age 20 to 24 (6.5%) and 25 to 34 (4.7%) and somewhat above those of adults age 35 to 49 (2.8%), while 12 to 15-year-olds experienced the lowest levels of dating violence (0.9%) of any age except 65 and older (0.1%). Given that intimate partner violence rises sharply as socioeconomic status falls and that teenagers and young adults suffer distinctly higher rates of poverty, teens experience fairly *low* rates of IPV.

Nor is dating abuse rising. *Intimate Partner Violence* also found that from 1993 to 2005, the proportion of teenage females reporting IPV fell by 70 percent. The most recent report, through 2008, reports that IPV continues to decline. Though estimates are provided only for general ages, teens age

12-17 suffered IPV rates (1.7 cases per 1,000 females) less than half the rates of adults age 18 and older (4.5) in 2008. For those under age 25, females comprised 18 percent, and males 10 percent, of IPV murders.[15]

That is, the best information shows *young couples are experiencing low and declining rates of serious violence.* As discussed in previous chapters, the long-term measures available such as FBI Uniform Crime Reports, National Survey of Family Growth, Youth Risk Behavior Survey, and National Crime Victimization Survey variously agree that murder, rape, robbery, assault, sexual assault, and kidnapping involving younger and older teens has dropped dramatically over the last 10 to 20 years, most to all-time lows. Intimate partner violence has fallen the most dramatically.

Where, then, do the alarmingly large figures for teen violence come from? For an example of drastic problem inflation, consider the widely used Youth Dating Violence Survey (YDVS).[16] Those deploying the YDVS typically report that half or more of teens experience "dating violence," including not just real assault, but also "emotional violence" defined as follows: "Has a boy-friend/girlfriend ever ... (a) said things to hurt your feelings on purpose? (b) insulted you in front of others? (c) not let you do things with other people? (d) told you that you could not talk to someone of the opposite sex? (e) put down your looks? (f) made you tell him/her where you were every minute of the day? (g) did something just to make you jealous? or (h) threatened to start dating someone else?"

This is ridiculous. By the YDVS's vague, scattershot questions asking whether some partner ever did something—even mildly, even once, regardless of context—it is highly likely that 100 percent of adult marriages would be defined as emotionally violent. Telling a partner you do not like the shoes he is wearing, saying a partner makes bad coffee in front of her sister, or going over the day's activities in detail (even for fun) is considered "emotional violence"—as is just about any breakup.

The most crushing proof of how self-serving interests have hijacked and hyped "teen dating violence" is provided by a 2008 survey commissioned by Liz Claiborne Inc., whose spokeswoman then abjectly misrepresented their own survey with the help of fawning news coverage.[17] "One in three teens reports knowing a friend or peer who has been hit, punched, kicked, slapped or physically hurt by their dating partner," a representative of Liz Claiborne stated to the press. "The number of 'tweens [ages 11 to 12] in abusive relationships (is) staggering." The Attorney General's 2008 resolution agreed: "Teen dating violence has become a prevalent problem in high schools, junior high schools and middle schools throughout our country ... Recent studies have shown that teen dating violence is starting" as young as ages "11 to 14."

But Liz Claiborne's survey actually found *nothing of the sort.* I was fortunate to obtain a copy of the original survey,[18] which Claiborne had not provided with its press release—and even more appallingly, news reporters covering the issue (with one exception[19]) showed no evidence of having read it. Liz Claiborne's survey actually found that 2 percent of 11-to-14-year-olds (14 males and 7 females out of the 1,043 surveyed) reported *ever* having had a partner "hit, slap, punch, choke, or kick" them even once. Further, 1 percent reported having been pressured into sexual activity (a total of 5 males and 8 females; whether these duplicated some of those physically abused is not shown).

As with the YDVS, Liz Claiborne's employed wild problem-inflating techniques—several of which carry harmful implications—to drastically exaggerate the prevalence of teen dating violence. Like other lobbies, Liz Claiborne extended the definition of "teen dating violence" far beyond the National Association of Attorneys' General criterion of "a pattern of controlling and abusive behavior of one person over another within a romantic relationship including verbal, emotional, physical, sexual, and financial abuse."

Liz Claiborne's first problem-inflation trick was to include figures for 20-to-24 year-olds (an age group with considerably higher violence rates) as "teenage dating violence." Second, it repeated higher 1990s numbers rather than the most recent, dramatically lower numbers. Third, it cited one-time behaviors rather than those documenting a *pattern of controlling and abusive behavior.*" Liz Claiborne's fourth problem-inflation technique was to emphasize not the small numbers of teens who reported *really having been abused*, but secondhand *guesses* by teens in response to speculative questions as to whether "people your age" might suffer abuse by dating partners.

Liz Claiborne's fifth and most disturbing exaggeration technique was to expand the definitions of "relationship" and "abuse" far beyond behaviors normally associated with the terms. In Claiborne's survey, a "relationship" included not just regular dating, but "sitting next to each other in school," "admitting that he/she likes the other person," "flirting," and "calling or texting each other regularly." I am not joking. A boy and girl sitting next to each other in school is a "relationship."

Even worse was Liz Claiborne's definition of an abusive relationship. "Abuse" included partners who "made you feel bad or embarrassed about yourself," "made you feel nervous about doing something he/she doesn't like," "hurt you with words," or "tried to tell you how to dress"—even once. So, a boy tells a girl sitting next to him at school, "wow, you did bad on that test," or a girl texts a boy, "why don't you wear that black shirt more often?" . . . that's "dating violence," according the Liz Claiborne.

Not content with these huge exaggerations, Liz Claiborne's press statements cited alarming "dating abuse" numbers that came from tiny subsamples of teens, not the whole sample. For example, consider Claiborne's statement, "69 percent of all teens who had sex by age 14 said they have gone through one or more types of abuse in a relationship." Having "sex," by Liz Claiborne's definition, referred to not just intercourse or oral sex, but ever "having gone further than kissing and making out." Thus, the "69 percent" figure actually referred to just 30 of the 1,043 youths surveyed who had experienced even the mildest negative interaction with a partner with whom they had gone further than kissing or making out.

As for real emotional abuse, Claiborne's survey found that just 3 percent of teens had "been concerned about [one's] safety (being hurt physically because of him/her)," and 2 percent reported that a dating or hookup partner actually had "threatened to hurt you or himself/herself if you were to break up." Nor did the survey confirm Claiborne's and news media insistence that modern technology has opened up vast new theaters of meanness. Only 2 percent of 11-to-12-year-olds and 7 percent of 13-to-14-year-olds had ever had a partner say anything "really mean" about them using cell phones, text messages, instant messaging, social sites, blogs, or other Internet tools *even one time.*

If program advocates' own recent survey is credible, then, younger teens' opposite-sex relationships and even friendships and acquaintances are remarkably *nonviolent.* Abuses appear to be rare and dropping, not epidemic and rising. Why, then, are those who claim to want to reduce teen dating violence so hell-bent to convince teenagers that violence is *normative* in relationships?

Schools should not be teaching propaganda from self-interested corporations and lobbies. Schools should not be party to "teen dating violence" interest groups' degrading stereotypes of young people as violent and cruel. Nor should schools adopt interest groups' wrongheaded definitions of "abuse" to teach students the unrealistic lesson that normal, occasional disagreements and unharmonious feelings constitute "abuse." Real relationships include some anger and rough spots.

By ignoring or downplaying uncomfortable precursors such as parents' and community violence, programs obscure important causes. For example, Claiborne representatives blame 'tweens' "early sexual experimentation" as the *cause* of "increased levels of teen dating violence and abuse," even though its survey does not establish any such cause and effect. However, a solid body of research indicates that growing up in violent homes and suffering childhood violence and sexual abuse, usually inflicted by parents or caretakers, is the most reliable predictor of early sexual activity, violence, and abuse.[20]

Dating violence is not increasing or "epidemic" among high school students but does affect a fraction. It is not a distinct form of violence, but part of a continuum that includes abusive parents and violent homes and communities. For most schools, targeted referral and counseling training, services, and curriculums that include domestic and dating violence as one type of health risk represent the most viable educational approach.

ONLINE PREDATORS INVADING YOUR CHILD'S BEDROOM!

"The Internet and cell phones and texting and sexting and Twittering and blogging—this is very, very dangerous," a Phoenix police detective declared in a national news story posted by the Associated Press (June 30, 2009).[21] He was referring to the case of a man who posted a video online of his sexual assault on an unconscious woman.

Really? Blogging is dangerous? The notion that Internet and cell phone technology—in fact, all forms of these new media—somehow is to blame for a violent criminal's sexual assault and video is another example of grown-ups gone haywire. This loony quip was deemed sage enough to be presented by the reporter and local and national news editors without the slightest questioning or balance. It made as much sense as cops and reporters referring to a child-porn magazine announcing: "These cameras and film and printers and paper are very, very dangerous."

Modern Americans' paranoia toward cyberspace resembles sixteenth-century colonists' terror toward dark forests filled with witches and goblins. *Dateline MSNBC*'s "To Catch a Predator" Web page brims with panic, bannering, "Enemies in your home," "Most teens have met strangers online," "Why are kids still surfing in the bedroom?," "Abduction protection," and, "What you don't know can hurt your kids."[22] One gets the impression of hairy hands grasping right out of screens.[23]

Experts, led by Enough Is Enough's Donna Rice Hughes (yes, the former stripper of famed extramarital romp with ex-Senator Gary Hart that derailed his 1988 presidential campaign), issue "facts," mostly consisting of alarms that legions of violent perverts are trolling through online chatrooms and social sites to snatch foolish children from suburban bedrooms. Coincidentally, they also hawk programs and software to protect kids from what turns out to be a largely nonexistent menace.

Are kids really threatened by a new pack of cyberpredators? Once again, begin with the problem-inflating "survey." "Most teens say they've met strangers online," the MSNBC page[24] blares of Internet users age 14 to 18:

- Some 66 percent say they have met "someone online via e-mail, instant messenger, chat room, etc."
- Some 58 percent of those (that is, 38% of the teens surveyed) say someone they met online asked to meet them in person.
- Some 29 percent have "had a scary online experience, or an online experience that has made (them) feel uncomfortable in any way."
- Some 47 percent said yes to: "Do you talk about yourself or personal things online?"
- Some 49 percent said yes to: "Have you ever done anything online that you would not want your parents to know about?"

These questions are *idiotic*. Met "someone online"? Who hasn't? I, for one, am regularly invited by Senegalese royalty to meet so we can share in riches. "Talk about yourself" online? Who hasn't? Share "personal things"? Like one's email address? Had "an online experience" that was "uncomfortable any way"? *Any way?* What do these questions even mean? And only 49 percent of teens age 14 to 18 have *ever* done anything online they would not want their parents to know about? How many at MSNBC could honestly answer that they have *never* done anything on the Internet they would not want their own parents—or spouse, or children—to know about? MSNBC's survey yields nothing useful to understand teens' online contact with potential predators. It simply ropes in billions of routine interactions such as contacts involving students seeking information for studies, meetings for sports or school or church activities, and other non-rapist exchanges. It is designed *not* to ferret out real dangers, whose numbers are disappointingly small.

What is the real online danger to teens? How many children and teens actually have been raped, sexually abused, abducted, or otherwise violently victimized by a stranger they met online? How big a threat does unsupervised Internet use pose compared to other environments children and teens routinely occupy, such as homes, churches, schools, and streets? It is curious that, other than a few isolated cases of youths murdered or abducted by online acquaintances here and there over many years, there is no comprehensive assessment of real dangers anywhere on Dateline's page or the program's other alarmist sites. Nor did they respond to my information requests.

The reason for the obfuscation: there is no evidence that the Internet is particularly dangerous or that online formats are the source of some new peril. There are hazards to online contacts, just as for any medium. If a predator met a victim by posting a phony job offer on a bulletin board (as has happened in actual cases), would reporters and police blame fiberboard and post-it note manufacturers?

That interest groups and media reports cannot cite real dangers is not for lack of studies. Researchers at the University of New Hampshire's Crimes against Children Research Center (CACRC)[25] live in the real world of real outcomes. Their 2009 study, "Trends in Arrests of 'Online Predators,'" based on reports from a random sample of 2,500 law enforcement agencies nationwide supplemented by interviews for specific offenses, concluded: "The facts do not suggest that the Internet is facilitating an epidemic of sex crimes against youth."[26] In fact, sex offenses against youths *declined* sharply from 2000 to 2006 as Internet use burgeoned. "Arrests of online predators in 2006 constituted about 1 percent of all arrests for sex crimes committed against children and youth" and "there was no evidence that online predators were stalking or abducting unsuspecting victims based on information they posted at social networking sites," the CACRC report stated.

Moreover, of the small number of victimizations of young people by online predators, just 5 percent involved any kind of violence. Nearly all the cases involved meetings at which a voluntary romantic or sexual encounter occurred, the type of adult-youth liaison that has been routine for centuries. Evidently well aware of the news media and interest groups' penchant for creating panics by pulling isolated phrases from reports out of context, the CACRC authors included an unusually strong disclaimer:

> The findings here should emphatically NOT be interpreted to suggest that the Internet is a dangerous environment for children or youth or that the Internet is ridden with sex crimes or becoming more dangerous. The levels of arrests of online predators revealed in this study are quite small compared to total arrests for sex crimes as evidenced by national crime data. Moreover, the growing number of arrests of online predators is best interpreted as a product of the increasing range of the Internet and the increasing aggressiveness of law enforcement activity online.

In another summary titled, "Are 1 in 7 youth threatened by 'online predators?' "[27] the CACRC took on the popular myths spun by interest, net-nanny peddlers, and the news media:

> Articles about online dangers frequently cite statistics from a 2005 University of New Hampshire study that 13 percent of youth were sexually solicited by online predators. (This statistic is sometimes referenced as coming from the National Center on Missing and Exploited Children, which funded and published the study.)
>
> As the authors of the research upon which these numbers are based, we believe these statistics often have been misunderstood. The following points are important caveats that those using or quoting this statistic need to understand in order to avoid further confusion.
>
> 1. These solicitations did not necessarily come from "online predators." . . .
> 2. These solicitations were not necessarily devious or intended to lure. . . .
> 3. Most recipients did not view the solicitations as serious or threatening. . . .
> 4. Almost all youth handled unwanted solicitations easily and effectively. Most reacted by blocking or ignoring solicitors, leaving sites, or telling solicitors to stop.
> 5. Extremely few youth (only 2 in the sample of 1,501 youths) were actually sexually victimized by someone they met online.

As for "the more serious types of sexual solicitations," the CACRC's studies found these to be extremely rare:

> • 1 in 25 youth (about 4%) got "aggressive" sexual solicitations that included attempts to contact the youth offline. These are the episodes most likely to result in actual victimizations. (About one-quarter of these aggressive solicitations came from people the youth knew in person, mostly other youth.)

- 1 in 25 youth (about 4%) were solicited to take sexual pictures of themselves.
- 1 in 25 youth (about 4%) said they were upset or distressed as a result of an online solicitation. Whether or not the solicitors were online predators, these are the youth most immediately harmed by the solicitations themselves. . . .

In reality, then, *the Internet is one of the safest environments children and teens can use unsupervised.* Consider the hazards young people face in other venues.

PARENT, TEACHER, PRIEST . . . THE REAL PREDATORS?

How do we compare the small dangers of the Internet with those of traditional institutions in society to which teenagers and children are exposed by the tens of millions every day? For example, the CACRC's reports for the U.S. Department of Health and Human Services find over 200,000 substantiated cases of violent, sexual, and multiple-abuse victimizations toward youths (including around 80,000 toward teens age 12 to 17) every year, overwhelmingly inflicted by their parents.[28] While the CACRC found around 1,600 pre-teen children and 100 juvenile teens murdered by their parents in 2008, it could confirm no cases of a child or teen murdered by an online predator. Of the 913 children aged 0 to 1 and 1,142 teens aged 12 to 17 who were murdered by all assailants in 2006, thousands of law enforcement agencies and academic investigation could not trace a single one to an Internet predator.

While, other than for homicide, the numbers of victimizations of children in all locales are underestimates of the true numbers (many cases are never reported or substantiated), victimizations via the Internet are far, far lower than at home, in school, at church, and in other routine environments. Note the irony in the following statement about the dangers of Internet pedophiles by an officer who posed as a young girl for the London Metropolitan Police's paedophile unit: "People don't realise the scale of this problem . . . the people we arrest are from all walks of society. They are doctors, lawyers, teachers, businessmen and even policemen."[29] *Dateline NBC*'s profiles likewise show the online predators they have caught have included teachers, principals, social workers, clergy, police, psychologists, medical personnel, businessmen, and parents. All of these online predators quite likely have direct contact with children in their daily lives. If the same logic were applied to more traditional institutions in society, we would conclude with even more alacrity that protecting children from pedophiles and predators requires keeping children away not just from their own families, but from churches and schools. Yet, we do not see police, reporters, "experts," or Enough Is Enough warning that children are in vast danger when they are with their parents, cops, teachers, businessmen, doctors, or clergy.

Well, why not? Suppose administrators of an Internet social site admitted they had looked the other way as thousands of confirmed pedophiles on their site sexually and violently abused thousands of children and youths for years? More recent reports of the extent of sexual abuse of youths in churches and schools reveal dangers far more serious than anything connected to the Internet.

At the request of Catholic bishops, an investigation by the John Jay College of Criminal Justice estimated 11,000 sexual abuse allegations had been made against 4,392 priests in the United States covering the 1950 to 2002 period.[30] "The problem was indeed widespread and affected more than 95 percent of the dioceses and approximately 60 percent of religious communities," the report lamented. Indeed, in 2008, the Vatican itself agreed that the scandal was serious, involving perhaps "1 percent (that is, 5,000) of the over 500,000 Roman Catholic priests worldwide." A 2009 report on Ireland's Catholic Church likewise found rape, sexual assault, and physical violence against thousands of children in the care of nuns and priests was "endemic" over several decades—as was church officials' and law enforcement's rampant cover-ups of the scandal.[31] Similar situations in other denominations have been suggested, but so far only isolated cases have been confirmed.

It is not just the Church. What about documented sexual relationships between teachers or school personnel with their students? There are many studies on that topic. In 1991, for example, a survey of high school seniors in North Carolina found 82 percent of female students and one-fifth of male students had experienced sexual harassment at least once by school personnel, and 13 percent of students actually had sexual relations with a teacher while in junior or senior high.[32] Are students just making up hot-for-teacher tales? A comprehensive study of 225 school districts published in *Phi Delta Kappan* in 1995 concluded that false allegations by students were rare; in fact, students were much more likely not to report sexual incidents with school personnel.[33]

An October 20, 2007, Associated Press survey of school disciplinary records in all 50 states found more than 500 teachers and school personnel every year (a total of 2,570 from 2001 through 2005) had their credentials suspended or revoked after allegations of sexual misconduct, two-thirds of them involving students and 20 percent non-student youths.[34] "Students in America's schools are groped. They're raped. They're pursued, seduced and think they're in love," the AP story declared of "a widespread problem in American schools: sexual misconduct by the very teachers who are supposed to be nurturing the nation's children." "Too often, problem teachers are allowed to leave quietly," the AP story lamented. "That can mean future abuse for another student and another school district." The story regaled a plethora of cases, from a 37-year-old speech teacher charged with sexual assault and abuse of three students, aged 16, 16, and 15, to a 23-year-old junior-high math teacher sentenced to three years in prison for having oral sex with a ninth-grader.

"One report mandated by Congress estimated that as many as 4.5 million students, out of roughly 50 million in American schools, are subject to sexual misconduct by an employee of a school sometime between kindergarten and 12th grade," the AP continued. "That figure includes verbal harassment that's sexual in nature." Note, once again, the problem inflators. For example, one-time verbal harassment that's sexual in nature would include things like Edward James Olmos's famous insult in *Stand and Deliver* that a voluptuous girl "gotta do some work from the neck up."

Such news stories are rare, of course. More typically, schools, reporters, and experts find it easier to focus on student-student situations. Quite a few authors and reporters continue to cite the American Association of University Women's (AAUW) *Hostile Hallways* reports[35] to deplore sexual harassment at school as just a student peer problem. But these reports found something far more unsettling. The 1993 report found that 18 percent of students (25% of girls and 10% of boys) who were sexually harassed at school "cite adults as the perpetrators . . . a school employee (such as a teacher, coach, bus driver, teacher's aide, security guard, principal, or counselor")." In its 2001 update, the AAUW found that "a large number of students report that teachers and other school employees sexually harass students, although this number has declined since 1993 (38% today versus 44% in 1993)." It also found that 37 percent of students reported incidents of students sexually harassing teachers and other school employees, and 30 percent reported incidents of teachers and staff sexually harassing each other (the obvious cases, one suspects).

Yet again, what is depicted as a youth problem turns out to involve adults as well, and with considerable interage reciprocity. Given that adults comprise only a small percentage of individuals on school grounds at any time, student experiences with sexual harassment involving teachers and staff is extraordinary. Further, while the vast majority of harassment by peers consisted of verbal comments (the most common was being called "gay"), adult harassers were much more likely to sexually proposition or physically molest students.

One can extend paranoia indefinitely. Are kids safe going to the doctor? In December 2009, a Delaware pediatrician was arrested and charged with molesting 100 or more patients as young as six months old, many of which he videotaped.[36] If these charges are accurate, this one pediatrician represented more of a sexual violence threat to children and teens than all the Internet predators combined. Talk about an issue *Dateline NBC* and the American Academy of Pediatrics AREN'T going to raise!

Indeed, what "To Catch a Predator" has found is that there are lots of adults, mostly men, in any community seeking sex with much younger teens. That is no shock; birth records by age of mother and father going back a century already show that. But the best evidence shows very few teens have been victimized by online predators. As the CACRC notes, teens are not stupid. Youngsters willing to meet adult strangers in secluded places are vanishingly small in number and usually had prior problems. The irony, statistically, is that any adult assigned to supervise a youth's Internet use is more likely to abuse him or her than someone the youth meets online.

SEXTING

The furor over "sexting" is more disturbing still, since it represents efforts by adults in official capacity *to inflict harm on young people* for largely harmless behaviors—backdropped by a heavy-media breathing. On CNN's tabloid show, Headline News, at the moment (October 26, 2009), the banner line trumpets, "Are Parents in Denial about Sexting?" as some official-type is raising the umpteenth alarm of this "new behavior by children." National Public Radio broadcast five stories on sexting in 2009.[37] The alarm concerns the fact that teens, someone discovered, sometimes send messages containing sexual references and, very occasionally, sexy photos to their boyfriends/girlfriends via private cell phones. Moral outrage seems to obligate school authorities and cops to confiscate phones and rummage private message files for anything racy. If such is found, authorities threaten not just school disciplinary action, but turning the "sexters" over to prosecutors for criminal charges, jail, and permanent records as sex offenders.

I have a better idea. Why don't grownups—school principals, cops, prosecutors, other self-deputized sex police—*not* snoop through teens' private cell phones salivating for hot pictures and sexy talk not intended for their eyes? The official rationale for voyeurism seems to be that stupid kids *hypothetically* risk ruining their lives should their private lives or parts transmitted via cell phone be diverted to public online sites. The official solution threatens to *assuredly* ruin their lives through charging youths sending private messages with "child pornography." Official pedophilia is what I call this latest excuse for grown men to leer at teen photos and love notes under the color of authority.

The hundreds of press stories on this supposedly mammoth new threat to teens that I have seen are completely identical. So I might as well pick the local, *Daily Oklahoman*'s July 31, 2009, front pager ("New danger for Oklahoma kids: 'Sexting.' School officials, police fight increasing trend; expert says consequences can include jail"):

> "Sexting"—sending sexually explicit content on a cell phone—is making news . . . While 70 percent of the senders say the message is directed to a boyfriend or girlfriend, [a local high school] principal said confidentiality is never present in today's technology-based world. . . .

Amid paragraphs featuring the usual shriekfest about sexting's "dangers" (ones, it turns out, that are created by officials themselves) and a hyper-inflated survey from the National Campaign to Prevent Teen Pregnancy (see below), we finally get *one* example, and it is an odd one: "a married man, heavily involved in his church, was caught having a sexual affair with a 15-year-old." Interestingly, phone text records helped authorities document their case against the man.

Why is "sexting" depicted as "the danger"? If this story is serious, shouldn't authorities be warning about teens associating with churchgoing men? And why would we trust school officials to snoop into student-student texting given accounts of thousands of sexual improprieties inflicted on students by school personnel?

The National Campaign to Prevent Teen and Unplanned Pregnancy's[38] deceptive publicity grab cited in the news story provided more worse-than-meaningless survey numbers. Its survey included "teens" all the way up to age 26, one-time behaviors, and vague questions about "suggestive" messages and "semi-nude photos," all conveniently undefined. Even with these efforts to exaggerate numbers, the survey found only 40 percent of teens had ever sent a "suggestive text message" to anyone. That is unbelievably *few*.

A September 2009 AP-MTV poll by Knowledge Network, setting off yet another press stampede, was even more ludicrous. Under the breathless warning, "Think your kid is not 'sexting'? Think again," the Associated Press declared, "More than a quarter of young people have been involved in sexting in some form . . . despite sometimes grim consequences for those who do it."[39] The AP's problem-inflators were particularly crude. The poll surveyed 14 to 24 year-olds (which the story referred to as "teens"), included one-time incidents, tossed in online cases ("sexting" is supposed to refer only to cell phone messages), and adopted wildly broad definitions. Here is what the poll actually asked and found about its sample:

- Involved in some type of sexting, 30 percent
- Someone I know sent me messages with sexual words, 29 percent
- Someone sent me naked pictures or videos of themselves, 18 percent
- Someone sent me naked pictures or videos of someone else that I know personally, 8 percent
- Participated in a webcam chat during which someone else performed sexual activities, 7 percent

How could anyone be online and/or possess a cell phone and never once get a message with any sexual word in it at all? If you received a message mentioning sex from someone you knew, or if the pix Mimi in Miami sent out to, oh, 60 million e-mail addresses peddling her webcam site got through the spam filter, you qualify by this poll's definition as a "sexter." As for anything that approaches what "sexting" is supposed to mean, only 7 percent to 8 percent of persons age 14 to 24 ever participated, even once, in any virtual situation involving someone else's nudity or "sexual activities" (undefined). How many teenagers did so with cell phones is not reported, but the percentages would be smaller.

An ethically reported AP story should have read, "Very few young people, even including those in their early twenties, have engaged in any personal sexting involving depictions of sexual activity or nudity." But then it would not have been a fun story. The AP could not have quoted some experts like Kathleen Bogle (of *Hooking Up* fame) reciting boilerplate stereotypes about how brainless young people are. Yet again ... do these reporters and experts *think* before they opine? Do they realize that "8 percent" is not *all* young people, but a *tiny fraction*?

Nearly all of the consequences of sexting deplored in this article and elsewhere are caused by the bad reactions of grownups like principals, cops, prosecutors, employers, college admitters, and the like who might come across pictures and texts not meant for their eyes and suffer neopuritan meltdown. Here is yet more of the latest foolishness:

> A new survey from the Pew Research Center's Internet & American Life Project found that 4 percent of cell-owning teens aged 12 to 17 say they have sent sexually suggestive nude or nearly nude images or videos of themselves to someone else via text messaging, a practice also known as "sexting." ... Teens explained to us how sexually suggestive images have become a form of relationship currency," said Amanda Lenhart, Senior Research Specialist and author of the report.[40]

Pew researchers ... *think. Not* a teenage "form of relationship currency." *Four percent.*

Poor judgment by reporters, editors, and their official and expert sources in blaring ever-new teen "crises" such as "sexting" is a national epidemic. Note how two Make-It-Up local news stories ballooned across the country due to the anything-goes attitudes even supposedly well-informed, national trade-magazine editors (in this case, those at *Youth Today*'s "Press Watch") display:

Teen Dating Abuse on the Rise, Experts Say
Youth Today, May 2008

With the advent of 24/7 communication via cell phones, BlackBerries, laptops and social networking sites, mental and emotional abuse can continue even when the couple isn't physically together, in the form of nonstop calls, constant texting and public cyberbullying. "These kids just can't get away from their abusers," says Jane Randel, vice president of communications at Liz Claiborne, which conducted a poll on dating abuse.

Teens Get More Exposure Than They Intended
Youth Today, August 2008

Some youths are using their cell phone cameras to send nude photographs of themselves to boyfriends or girlfriends, occasionally resulting in legal consequences. The pictures are often passed on to others, or posted on the Internet, which has led to the prosecution of youths as young as age 16 in several states. Schools have confiscated phones in order to halt the distribution of such pictures. While some psychologists say the phenomenon is just an example of youthful hormones, others say it's an example of youthful exhibitionism.[41]

"Kids just can't get away from their abusers?" I own the world's simplest cell phone, I never read the guidebook, and I know at least three options to avoid unwanted phone calls. Your more sophisticated teen texter knows many more. One could better argue that teens could not escape abusers in the 1950s, 1960s, and 1970s, when just about everyone's *home phone number* (richer homes helpfully added a "teenager's phone") alongside *home addresses* were listed alphabetically in a big directory (known as the Phone Book) any predator could access. Myths that adolescents believe they are "invulnerable" and are ruled by "hormones" have long been debunked, and "youthful exhibitionism" is just made up.[42] These were youths' *private* messages that only came to light due to the exhibitionist zeal of officials, news reporters, and editors.

It is true that while in 1955, your backseat boff was high school hallway currency guaranteed to get around town via gossip networks, today one's texted dishabille, posted MySpace revelation, or chatroom quip potentially can bounce to Katmandu and endure 4ever. But, what, practically, does this mean to the younger citizens supposedly so much at risk of becoming permanent damaged goods that schools, cops, and prosecutors are champing to ruin their lives with criminal records to "protect" them? Journalist JoAnn Wypijewski, reflecting on dozens of cases in which teenaged texters faced criminal charges as child pornographers for, in effect, *privately exploiting themselves* is one of the few to reverse the lens.[43] "The recent attention to teen 'sexting' has focused quite a lot on the presumed self-exploitation of kids, not so much on the prurient reflex of grown-ups who spy on and punish them," Wypijewski writes.

One prosecutor, Wyoming County, Pennsylvania, District Attorney George Skumanick, Jr., branded photos such as those of two girls in training bras, another in a bathing suit, and one taken by a 16-year-old girl of herself emerging toweled from the shower as "provocative" (by what criterion? his own tumescence?). Prosecution entails exposing such private photos of girls to the dozens of cops, investigators, jurors, experts, witnesses, judges, and others necessary to sustain the prosecution. One of the girls photographed posing in her bathing suit was allowed to submit for prosecutors' approval an essay on "why it was wrong," how her brazenness would "affect the victim? The school? The community?" and "what it means to be a girl in today's society."

Under this self-exploitation logic, then, is a juvenile who sees himself or herself naked guilty of consuming child pornography as well? Is masturbation by youths prosecutable as child sexual abuse? Don't laugh. These insanities are not farfetched given prosecutors' fanaticism and renewed crusades in evangelical texts such as "Every Young Woman's Battle" to stop the "shame" of masturbation. Concludes Wypijewski:

> It is just possible that the 15-year-olds are envisioning, however inchoately, a saner world than the one the grown-ups lecturing them have constructed, one where their life chances won't be ruined by a "compromising" photograph on the Internet. If sexting really is as common as is claimed, it's more likely to proliferate than to abate, and then the issue won't be scandal or embarrassment but banality.

Indeed, grownups routinely excuse those among our number, from Dr. Laura Schlessinger to former Miss USA Carrie Prejean and many, *many* in between whose provocative photos and revelations in their permanent records hardly wrecked their careers. Even major sex scandals have not derailed the many prominent men caught with pants down, love children abounding, and lying denials and bribes run amuck. Who, in the Internet age, cares about one more topless shower picture? Even by the information hysterics dispense, "sexting" is a thoroughly moronic non-issue reflecting grownup craziness whenever teens intersect with new technology.

ANATOMY OF A BAD SEX STUDY

Then there's that old culture-warhorse, TV sex. Enter the famous Rand Corporation "study" published in the November 2008 issue of the pseudo-journal *Pediatrics* announcing that teenagers who watch the sexiest TV shows are twice as likely to get pregnant or cause a pregnancy than teens who watch the least.[44] By the time Rand researchers flooded the media, *Friends*, *Sex and the City*, and *That '70s Show* stood accused of causing what would amount to millions of teenage pregnancies over the last decade.

The Rand study and the media distortions were so transparently atrocious they should have brought thundering condemnations from academic authorities. Yet, the only reporter I could find who presented any critical scrutiny of the report was Kim Masters of National Public Radio's *All Things Considered*.[45] The rest of the media acted as a single-celled protoplasm. "Study first to link TV sex to real teen pregnancies" (*Washington Post*) and "Teen pregnancy tied to viewing sexy TV shows" (*Associated Press*) headlined the robot army of cloned stories. In a particularly numbskull quip, *Time* praised the study for explaining "in part why the U.S. teen pregnancy rate is double that of other industrialized nations."[46] (Everyone knows there is no sex on French, Swedish, or Japanese TV.) *Youth Today*'s editors reproduced the study's silliest chart along with an uncritical recapitulation of Rand's claims as if they were serious.[47] Even the National Campaign was more (though barely) analytical.[48]

Media toadying was crazy for a dozen reasons. First, real-life trends strongly contradicted Rand's claims. While Rand's lead researcher declared that "sexual content on television has doubled in the last few years,"[49] Centers for Disease Control figures showed teen pregnancy rates plummeted by 20 percent since 2000 and by 50 percent since 1990. Today, pregnancy rates among teens are much lower than the first tabulations back in 1973, when *All in the Family* and *The Waltons* ruled television. How did a doubly sexy media produce a halved teen pregnancy rate?

Second, real-life pregnancy patterns contradicted Rand's claims. Are black and Hispanic youths dramatically more likely than white kids to emulate white TV stars? Teen pregnancy rates closely parallel pregnancy rates among adults in their families and communities. How do teens watching sexy TV shows make *grownups around them* get pregnant?

Third, Rand's study suffered mammoth methodology flaws, starting with a crippling loss of subjects. Of the 2,000 youths aged 12 to 17 originally sampled, one-third dropped out. Of the 1,315 remaining, just 91 (58 girls and 33 boys), or 7 percent, had experienced or caused a pregnancy over the three-year study period, a remarkably low rate. Naturally, no one reported that.

When it came to analysis, Rand failed to report the television habits of the 600 teens who had never had sex. That is suspicious. Would presenting the TV viewing habits of the no-sex teens, a highly relevant subsample, have messed up the findings? That left around 700 subjects, one-third of the original sample, on which the findings were based.

Rand then chose an odd set of variables to include. Its researchers failed to analyze straightforward factors of interest, such as their subjects' poverty levels, age at puberty, parents' pregnancy behaviors, abuse histories, and other crucial factors associated with teen pregnancy. The variables they did include yielded very strange results. In both simple and multiple analyses, Rand found Hispanic ethnicity, lower parental education level, lower school performance, and older age were *not* associated with greater odds of having experienced pregnancy compared to non-Hispanic youth, children of better educated parents, students with higher school achievement, and younger teens. That is absolutely nuts. It defies rational belief.

Then, Rand's multivariate regression—a mathematical technique that weighs the factors in combination with each other—actually found that even for its weird sample and variable set, living in a one-parent household (reflecting family instability) boosted teen pregnancy rates the most, followed by being African American (reflecting poverty), and being female (reflecting impregnation by adult men), each of which were many times more important than television-viewing habits. Yes, once again, a study found socioeconomics and adult behaviors were by far the biggest factors in teen pregnancy. Once again, that finding was ignored.

Rand also found that teens who watched lots of television in general had significantly *fewer* pregnancies—a stronger finding than their dubious one on sexy television shows. None of the media reports I saw mentioned that weirdo result, either.

Then came the biggest irony: the Rand study's numbers suggested that watching sex on television was a trivial factor. This can be estimated (little about this study can be determined in clear-cut fashion) from the Beta coefficients, which the study did present. Beta values weigh how much a given change in each variable (say, the hours spent watching television) is associated with change in the variable of concern (teen pregnancy rate). Compared to the Beta values for much more important factors such as family structure, race, and gender (and other variables the study sample was too erratic to evaluate), *watching sex on television explained just about nothing.*

How, then, did Rand researchers hype the outlandish fallacy that teens who watched the most sex on television are twice as pregnancy-prone as those who watched the least? Enter the lethal combination of statistical fraud and news-media sensationalism. After initially including 12 factors in their calculations, researchers then excluded the other 11 factors and pretended sex on television was the *only* cause. Using this elementary trick, of course, researchers can inflate any factor they want, no matter how silly or small, into the major cause of whatever behavior they study. For example, Rand researchers could have argued (with more justification) that if parents let their teens watch *more* television in general, teen pregnancy rates would fall sharply.

The proper conclusion from the Rand study, then, is: don't worry about teens watching television. To reduce teen pregnancy, Americans should concentrate on strengthening families and reducing the high levels of youth poverty connected to high rates of pregnancies among minority teens. But sex on television is a hot topic. Journal and news editors favor sensational, attention-grabbing fare. Who wants to see news reports about teens' complex real-life problems?

More to the point, Rand's study trampled a host of basic validity and ethical standards. This was a disgraceful piece of work, and *Pediatrics* revealed uncommonly low standards in publishing it. Indeed, media causality research has been a dubious field employing substandard methods from the beginning. Researcher bias, laboratory artifacts, short-term time frames emphasizing immediate over long-term effects, the inability to recreate real-world settings, and studies geared for news-tabloid splashes (of which Rand's is only the latest example) have plagued efforts to determine the complex ways in which media and real-life behaviors interact. Media-effects research is so weak that the same techniques used to claim sexy television and violent games and media cause youths to act badly also have been used, in previous studies by premier researchers, to show that programs like *Sesame Street* and *Mr. Rogers' Neighborhood* make children more aggressive.[50] The most reliable predictor of whether a study will find this or that media make teens act in more sexualized and violent ways is whether the researcher's record indicates *belief* that the study will find those results. It is time, in short, to turn off the tube and get back to the real world.

WHAT'S BEHIND GROWNUPS' ANTI-YOUTH RAGE?

Today's craziness is extreme. Teenagers—even older teens—sitting next to each other, talking, kissing, sending mildly risqué messages, posting bathing-suit photos, having normal boy-girl disagreements, watching a PG television show, and having the most routine exchanges online are met with howling, punishing fear crusades by major interest groups, academics, politicians, police, and school officials, each guaranteed worshipful news media hype. When fatuous panics like online predators, *Friends'* igniting teen pregnancy, "hooking up," and "sexting" banish serious issues affecting millions of young people from media and policy forums, there's solid reason to question whether American adults (at least, their official and media versions) are capable of ratiocination about teenage sex and pregnancy.

Today's endless series of youth-and-technology "crises" and bad studies such as Rand's that trivialize real problems under a barrage of frivolous panics are symptomatic of larger disturbances. When officials declare their intention to inflict lifelong harm on teenagers over what private messages they send to each other, which is what the "sexting" furor amounts to, it is time to start dismantling the damage culture war and privatized policy interests are doing to young people and basic grownup decency.

By their own words, many commentators seem enraged at teenagers. Psychologist Michael Bradley brands teens "crazy," "stupid," "nuts," and "brain damaged" in frenzied repetition on nearly every page of his popular *Yes! Your Teen IS Crazy!*.[51] In major news media, reporters and commentators have lambasted adolescents as "reckless," "irrational," "crazy," "stupid," and even "alien"—not just wayward individuals, but the entire generation. The cruelty with which many popular authors vilify teenagers for causing adults' vexation while dismissing what adult did to teens borders on barbaric. In *Dirty: A Search for Answers Inside America's Teenage Drug Epidemic* (2003), angry parent Meredith Maran[52] displays a callous intolerance toward young people I find again and again in commentaries on youth. "How did this home produce a twelve-year-old crack dealer, a two-hundred-dollar-a-trick teenage prostitute, the possibly pregnant girlfriend of a boy from the Rodeo projects?" Maran unloads on one of her young interviewees. "Which part of 'intact, upper-middle-class, college-educated, suburban nuclear family' didn't [teenager] Zalika understand?" I wanted to yell at Maran in the same tone to reread *her own words* a few dozen pages earlier detailing the "part" involving Zalika's and her siblings' father, who repeatedly beat his daughter violently and whose sordid serial affairs poisoned their childhoods with bitter family conflict, "yelling," and "nonstop drama." That part, maybe?

The degrading, prejudicial tactics authors and commentators routinely inflict on teenagers represent adult bullying, a form of hate speech we would not tolerate if directed at other groups in society. "We wouldn't dare make the same sweeping generalizations about equally appalling adult behavior," University of Southern California sociologist Karen Sternheimer observes of the easy condemnations of teenagers.[53] Sternheimer's excellent *Connecting Social Problems and Popular Culture* (2009) presents a much more complex, research-based—and highly readable—discussion of teens' responses to the widely varied ways sex is presented across the complex, varied media they encounter. Why do professional and academic research communities, which would stand forcefully against racist, sexist, and related bigotry, remain largely silent in today's anything-goes climate governing malignings toward young people?

The reason is that progressive interests who might ordinarily embrace the cause of economic equality and greater opportunities for young people, ending racial and gender stigmas toward youth, and advocating liberalized views of sexuality have a bigger fish to fry. The never-ending war between those who promote comprehensive sexuality education and the "abstinence only" ayatollahs has sucked every molecule of oxygen from what should be a truly dynamic debate over America's multicultural future.

Chapter Ten

WILL SEX-ED SAVE THE DAY?

For 99 percent of those involved in America's "teen pregnancy" debate today, one's worth as a gentleman, scholar, and occupant of space on this earth hinges on the answer to just one question: do you support "comprehensive sexuality" or "abstinence only" education? That is it. That is the great golden Ra around which all teenage sexuality discourse orbits. Each new teenage event, statistic, or entry into the discussion is assayed for its value in advancing sex education or abstinence.

As I said at the outset, I support straightforward sex education. "Values" preaching insults adult and youth alike. Young people learn adult values by observing adult *behaviors*. "Children have never been very good at listening to their elders, but they have never failed to imitate them," as James Baldwin put it. Preaching phony pieties contrived as "abstinence education"—or "abstinence lite," in which contraception is barely murmured—presumes an absolute morality teens readily see grownups do not practice and weakens the incentive for adults to improve our behaviors to serve as good models for children. Abstinence education in an abstinence-valuing society is unnecessary. Abstinence education in a non-abstinence-valuing adult society is immoral.

Perhaps, 30 or 60 or 100 years ago, when classrooms were youths' only source of reliable information on sex, this spectacle could have been viewed benignly. Today, the sex-ed-versus-abstinence Hatfield-McCoy feud has become a destructive obsession, as if nothing else on earth mattered except which side "wins" this chalkboard war. *It does not matter.* This is the global Internet age. School sex-ed is yesterday's rumble. Its obsolete framings drag teenage sexuality discourse backwards into the sexism, racism, and scapegoating of the past.

Teens now have far better, more objective, and more diverse sources of information on sexuality than local school-board politics will permit. It is not what schools teach or preach, but how adults act—toward young people, toward our own sexuality—that is the pivotal issue now demanding attention.

Still, having been there, I understand why 1990s liberals lapsed into deception after suffering two decades of defeats at the hands of bullying and lying by anti-sex-education forces. Politically, liberals could no longer affirm the sexuality of darker-skinned teenagers to fearful white voters and policymakers. To survive, sex-ed advocates fired back against conservatives in kind, attacking abstinence-only regimes with fear campaigns upholding sex education as the true savior of teens from deadly sex (and America from swarthy babies). "Abstinence-only education" is "better known as the best teen pregnancy and STD delivery system politicians have ever devised," summed up Rachel Maddow's September 9, 2009, MSNBC show. Abstinence-only is producing "skyrocketing" teen pregnancy, liberals shrilled, even though teen pregnancy was not rising, let alone skyrocketing, and abstinence education was too trivial to be blamed or credited for much of anything.

Make-It-Up is everyone's game now. "Comprehensive sexuality" versus "abstinence-only" brawling has sunk into mirror-image illogic. Of the hundreds of studies published on sex education, both sides have culled a handful, mostly by partisans, insisting that only their favored approach reduces the numbers of teenagers having sex and getting pregnant. This century-long debate long ago left teenagers and reality behind and now quarrels within its own echo chamber of wrongheaded talking points.

The only meaningful values education that adults provide for teenagers consists of the real sexual behaviors adults practice. Propagandizing teens through abstinence-only and "abstinence-plus" lectures that (in the words of the Adolescent Family Life Act) Americans' "expected standard" is chastity outside of marriage—a standard teens can see adults do not value in their own conduct—is pointless. No wonder studies repeatedly find it does not accomplish much of anything.

Viewing the literature as a whole, comprehensive sexuality education is not connected to major effects on teens' sexual outcomes. The Alan Guttmacher Institute's famous study of European programs,[1] detailed in Chapter 1, found that higher socioeconomic status, not the highest-rated sex education and services, linked to lower teen birth rates. In the United States, exhaustive research has identified only a handful of "teen pregnancy" prevention regimes with even tentatively positive results from controlled scientific evaluations—and these relied on self-reporting surveys rather than outcomes records. A 2007 analysis, examined in detail later in this chapter, used woefully weak criteria to find that *even under the most optimistic assumptions*, sexuality education could affect only a fraction of teen pregnancy rates and other outcomes.

I believe progressives have had a solemn duty to confront elected and institutional officials with a sobering reality: teen pregnancy is a product of the adult mores and economic system a nation imposes on its young people, not a technical matter for better instruction and moral cajoling to fix. Progressives have failed that duty, increasingly abjectly, in recent years. Instead, interest groups have studied and restudied and re-restudied programs endlessly to uncover something that "works."

Even this fervor focuses on the wrong question. In the real world, comprehensive sexuality education that accurately details biological and contraceptive facts and offers informed, confidential access to contraceptives and abortion is a non-negotiable right. Teenagers are part of the adult sexual world. Despite occasional "statutory rape" prosecutions of adult men and a few adult women in egregious cases, consensual sex between adults and teenagers is tacitly condoned. In California, for example, adult men aged 20 and older father 8,000 to 10,000 babies each year, as well as engage in countless hundreds of thousands or millions of non-reproductive sexual liaisons with girls age 17 and younger.

Since American authorities clearly have little inclination to prevent adult-teen sex (short of reinstituting stocks and stonings), we have an obligation to make sure teens are equipped to protect themselves. Teenagers have a practical right to accurate, explicit information necessary to consent to or reject relationships with peers and adults as well as the science to prevent unwanted consequences. Sex education should not be evaluated by the narrow criterion of whether it "delays teenage sex" or "prevents teen pregnancy," but by its success in imparting practical knowledge. A school mathematics curriculum is successful if it teaches a student to do math, not by whether the student later uses it to discover a brilliant new theory or to cheat on taxes. Health education and clinics for young people should not be branded failures or successes depending on whether the teen birth rate in their bailiwicks rises or falls.

ONE-TRACK MINDS

Unfortunately, discussion is going in the wrong direction. Many advocacy groups misrepresent sexuality education, abstinence education, and related programs aimed at teenagers as pivotal factors in pregnancy rates, and the political and media campaigns for these approaches have become ever more unreal. For example, in September 2004, Los Angeles's Get Real! and the San Francisco Bay Area's California Adolescent Health Collaborative issued a "Reality Check" report ranking California's 55 largest cities (all those with populations of more than 100,000) in providing services to teens and preventing teen births.[2] The report rated Berkeley as "California's most teenager-healthy city" for providing teens with the greatest access to health and prevention services, including "a health center that readily hands out advice and condoms" to youths, credited with producing "the state's lowest birth rate among teen mothers."[3] In "Berkeley High: A Sex Ed Success Story," Planned Parenthood also argued that Berkeley's "comprehensive sex education programs that are proven to work" and "web of support" have resulted in the fact that "for eight years running, Berkeley has had the lowest teen pregnancy rate in the state"[4] (by which the group meant "birth rate").

However, Berkeley did *not* have California's lowest teen birth rate. The state's Center for Health Statistics' 2002 report showed that Berkeley ranked fifth from the lowest in teen birth rates among California's cities of more than 100,000 population.[5] In fact, Berkeley had a higher teen birth rate (16.2 births per 1,000 females aged 15 to 19) than three cities ranked as among the *worst* in youth services (Irvine, Glendale, and Santa Clarita). The city with the state's lowest teen birth rate, Irvine (3.3 births per 1,000 females aged 15 to 19), not only ranked second worst in services to youth, its schools taught a "family life" curriculum stressing conservative "universal moral values," anchored by such films as, *Why Abstinence? The Price Tag of Casual Sex.* If only programmatic approaches were compared and other factors ignored, the opposite conclusion could be argued from Get Real!'s "Reality Check" data: that teaching abstinence from sex produces lower teen birth rates.

That also would be misleading. The common reason Berkeley and Irvine have low teen birth rates, which no one cited, is that both are affluent cities dominated by large universities. Eighteen- and 19-year-olds enrolled at the University of California, Irvine, and U.C., Berkeley, have minuscule birth rates, bringing down the entire city's teen birth rate. But none of the interests or the news reporter proved to be concerned about accuracy.

The matter got uglier when I reanalyzed Get Real!'s data for all of California's 55 largest cities for the 1990 to 2002 period for a paper published in the *Californian Journal for Health Promotion.*[6] My analysis included levels of health and development services to youth, socioeconomic factors such as poverty, and environmental factors such adult birth rates or rates of and changes in births to teenage mothers. My main finding was that teenage birth rates vary a staggering *30-fold* from California's richest to its poorest city, rendering discussion of influences other than those related to poverty largely irrelevant. Indeed, the regression analysis showed socioeconomic and environmental factors, chiefly adult birth rates and youth poverty rates, were associated with nearly 90 percent of the variance in teen birth rates by city, leaving little room for other factors.

This finding was very similar to that of the national analysis by state and race presented in Chapter 1.*

My city-by-city analysis found no association between levels of health and development services to youth and lower rates of or greater reductions over time in teenage birth rates.[7] The reason for this apparently disappointing result actually was encouraging: California had done an exemplary job of targeting low-income populations with health services to compensate for richer teens' greater access to private health care. These services did appear effective in better health and related outcomes among poorer teens . . . but not lower birth rates.

Even within cities with the same education regimes, birth rates vary dramatically. San Francisco schools offer the most comprehensive sexuality education programs anywhere, and family planning clinics are abundantly available to teens. Yet, the birth rate among teenagers in San Francisco[8] varies nearly 3,000 percent by district (Table 10.1). While there are some intriguing anomalies (note ZIP codes 94132 and 94133), birth rates strongly grade with poverty.

SUPPRESSING REALISTIC DISCUSSION

A handful of researchers do take a socioeconomic view that poorer young women have higher birth rates because of the conditions imposed by poverty itself, including the lack of financial assets necessary to pursue higher education and career options, extended-family structures that provide more caregivers for children of young mothers, and economic advantages to poorer women of having children earlier in life. In this view, discussed in Chapters 3 and 4, teens' births are a rational response to social inequality and are directly related to the sexual behaviors of adults of similar status.

However, the predominant view expressed by major American teen-pregnancy prevention groups might be called "program panacea." This view holds that teenagers' sexual behaviors can be treated separately from those of adults, and high teen birth rates can be remedied simply by enhancing poorer youths' access to abstinence/sexuality education, contraceptive services, and youth development programs. Programmatic approaches, they argue, can be credited with the low rates of teen births in European countries, variations in teen birth rates among American states, and the large decline in teen births in the United States from 1991 to 2005. While the National Campaign to Prevent Teen and Unplanned Pregnancy and other groups involved in the debate advocate expanded investment in education curricula and

---

*Norman Constantine of the Public Health Institute (which provides research to generally liberal interest groups) made a thoroughly groundless attack on my study, as those interested may judge by examining the exchange in CJHP.

Table 10.1   San Francisco Births by ZIP Code, 2004–2008

ZIP code	All	Mother <20	Teen birth rate*	Youth poverty rate
94102	1,035	85	52.4	33.8%
94124	2,722	324	47.5	27.0%
94107	1,572	42	43.0	44.1%
94103	1,079	71	39.5	22.6%
94110	4,851	278	35.1	23.0%
94109	2,073	58	26.5	17.5%
94134	2,647	165	26.4	14.6%
94112	5,034	254	26.1	14.0%
94115	1,777	58	25.2	27.0%
94117	1,925	27	22.6	17.8%
94108	472	11	13.8	17.3%
94132	1,145	31	12.2	7.9%
94133	1,112	20	10.7	17.2%
94129	279	1	9.6	0.0%
94114	1,581	9	8.7	6.8%
94131	1,701	16	8.4	5.5%
94118	2,324	23	6.5	3.6%
94123	1,539	3	5.2	0.0%
94122	2,940	19	3.4	9.5%
94121	2,091	16	3.3	8.0%
94127	998	6	2.3	2.8%
94116	2,047	10	1.8	3.4%
City	43,487	1,539	21.4	14.9%

*Average annual births by mothers under age 20 per 1,000 females age 15 to 19 in each ZIP code with at least 100 teens.

Source: Center for Health Statistics (2009).

programmatic measures, none I can find proposes redistributive policies such as stronger social insurance programs to boost incomes of low-income families (as we do for the elderly) as a strategy to reduce teen birth rates. But if only major investments to reduce the high rates of poverty suffered by American youth will bring down the birth rate among teens in the long term, overpromotion of educational and program solutions gives policymakers another excuse to avoid politically difficult economic reforms.

For examples of program-panacea logic, The National Campaign's prevention initiative, called "Putting What Works to Work," advocates only a variety of education, service, and program initiatives.[9] As noted in Chapter 4, the National Campaign initially cited poverty, poor schools, and lack of opportunity as major factors in teen pregnancy a decade ago, then backtracked. Now, finding mention of these factors on its Web site is all but impossible.

Another lobby, Advocates for Youth, concedes that "most teenage mothers come from socially and/or economically disadvantaged backgrounds," but credits only "easy access to sexual health information and services" as the cause of "better sexual health outcomes" in European nations.[10] The Sexuality Information and Education Council of the United States (SIECUS) appears to be retreating from acknowledging economic factors. My review in 2005 found SIECUS at least mentioned that coming from "low-income families" was one in a lengthy list of risks leading to higher odds of teen pregnancy en route to advocating only programs and educational remedies. But my most recent Web site search in 2009 found no mention of socioeconomic contexts. Now, SIECUS's solution simply boils down to: "Young people should have access to the information, skills, and services they need to prevent unintended pregnancy."[11]

The National Abortion Rights League (NARAL-Pro-Choice America) does not even mention poverty or related solutions. Instead, NARAL poses only "honest, age-appropriate, and medically accurate sex education that promotes abstinence and provides young people with the information they need to protect themselves" as the solution to "unacceptably high rates of teen pregnancy, sexually transmitted diseases (STDs), and HIV/AIDS infections."[12] The California Adolescent Health Collaborative (CAHC) acknowledges that "teen births are more prevalent among populations of lower socio-economic status," but none of its policy recommendations includes measures to reduce youth poverty.[13] Instead, CAHC's "strategies to reduce teen pregnancy and STIs" are to "provide teens with the information, skills, and support they need to practice safe sexual behavior, including abstinence ... increase access to reproductive health care ... increase the role males play in preventing adolescent pregnancy ... " and "decrease glamorization of irresponsible sexual behavior in the media."

Likewise, the Public Health Institute (PHI), in a 2003 report funded by the California Wellness Foundation, notes that "one of the best predictors of teen birth rates are poverty rates."[14] Yet, neither organization advocates measures to reduce adolescent poverty. Instead, the PHI credits only "state funded reproductive health ... and teen pregnancy prevention programs" and "program and policy grant initiatives funded by philanthropic foundations in California" as "the solution" for reducing teenage motherhood. While Wellness advocates what appears to be a promising "Get Real! ... campaign aimed at the adults who control the environments of children and teens," it turns out the campaign is confined to urging "educators and community leaders to use their influence to help teens prevent pregnancies by offering comprehensive sexuality education, as well as access to contraceptives."[15] Even those, such as the Alan Guttmacher Institute, that cite a combination of socioeconomic and programmatic factors in research papers typically recommend only programmatic solutions: "Societal assistance to teenagers in their transition to adulthood, combined with acceptance of teenage sexual relationships, clear expectations for responsible sexual behavior and access to sexual and reproductive health services leads to lower rates of teenage pregnancy."[16]

It is abundantly clear that liberal interest groups are very reluctant to discuss, let alone promote, measures to address poverty, disadvantage, adult sexual behaviors, and family environments that define teen pregnancy rates. That means, as we have seen, that 90 percent of the factors influencing teenage outcomes are taken off the table before the discussion begins. Today's endlessly virulent debate has erupted over factors that might influence a fraction of the remaining 10 percent.

Indeed, there is not even much of a debate any more now that both sides have retreated into their parallel echo chambers. Given the hundreds of studies now available, a handful can be selected to show whatever effect from either abstinence or sexuality education is desired. Advocates who have become adept at demolishing flawed claims by their opponents then turn around and accept the same flawed logic to defend their own agendas.

Taken as a whole, the large body of research on the effectiveness of various sexuality, abstinence, and contraceptive education and programs in reducing births by teen mothers has been inconsistent and inconclusive.[17] Even the few studies claiming to find some modest results[18] typically suffer from method glitches such as selection biases between test and control groups, low sample retention, and lack of replication of results for programs found effective in single studies. All of these studies rely on self reports, which may mean nothing more than that programs are effective in changing a small number of students' answers on pencil-and-paper tests (see Chapter 5). After all, if teens hear for weeks in school programs that teen sex and pregnancy are bad, and school is a place where you learn to give right answers, then the right answers on the program follow-up survey must be, "No, I am not having sex," and "No, I am not pregnant." When the studies themselves are conducted by partisans, regardless of which side they are on, a host of confounds come into play.

ABSTINENCE FAILURES

Abstinence-only education's stated premise in the Adolescent Family Life Act that created it is that Americans subscribe to a "standard" that reserves sex solely for marriage. This joke is not even funny. The National Center for Health Statistics' 2002 Sexual Behavior survey[19] found American heterosexual men aged 40 to 44 (the age to be dads of teens) reported having had a median of 8.2 female sexual partners in their lives. Five in six had had sex with three or more, 58 percent with seven or more, and one-third with 15 or more women in their lives. Heterosexual women that age reported a median of

3.8 male sexual partners, with two-thirds having had sex with three or more men, 30 percent with seven or more, and 11 percent with 15 or more men in their lives. (I know; I cannot explain these discrepancies by gender either, and the usual caveats about surveys apply to this one.) Contrary to the snide asides about "adolescent promiscuity," the vast bulk of promiscuity takes place in adulthood.

Still, one of the most vigorous advocates of abstinence-only education, the Family Research Council (FRC), insists:

> The context for the full expression of human sexuality is within the bonds of marriage between one man and one woman. Upholding this standard of sexual behavior would help to reverse many of the destructive aspects of the sexual revolution, including sexually transmitted disease rates of epidemic proportion, high out-of-wedlock birth rates, adultery, and homosexuality . . . In accordance with this position, the best sexuality education embraces sexual abstinence outside of marriage.[20]

The FRC at least might have acknowledged that many prominent advocates of abstinence-only preaching sport records charitably described as abstinence-challenged.

Attempting to qualify the AFLA standard to mean that chastity is expected of teens while promiscuity is tolerated for adults is even more grossly immoral, not just because it is self-serving, but because whatever age is chosen as "adult" will include many over that age having sex with those under that age. Such logic winds up pushing the worse-than-1950s sexist double standard the Urban Institute's tortured analysis floated: that it is socially acceptable for older adult men to impregnate younger teen girls but unacceptable for younger teen girls to have sex or get pregnant.

As places of education, schools have an obligation to be truthful. The real "standard" is the one adults practice. A mature, values-respecting adult society does not lie to our kids by pretending to morals we do not observe. Other than a few claims by partisans, the bulk of research does not find abstinence-only effective at much of anything other than spending hundreds of millions of tax dollars to satisfy the needs of politicians and moralists to wax righteous. The consensus of studies seems to be that teens ignore it, and that is fortunate. The real lesson of abstinence-only "education" is that one's own sins may be excused by pretending to chaste standards while loudly berating the immorality of others.

Both sides eagerly leapt on the slight increases in older-teen birth rates in 2006 and 2007 as proof that the other side's approaches were to blame. "What we're really witnessing are the effects of contraceptive-focused sex education, often labeled as 'comprehensive sex education,'" stated FRC President Tony Perkins. "So-called comprehensive sex education falsely exaggerates the protective effect of condoms and promotes unsafe behavior. The results could not be clearer—an increase in STD rates in young people, and an increase in out-of-wedlock teenage pregnancies."[21]

FRC has pointed to "research" claiming abstinence programs such as Washington, D.C.'s Best Friends and Diamond Girls achieve fantastic results. (Sample: "Diamond girls are 120 times more likely to abstain from sex than their peers.") "Overall," the Heritage Foundation's Melissa Pardue, Christine Kim, and Robert Rector concluded, "16 of the 21 studies [analyzed] reported statistically significant positive results, such as delayed sexual initiation and reduced levels of early sexual activity, among youths who have received abstinence education."[22]

But examination finds this claim unconvincing. A number of the studies claiming the effectiveness of various educational and cajoleries were strictly in-house. The abstinence side largely cites studies by Robert Lerner (of Lerner and Nagai Quantitative Consulting, a consultant for conservative lobbies), Stanley Weed (of the Institute of Research & Evaluation, another right-wing consultant), and the Heritage Foundation's Kim and Rector. Only a tiny number of apparently independent studies affirmed abstinence's effectiveness, and then only in achieving small, temporary effects on the self-reported behaviors of certain subgroups.[23]

Weed did issue a review of 119 studies, the sum of which was that neither sex education nor sex education in combination with abstinence lectures could be shown to be effective:

> The common perception about the effectiveness of these two prevention strategies is not accurate. When judged against criteria of (1) sustained results, (2) broad-based impacts, and (3) real protection, there is little evidence that school-based comprehensive sex education strategies are effective. The evidence does not indicate that combining abstinence education with contraceptive-based education in the classroom is effective.[24]

Weed correctly pointed out some flaws in the National Campaign to Prevent Teen and Unplanned Pregnancy's own misleading in-house study (see below) claiming that by very weak criteria, the majority of sex education programs studied accomplished at least *some* result, no matter how small or temporary, by at least *some* standard of evaluation, no matter how low. However, Weed's counter-conclusion that "there is evidence that school-based abstinence education can be an effective prevention strategy" was based on an even smaller set of even more questionable and limited studies affirming only small, temporary effects.

IS SEXUALITY EDUCATION "EFFECTIVE," THEN?

The premier evaluator of sexuality education for the National Campaign to Prevent Teen and Unplanned Pregnancy is Douglas Kirby, of ETR

Associates (which once funded one of my research projects). Notes Kirby in his most recent review at this writing, *Emerging Answers 2007* for the National Campaign:

> There are many factors in young people's lives that affect their sexual behavior, for example, their own sexual drive and desire for intimacy, their family's values, their friends' values and behavior, their own attitudes and skills, the media, the monitoring of young people by their community, and opportunities for the future in their community.[25]

Kirby's ETR Associates is headquartered in Scott's Valley, California. There certainly are teen sex drives, families, peers, media, attitudes, skills, and opportunities (I cannot speak to the desire for intimacy) in affluent, red-wooded Scott's Valley, one node of the state's Silicon Coast (a techie, not implant, reference). What there is not in Scott's Valley is teen pregnancy. In the ZIP code (95066) in which ETR resides, just two of the 558 girls aged 12 to 19 gave birth in 2006—a rate comparable to that of the Netherlands. But drive 25 minutes downhill to Watsonville, a mostly Hispanic agricultural town with high poverty, and the teen birth rate rises to 12 times higher (see Chapter 4). Teen girls account for 13.5 percent of Watsonville's births, versus 1.4 percent of Scott's Valley's. One can find examples that contrast even more starkly. Motor through a populous district in nearby San Jose's Silicon tech neighborhoods, where just one in 100 births are by teens. Then drive up to Stockton in the Central Valley, where teens account for one in five births.

So, what exactly is Kirby saying in the context of his deploring of teen motherhood as a major social problem alongside gigantic variations in teen pregnancy rates by race? At the very end of Kirby's list is the acknowledgment that teens face varying "opportunities for the future." Perhaps, by this brief phrase, Kirby is referring to the fallout from poverty, a word that appears nowhere in his report except as something to be blamed on teenaged mothers' decisions to have babies. Does that mean Hispanic teens are to blame for poverty while Scott's Valley teens should be congratulated for their lack thereof?

Kirby and ETR have produced many excellent evaluations, but his *Emerging Answers* report is not one of them. The problems with his interpretation of his analysis are severe. The report's limited scope is evident in its introduction by National Campaign CEO Sarah Brown:

> It is unreasonable to expect any single curriculum or community program to make a serious dent in the problem of teen pregnancy on its own. Making true and lasting progress in preventing teen pregnancy requires a combination of community programs and broader efforts to influence values and popular culture, to engage parents and schools, to change the economic incentives that face teens, and more.

The National Campaign's truncated moral horizon does not confront national leaders with their obligation to reduce child poverty, in the same fashion that we now spend $400 billion per year to reduce poverty and boost incomes among the elderly. Nor does Brown mention family abuses or adult sexual behaviors, which powerfully influence teens' behaviors. The report is confined to teens aged 12 to 18 (though statistics for ages 19 to 24 are often tossed in to boost the numbers), which means two-thirds of the fathers of babies to teen mothers are excluded. Genuine issues, even in 2009, remain too uncomfortable and complicated to explore.

With all the big issues taken off the table, no wonder, then, that Kirby begins by admitting that *at best* programs can affect perhaps one-third of "sexual risk taking." Even by his own measures, the programs he evaluates do not come close even to that. Begin with his assessment of abstinence-only programs:

> Fewer than 10 rigorous studies of these programs have been carried out, and studies of two programs have provided modestly encouraging results. . . . There does not exist strong evidence that any particular abstinence program is effective at delaying sex or reducing sexual behavior. . . . In sum, studies of abstinence programs have not produced sufficient evidence to justify their widespread dissemination.

Then, move to his over-optimistic evaluation of abstinence-plus approaches: "Two-thirds of the 48 comprehensive programs that supported both absti-nence and the use of condoms and contraceptives for sexually active teens had positive behavioral effects," including 40 to 60 percent that reduced or delayed the initiation or frequency of sex, riskier sex, and unprotected sex. Here we run into the first big problem: Kirby's "positive behavioral effects" for school-based comprehensive sexuality education consisted solely of self-reported improvements, usually modest, in abstract matters such as "knowl-edge," "confidence," and "intention." That is fine, but there is no evaluation sub-stantiating whether these are connected to changes in real behavior outcomes. Even the supposed attitude changes fostered by comprehensive sexuality educa-tion programs were suspect. As National Campaign advisor and sex-ed critic Stanley Weed pointed out, when *Emerging Answers'* findings about comprehen-sive sexuality education (CSE) are examined in detail:

- No school-based CSE programs demonstrated a decrease in teen pregnancy or STD rates for any subgroup for any period of time.
- No school-based CSE programs had been shown to increase the number of teens who used condoms consistently for more than three months.
- Only two school-based CSE programs (as measured in five studies) delayed the onset of teen sexual intercourse for 12 months for the target population and only three programs increased frequency of condom use (but not consistent use) for the same time period.

- No school-based CSE programs demonstrated that they had increased both teen abstinence and condom use (by the sexually active) for the target population for any time period.
- Of the 25 school-based CSE programs that measured teen condom use, 64 percent did not increase condom use for any subgroup for any time period, even though the median follow-up time for these 16 programs was only four months.[26]

Even when the National Campaign evaluated just the 28 comprehensive sex education programs claimed to show the "strongest evidence of success" (*What Works 2008*)[27] evidence of success was sparse. Once again, all relied on self reports. Only eight of the programs even measured teen pregnancy rates as an outcome, and only three actually claimed reductions in self-reported pregnancy over a 12-month period. All of these were *community*, not school, programs. None of the school sex education programs were found to actually reduce teen pregnancy for any time period.

Kirby also lauded community-based (as opposed to school) programs to prevent pregnancy and STD, though his logic was peculiar. Four of the six studies of community programs found improvements in teens' self-reported knowledge and sexual behaviors, but these results were measured among *all* teens in the community, not just those exposed to the programs. Therefore, program effects cannot be judged.

Clinics themselves providing contraception and reproductive health services fared better, though their impact had to be inferred from the fact that "large numbers of young people obtain contraceptives from publicly funded clinics each year, and presumably those contraceptives prevent many pregnancies" though "the magnitude of the effect of publicly funded clinics on teen pregnancy is difficult to estimate." Kirby could be a bit stronger here. Teens do use contraception, evidently in increasing numbers, and they get it from somewhere. Taken as a whole—clinics, pharmacies, Internet suppliers, gas station restrooms—it is reasonable to conclude that contraception provision outlets contribute to reductions in pregnancy among all age groups and should be made available to teens without restriction.

Kirby also found the welfare reforms touted by the Clinton-Gingrich forces in the 1990s produced no demonstrable impact on adolescent childbearing. Oddly, for all the hollering about punishing and restricting teen mothers under welfare reform guidelines, Kirby found no studies of whether these were effective. However, comprehensive community programs that covered broader aspects of teens' lives did have some effects:

Perhaps the most intensive program, conducted over the longest time was the Children's Aid Society-Carrera Program (CAS-Carrera Program). This program recruited teens when they were about 13 to 15 years old and encouraged them to participate throughout high school. The CAS-Carrera Program operated five days a week and provided services in a wide range of areas: family life and sex education; general education, including individual academic assessment, tutoring, preparation for standardized exams, and assistance with college entrance; employment, including a job club, stipends, individual bank accounts, jobs, and career awareness; self-expression through the arts; individual sports; and comprehensive medical care, including mental health care, reproductive health services, and contraception when needed. In all of these areas, staff tried to create close, caring relationships with participants. They also sent a very clear message about avoiding unprotected sex and pregnancy.... A rigorous study found that the program was effective for girls, but not boys. Among girls in six sites in New York City, it delayed first sex, increased the use of condoms along with another effective method of contraception, and reduced pregnancy rates—for three years. However, in six other sites outside of New York City, not all of these favorable results for girls were obtained.

The costs of Children's Aid Society programs, about $5,000 per teen per year, resemble the investments other Western countries make to reduce youth poverty and provide these services as public entitlements.

What Kirby actually found, then, is that we do not know what caused recent pregnancy and childbirth declines among teens. The vast majority of the 1990s and early 2000s decline remains unexplained even if we accept his evaluations in their most optimistic light. Unfortunately, after his inconclusive set of findings, Kirby then lauded programs and educators with a thoroughly unwarranted conclusion that betrays the bias of the report and its funding agency. "For decades, dedicated adults have worked with teens to prevent unintended pregnancy," he writes. "Their efforts have been rewarded with declining rates of pregnancy and childbirth." But how, again, did "decades" of sex education and programs aimed at unmarried school-age teens produce the 1990s decline in births among *mostly older, married* teens?

WHAT IS "SEX EDUCATION," ANYWAY?

A 2008 study by University of Washington researchers in the *Journal of Adolescent Health*[28] appears to be the first to directly compare teenage sex, pregnancy, and STD rates among 15 to 19 year-olds who had received no sex education, abstinence-only education, and comprehensive sex education. The study included controls for some important external factors affecting teen pregnancy rates, such as poverty, race, and, family structure. Yet again, it found that socioeconomic status (family income level, in this case) and family structure ("intact" versus "non-intact") were the biggest factors predicting teen pregnancy rates.

Yet again, that conclusion was ignored by those who preferred to focus on the study's lesser finding that compared to youths who received no sex education of any kind, those who received comprehensive sex education were 60 percent less likely (a significant finding after other factors were controlled) and those who received abstinence-only 30 percent less likely (not statistically significant) to have become pregnant. This conclusion was hailed as "good findings" for sex education by reviewers[29] who tended to gloss over the study's problems.

This study was better done than most. But its chief difficulty was its very broad, somewhat inaccurate definition of sex education as "any formal instruction at school, church, a community center, or some other place about how to say no to sex." The study is not about the school curriculums that are objects of furious debate, but any "formal instruction" by anyone, anywhere. Those youths whose instruction included information on birth control were classified as having received "comprehensive sex education;" those whose instruction did not were classified as having received "abstinence only."

Youths who had received *some* kind of sex education were compared in terms of self-reported sexual activity, pregnancy, and STD rates to those who had not. Fewer than 10 percent of youths have never received any formal sex information from anyone, and they were far more likely to be very poor, female, black, rural, and from broken families. At its most generous interpretation, this study did indicate that trying to keep teens *completely* in the dark about sex does not prevent pregnancy, but its extremely broad definition of "sex education" as just about anything made it less applicable to the debate than would a more rigorous definition.

WHAT REDUCES TEEN PREGNANCY?

When long-term program evaluator Douglas Kirby estimates that even under the most impossibly optimistic assumptions, one-third of teen pregnancy could be prevented by programs and education—and then presents a report summarizing the best and latest research indicating that even this is questionable—then it is long past time for political and institutional leaders, the National Campaign, and other influential policymakers to stop quarreling over what indoctrinations and education to aim at teens. American experts damn well know what prevents what we mislabel as "teen pregnancy." They just do not have the decency or guts to say it.

I have looked at a number of natural community laboratories, variously termed, "Scott's Valley, California," "Georgetown, D.C.," "Irvine," and "White population, Marin County." These places boast fantastic teen pregnancy prevention programs, ones that would be the envy of Stockholm. In a country in which half of all adult pregnancies are unplanned, how on earth do these communities achieve such wondrous unfecundity among teens? Simple: they do not have 15 percent, 25 percent, or 40 percent of their teens growing up in poverty.

But are their successes due simply to their locations in liberal regions with good sex education and contraceptive clinics? Not necessarily. A broader insight can be gained from looking at my own, high-poverty, ultra-red, abstinence-only state, Oklahoma. The teen birth rate here, 70.4 per 1,000 females aged 15 to 19, is tenth highest among the states, 65 percent above the national average. Every race in Oklahoma has higher-than-average teen birth rates. Guttmacher lists just three abortion providers in the state. Oklahoma teens do not have much going for them in the way of externalities.

But curiously, one county—Cleveland—has very low teen birth rates not just among whites, but also among its 2,100 minority teen girls.[30] Tabulated separately by race, Cleveland County's rates are roughly half the national level for Native American and one-fourth the national average for black and Hispanic teens. Black and Hispanic teens in Cleveland County have birth rates lower than teens in the United Kingdom, in fact. What is unusual about this county? As you probably guessed, it is where the University of Oklahoma (Norman campus) is located, so that many of the county's 18-to-19-year-olds are university students. What is even more interesting is that the county ranks lowest for under-18 birth rates as well, indicating that younger teens (as in Berkeley and Irvine, California) also are influenced by the university's presence.

The National Campaign and its constituent lobbies are dedicated to preventing discussion of vital points like these. Left to themselves, as the rigid attitudes reported in sociologist Kristin Luker's *When Sex Goes to School: Warring Views on Sex—and Sex Education—Since the Sixties* (2006)[31] show, combatants are set to quarrel for another century even as schools' usefulness in this area has diminished markedly.

It is time for progressives to pursue much more promising modern developments. Conservatives have lost their battle to deny young people information. Teens today have unlimited access to sexual information that, fortunately, adults cannot effectively obstruct. There are now hundreds of Internet Web sites of every kind providing information on sexuality, and 90 percent-plus of teens have Internet access.

Today's youth are better served by consulting a variety of Web sites, especially those allowing interactive responses, than they are relying on politically whipped schools to provide accurate information on sexuality. Teens can find Web sites specific to their individualities, situations, and information needs that are much more useful than the generic curriculums emphasizing don't-do-it that schools are constrained to provide. In particular, schools are *never* going to address issues affecting gay and bisexual teens, or teens who enjoy sex and want information on how to enjoy it more (the kinds of subjects covered in lively fashion by Web sites such as those linked to the former TV show, *Dos Rombos*, cited in the introduction).

Schools are not where sex education is occurring, and that is a blessing. The ideal would be for schools to shift to sexuality education that emphasizes biological accuracy, skips preaching values, and refers students to reliable information and local services. The main task of sex-education advocates and their liberal allies now is to make sure those few teens without online capacity and local services have access to them without interference and to advance procedures to evaluate online information. And, finally, to stop squabbling with the fanatics over what schools preach and teach, and, instead, to turn to far more crucial issues such as young people's widespread social disadvantage and lack of opportunities that contribute infinitely more to pregnancy and STD rates. Redistribution of financial resources and restoration of education opportunities and public services commensurate to those Baby Boomers availed back in our day are by far the most critical needs.

However, if American leaders—especially progressive commentators and politicians—have sunk so far in greed and depravity that they no longer can summon the outrage to confront the fact that 14 million American children grow up in poverty, including 6 million in utter destitution, while average middle-aged household incomes top $100,000 annually, then we should at least have the decency to shut up about "teen sex" and "teen pregnancy." For the past 30 years, American leadership of both parties has seemed more concerned with ensuring that a millionaire grabs 2 million dollars than whether a poor child has access to good schools and universities, health care, employment opportunities, and pathways out of poverty. This book concludes with why older-generation attitudes, discussed in the context of teens and sexuality, are a far bigger threat to America's future than is now being acknowledged.

Chapter Eleven

THE CALAMITY OF CONSENSUS

President Barack Obama's call to use the "things we can agree on" to reconcile hot-button topics like teen pregnancy is the worst idea imaginable. He of all people ought to understand this. If Americans of the past had successfully pursued the consensus that all teen pregnancy must be prevented, he would not be here.

Obama's first book, *Dreams from My Father*,[1] is a remarkable compendium of idealism, even radical thought. It is especially startling on the topic of teenage mothers. Begin with his own, Stanley Ann Dunham, 17 years, 11 months old and unmarried when she became pregnant by fellow University of Hawaii student, 23-year-old Barack Obama, Sr. They split in 1964, when Barack Obama, Jr., was three. The future president's genesis had the standard horror markings: adult-teen sex, school-age pregnancy, father abandonment, unwed teen mom.

But far from sinking into poverty and maladaptive parenthood as modern consensus politics predicts, teenager Dunham proved an exemplary mother as she became a dynamic scholar. Briefly subsidized by government assistance (as were tens of millions of other Americans of all ages in the more generous 1950s and 1960s) and grandparent help with child care (hardly unusual), she soon married, obtained masters and Ph.D. degrees in anthropology, and vigorously pursued an international career.[2]

So, one expects better from President Obama than privatized-policy/culture-war sloganeering against teen mothers. At first, we get it. In the preface of *Dreams*, Obama admits that had he known his mother would die from cancer in 1995, his book would have been about her, "a celebration of the one who was the single constant in my life ... her joy, her capacity for wonder ... I know that she was the kindest, most generous spirit I have ever known, and that what is best in me I owe to her."

Obama's mother seems to be the shadow behind his respect for teen mothers as capable allies and leaders in his work for social justice in Chicago in the 1980s:

> They spoke without self-consciousness about pregnancy at fourteen or fifteen, the dropping out of school, the tenuous links to the fathers who slipped in and out of their lives. They told me about working the system, which involved mostly waiting: waiting to see the social worker, waiting at the currency exchange to cash their welfare checks, waiting for the bus that would take them to the nearest supermarket, five miles away, just to buy diapers on sale. They had mastered the tools for survival in their tightly bound worlds and made no apologies for it. They weren't cynical, though; that surprised me. They still had ambitions.

Indeed, their babies were the biggest reason for their ambitions and activism. Two young mothers who had teamed up, one caring for their children while the other attended community college and vice versa, caught Obama's attention. Concern for their children's health led them to join his challenge to the Chicago Housing Authority's toxic environment, helping to organize and lead community meetings that drew hundreds of residents to confront city officials. "I changed ... in a fundamental way," Obama wrote of these teenage mothers' influence on him. "It was the sort of change that's important not because it alters your concrete circumstances in some way (wealth, security, fame) but because it hints at what might be possible and therefore spurs you on. .... The former gangbanger, the teenage mother, had their own forms of validation ... providing the lawyer or doctor with an education from the streets."

Obama, in *Dreams*, bitterly resented the "frightening simplicities," "suffocating implications," and racialized codewords powerful white people used to blame inner-city poverty on inner-city immorality. His disdain extended to local black leaders, whose "fear and small greeds" placed protection of their cushy sinecures and corrupt bureaucracies like the CHA ahead of the desperate needs of their impoverished communities. "CHA ain't the problem," Obama scornfully quotes a complicit black pastor's evasion. "Problem is these young girls out here, engaging in all manner of fornication."

THE BARBARITY OF CONSENSUS

Unfortunately, refine that corrupt minister's sentiment a bit, and it would become akin to Obama's own a few years down the political road. Somewhere between his Chicago community days and his political campaigns, Obama's attitude toward teen mothers changed for the worse. "Everyone agrees that teen pregnancies place both mother and child at risk for all sorts of problems," he wrote in his campaign salvo, *The Audacity of Hope* (2006).[3] Any decrease in teen pregnancy "is unadulterated good news," he added. "The single biggest thing we could do to reduce . . . poverty is to encourage teenage girls to finish high school and avoid having children out of wedlock." Obama's past eloquence inveighing against the long history of "racial injustice," the "inequalities passed on from an elder generation that suffered under the brutal legacy of slavery and Jim Crow," the "inferior schools," "lack of basic services," and "legalized discrimination," now take second place to what he calls the worst culprit for African Americans' poverty: teenage girls' making babies. Or, as the reverend said, young girls fornicatin'.

But if that's the case, does Obama now believe his own unwed teen mother placed herself and him at risk, that her decision to have a child out of wedlock epitomized the biggest cause of poverty, and that preventing his own birth would have been "unadulterated good news"? I am guessing, no. A few pages on, without irony, he again lauds "my mother, whose love and clarity of spirit kept my sister's and my world centered," in contrast to "my father's irresponsibility toward his children." But in the view of the National Campaign to Prevent Teen and Unplanned Pregnancy, Obama's mother represented a "plague on the nation." If Obama now endorses popular stigma toward all parenting teenagers, how can he avoid stigmatizing his own mother?

It may seem unfair, given the fealty of family ties, to expect Obama to criticize his mom in the harsh terms he now inflicts on other people's teen mothers. But we could at least wish he had a bit more loyalty to his mother's work, which, according to a fellow anthropologist, "challenged popular perceptions regarding economically and politically marginalized groups, and countered the notions that the roots of poverty lie with the poor themselves."

Instead, Obama goes on to spend many pages and much speechifying deploring videogames, music lyrics, television, advertising images, Internet predators, and like stump-speech superficialities. These must be "the things we can agree on." The reason we can agree is the same reason we eat junk food—it is tasty, easy to swallow, and empty of substance.

As a means of designing policies to deal with social problems, seeking consensus is disastrous. In America, left-right agreement on hot-button issues rarely reflects wisdom-based synergy. It means an agreed-upon scapegoat has been identified to blame, which inevitably turns out to be the most powerless entity of the time—racial minorities and immigrants in the past; poorer teenage girls in today's falsely proclaimed "post racism" climate. We do not need yet another consortium of conventional combatants to issue yet another interest-friendly consensus-point report focused safely on blaming teens and their "culture" and pushing self-serving panaceas. Our privatized social-policy structure effectively silences discussion of real risk factors, a major reason the United States continues to lead the Western world in rates of unplanned pregnancy, STD, and a broad array of major risks among all ages.

Leadership of the type Obama once promised requires forcefully confronting exactly those issues dominant interests *do not* want raised. That is, leadership that will compel *dissensus*. We need objective analysis of original data to delineate the most important risk factors regardless of their political salability. We need to confront exactly those crucial realities all sides tacitly have agreed *not* to face. Today's teen pregnancy debate is not about the interests of teens, but the interests of interests. It's time to end the "teen pregnancy" discourse as we know it.

BAD CONSENSUS: THE PAST IS SUPERIOR TO THE PRESENT

The consensus most essential to the domination of the culture war and privatized social policy in issues such as teenage sex and teen pregnancy—as well as AIDS, drugs, crime, and other behavior issues—is the Nostalgia Myth. The Nostalgia Myth holds that younger generations are always inferior to older ones. The past is imagined as an Eden of high moral standards, caring communities, greater generations, better parenting, sweeter and safer children, and all-around contentment than the present.[4]

Most appealing to elders is the corollary: if the past is superior to the present, then older generations must be superior to younger ones. Modern young people are always lazier, stupider, sluttier, crueler, more alienated, more criminal, and just plain rottener than their elders. The ancient, gut-level axiom that the present is dangerous precisely in the ways it differs from the past, as represented by parents and grandparents whose bygone wisdom we must restore, governs virtually all American social policy debate. It is treated as inviolable doctrine, immune to logical analysis. It is the foundation for virtually all discussion of problems and remedies affecting young people.

The Nostalgia Myth is just that. Objectively, it can be shown that people did not act better and life was not safer back then. Subjectively, it can be argued with powerful evidence that "morals" were lower in the past, as evidenced by the prevalence and acceptance of racism, lynchings, family violence, barbaric working conditions, violent and exploitative prostitution trades, wanton environmental ruin, and other immoralities present standards have greatly reduced. News footage on the fiftieth anniversary of Little Rock's school integration riots, showing churchly white bigots screaming obscenities against little black kids trying to get to class . . . Is *this* the moral, family-values Fifties we elders long for?

Gut-level, evolutionary fear of change—of visible multicultures and diverse lifestyles, of girls and minorities asserting power, of the uncontrolled, unscreened, global information and contacts new technologies open up—intensifies the nostalgic yearning for the tribal past when "everyone kept to their own kind." The ultimate imperative of the Nostalgia Myth is to restore a tribal past, founded in yearning for the homogeneity of segregated ethnic, racial, and religious groups and the continuity in lifestyles and expectations from generation to generation, where change was slow and elders ruled.

Perhaps what we long for is not the sum of past reality, but the part that seemed predictable and familiar. White Americans, at least, imagine the suburban Midwestern pastoralism of *Father Knows Best*, a popular 1950s television sitcom in which patriarch Jim Anderson and sensible wife Margaret serenely mellowed the sweet screwups of their teen and 'tween children—Betty ("Princess"), James Jr. ("Bud"), and Kathy ("Kitten"). But even that was delusion. In real life, Father (Robert Young) suffered from severe alcoholism and depression and Kitten (Lauren Chapin) was enduring a childhood of sexual and violent abuse. Young and Chapin candidly admitted their demons later in life to help others with similar addiction, abuse, and depression problems. Similarly, the star of *The Patty Duke Show* later revealed a childhood of violent, alcoholic father, depressed and violent mother, her own sexual and emotional abuse at the hands of her managers, and her anorexia, heavy drinking, drug overdose, and depression. The moral superiority of the present is that personal afflictions once rendered unspeakable by cruel codes of silence now can be openly acknowledged.

The edgier 1950s comedy, *I Love Lucy*, was backdropped by her husband (on the show and in real life) Desi Arnaz's offscreen drinking, drug abuse, and infidelity, leading to their divorce. These volatilities were hinted in the show's marital jealousies, Cuban husband "Ricky's" barely controlled temper, and innuendo, the most maudlin of which was the euphemism "expecting" ("'spectin'," as Ricky said it) for Lucy's onscreen and real-life pregnancy.[5] The culture-war legend is that since these innocent-media days when the outer pretense of serenity hid real-life crises, sophisticated corporate stealth-media and permissiveness have stolen our children, sexualizing them in kindergarten and driving them to 'tween sex, and high school and college orgies, drunkenness, rape, and suicide. This legend defies rational scrutiny. True, you see less violence and far less sex, especially of a realistic and explicit kind, in media of 40 and 50 years ago, yet there were much higher levels of violent death, serious crime, self-destructive behaviors of every kind, dropout, and pregnancy among teenagers—especially younger teenagers—back then than now. Meanwhile, the mammoth increases in middle-aged drug abuse, crime, imprisonment, family disintegration, AIDS, and related ills have become taboo issues. Perhaps these disturbing older-generation crises cannot be mentioned for fear of bringing down the entire Nostalgia Myth house of cards.

BAD CONSENSUS: "THEY ARE NOT LIKE US"

Instead, the easy consensus among interest groups across the spectrum indulges the myth that teenagers (especially modern ones) are very different, in bad ways, from adults. After absorbing what seems like several tons of literature on "teenage sex" and "teen pregnancy" (I now understand puritan Anthony Comstock's urge to burn), the basic consensus I perceive is this: *adults love to call teenagers stupid.* It is good politics, good media. It makes us glow.

Here's today's teen pregnancy discourse, stripped down: Teenagers are so stupid they have ignorant sex absent preparation to do it safely. They are so stupid they wantonly get knocked up, diseases, AIDS, and dead. They are so stupid they recklessly destroy their futures and societies by having stupid babies they are too stupid to raise right. Teenagers are so stupid that just *watching* a TV show *mentioning* sex or seeing some silly images in an ad, a videogame, a movie, or some celebrity example drives them to have stupid sex and cause millions of stupid pregnancies. We smart adults must "educate" them, constantly watch them, and "send them messages," which, very likely, they will be too stupid to heed. This image peddled to the public and policymakers by scores of major organizations and media on all sides is illustrated by their publicity statements on the National Day to Prevent Teen Pregnancy (May 6 in 2009):

- Join the American Academy of Pediatrics and more than 200 other national organizations in promoting the National Day to Prevent Teen Pregnancy, a campaign geared towards teens to avoid too-early pregnancy and parenthood (American Academy of Pediatrics).
- The purpose of the day is straightforward: too many teens still think, "It cannot happen to me" (National School Boards Association).
- The number of teens having children is on the rise again and we need your help to turn this troubling trend back around. A great way to start is by getting smart about the risks (National Campaign to Prevent Teen and Unplanned Pregnancy).[6]

Stupefying stuff. Search the Web sites of various lobbies diligently and you (might) find (a bit more) complexity. But the public face—and therefore the media face—of the issue reflects the consensus that the problem is just stupid teens needing to "get smart" about the risks.

One of the most destructive stampedes in policy forums, lobbying agendas, and news media splashes across the country is toward supposedly new findings disparaging the "teenage brain." The latest "teen brain" fad (these have come along regularly for at least the last century) purports to combine cerebral neuroscannings with developmental psychology to pronounce teenagers' brains biologically prone to risk and incapable of rational self control.

Unfortunately, a collection of excitable academic grantees and lobbying groups have cajoled news reporters into creating a false consensus that resurrecting nineteenth-century biodeterminism (the obsolete consensus that certain races, immigrant groups, and women were limited by innate, unchangeable biological flaws) represents some "new science." Biodeterminist science has followed official prejudice with clockwork regularity so often in our history that one would think skepticism would now be the rule. Indeed, responsible neuro-scientists, as we will see, have warned against jumping to hasty conclusions about brain structures and behavior.

Teen-brain "science" has the capacity to do profound damage to rational approaches to sexual issues involving adolescents. If teens really are as brain-less as the disparagers claim, then sex education is useless and unsupervised personal interactions must be replaced by a 24-7 system of adult regulation. For example, consider the popular book by *New York Times* science and health editor, Barbara Strauch (*The Primal Teen: What the New Discoveries About the Teenage Brain Tell Us About Our Kids*, 2004).[7] Strauch insists that teenagers think with a "primitive . . . crocodile-like" region of their brains; the mature, adult brain isn't up and running until the late twenties.

Strauch begins with hackneyed stereotypes, 90 percent of which are negative: teenagers are a "pain in the neck," "odd," "wacky," "weird," "slam doors," "forget to call home," "wild," "crazy," "drink themselves silly," and "acting *that* way." Strauch follows with formulaic references to school shootings and anecdotes of teenage tantrums, crime, volatility, self-involvement, drugs, "pouting in their rooms," "sneaking out windows," "stomping their feet," "making LSD in the school science lab," "pierced eyebrows," "orange-spiked hair," and "brief insanity." Can someone who peddles this cartoonish junk really be the *science editor* for the nation's flagship newspaper?

Strauch's is just one in a lockstep march of identical books (*WHY Do They Act That Way?; Parenting the Teenage Brain; Secrets of the Teenage Brain; Yes! Your Teen IS Crazy!*; to name a few). It seems futile to repeat that Strauch and peer authors are slandering 30 million people from Hmong migrant workers to Scarsdale preppies with typecasts that few teenagers actually embody and/or adults also display. In real life, it goes both ways. Youths witness plenty of door slamming, foot stomping, pouting, tantrums, insanity, and worse-than-silly drinking amongst their elders (divorce rate, 50%). A few teenagers with orange hair? How about 8 million medically unnecessary cosmetic surgeries and alterations on middle-agers every year?

Strauch's reporting is stenography. In "The Age of Impulse" chapter, she declares that stereotyping teenagers as "impulsive . . . just happens to be true." What just happens to be true is that Strauch did not investigate whether it was true. What is the evidence that teenagers, more than adults, act impulsively—the same characterization leading scientists once used to describe "atavistic" black men and "hot blooded" Latins? Or, to invoke another of Strauch's stereo-types, harbor "feelings of immortality" that lead them to engage in excessive "risk taking" and "doing dumb things"—a myth that has been extensively debunked?[8]

"One big stumbling block in studying the brains of teenagers has been that relatively few of them die," Strauch declares, missing the irony.

Strauch's old-journalism, source-dictated, melodramatic technique is hopelessly inadequate to cover modern youth issues. She gushes over pompous claims by a few self-praising researchers that their sketchy notions amount to a monumental scientific revolution. She fails to interview conscientious experts who admit that our knowledge of how brain organization affects real-world behavior is woefully lacking.

Moving beyond media and popular-author treatments of "teen brain" issues, the popular-psychology case sounds more erudite but is not much better. "'If kids are as smart as adults, why do they do such dumb things?'" psychologist, text author, and McArthur Foundation grantee Lawrence Steinberg asks,[9] presaging his explanation:

> The temporal gap between puberty, which impels adolescents toward thrill-seeking, and the slow maturation of the cognitive control system, which regulates these impulses, makes adolescence a time of heightened vulnerability for risky behavior. ... Risk-taking is the product of a competition between the socio-emotional and cognitive control networks ... and adolescence is a period in which the former abruptly becomes more assertive at puberty while the latter gains strength only gradually, over a longer period of time.[10]

Is this straight-line biodeterminism accurate? No. Ambiguous brain neuroscannings purporting to show that teens "think" with a more primitive brain region called the amygdala while adults consult the lofty cerebral cortex, along with other neuroscannings showing just the opposite, all are interpreted as documenting adolescent brain inferiority. While Strauch declares the amygdala a "crocodile-like" brain area promoting greater adolescent rashness, neuroscientists point out that the complex amygdala actually "inhibits the midbrain aggressive patterns of behavior" and promotes more caution.[11]

In the scientific literature, the views presented by Strauch, Steinberg, and others as scientific consensus are strongly disputed. Asked, "How much do we know about the relationship between the anatomy or biology of the brain and behavior?" Kurt W. Fischer, director of the Mind, Brain, & Education Program at the Harvard Graduate School of Education replied,

> We do not know very much! ... Most of the recent advances in brain science have involved knowledge of the biology of single neurons and synapses, not knowledge of patterns of connection and other aspects of the brain as a system ... but we have a very long way to go, ... People naturally want to use brain science to inform policy and practice, but our limited knowledge of the brain places extreme limits on that effort.[12]

Daniel Siegel, of UCLA's Center for Culture, Brain, and Development and director of the Center for Human Development, agreed: "We are just beginning to identify how systems in the brain work together in an integrated fashion to create complex mental processes." Richard Lerner, director of Tufts University's Institute for Applied Research in Youth Development, likewise points out that brain research is "in its infancy" and "it's way too premature to make those specific links" between biology and behavior.[13]

"Intelligence, reasoning ability, and some important aspects of memory all peak between ages thirteen and fifteen and decline thereafter," pointed out Robert Epstein, contributing editor to *Scientific American Mind* and director emeritus of the Cambridge Center for Behavioral Studies.[14] In an interesting twist, a team led by Emory University School of Medicine researchers found that "rather than having immature cortices, adolescents who engage in dangerous activities have frontal white matter tracts that are more adult in form than their more conservative peers."[15] "I couldn't really find any link between brain development and adolescent risk-taking," the study's lead author declared.

Ironically, if middle-agers were a hated outgroup instead of our most powerful constituency, scientists would pin the blame for rising midlife pathologies on the deterioration in the middle-aged brain. The severe loss of memory and learning genes that begin wasting away after age 25 or so has been documented most alarmingly by detailed brain scans published in the June 2004 *Nature*: "The ageing of the human brain is a cause of cognitive decline in the elderly . . . DNA damage may reduce the expression of selectively vulnerable genes involved in learning, memory and neuronal survival, initiating a programme of brain ageing that starts early in adult life" (British spelling).[16] In short, there's no "mature adult brain" that emerges after adolescence. Brains change across the life span with great individual variance and not necessarily in the direction of superior cognition. Some of the most dynamic research has emerged from Strathclyde University community education professor Howard Sercombe and neurologist Tomas Paus of the University of Nottingham's Brain and Body Center, who note:

> The brains of young people are not radically different from adults in structure. There is no great difference in capacity between young people and adults. There is a difference, however, in the degree of myelination, which makes brains more reliable and efficient in their reactions and responses but less flexible and less available for new learning. . . . Brain research, and fMRI in particular, is vulnerable to oversimplification, over-interpretation, and the confirmation of prior prejudice. Especially in media reports, huge claims have been made about differences in human capacity based on tenuous, and often small, observations of differences in brain activity or structure in different populations.[17]

However premature at best and bigoted at worst, "teen brain" demonization has prairie-fired through lobbies and institutions that control media discussion. Teen-brain dysfunction is good business and a political gold mine. Big agendas, left to right, can be effortlessly advanced by invoking the "cognitive limitations of the adolescent brain." The veneer of bioscience can be fronted to deny the importance of economic disadvantage, bad schools, adult abuses, adult behaviors, and teenage individuality. It also is supremely satisfying for grownups to declare our brains the apex of all evolution. The current dogma is finally receiving some debate—see the January 2010 *Journal of Adolescent Research* for a four-way exchange.[18]

The "teen brain" fad has serious implications for teen sexuality issues. If adolescents are incapable of responsible decision making (many researchers liken them to preteen children), then adult men who have sex with teens, even 18 or 19 year-olds, should be prosecuted as if they had raped toddlers. If young adults remain cognitively flawed well into their twenties, then President Clinton was a rapist for taking advantage of Monica Lewinsky's underdeveloped 21-year-old cognition. The ages of consent and marriage should be raised to at least 25, if not 30. Sex education should be abolished. You cannot educate "crocodiles" (to borrow Strauch's term). The only solution would be to harshly force absolute abstinence on everyone under age 20, or perhaps even 25, by all means necessary, from a steady regime of abstinence lectures to criminal penalties. Perhaps we should return to the pre-1970 days when girls were incarcerated for promiscuity. That is how extreme the implications of teen-brain notions have become.

BAD CONSENSUS: ADULTS SHOULD FORCE TEENAGE MOTHERHOOD

If teenagers are this stupid, then adults must make every important decision for them. One of the most destructive areas of consensus flowing from this assumption has been laws requiring the notification or consent of parents before girls under age 18 can obtain abortions. It is fine for grownups to have sex with "underage girls" as young as 15, say legislators in 36 states. But "underage girls" are too immature to get an abortion, say legislators in the 37 states which require parental notification or consent for minor girls' abortions. (In six more states, laws are enjoined pending judicial review.) In California, three efforts to pass a parental consent law at the ballot box have failed, but exit polls indicate that is only because voters under age 30, the most supportive of legal abortion choice of any age group,[19] were vigorously opposed. California's most recent exit poll[20] found that just 34 percent of voters age 18 to 24 and 38 percent of those age 18 to 29 in the 2008 election favored Proposition 4 to require that parents be notified before a girl under age 18 could obtain an abortion. Voters over age 30 were evenly split, indicating that as in previous elections, younger voters effectively overruled older ones to preserve abortion rights.

The logic of parental consent/notification laws is this: if a "minor" girl is judged too incompetent to get an abortion, the solution is to manufacture a punishing legal runaround to force her to become a mother. They originated in liberal, Democrat-dominated Minnesota and Massachusetts in the 1980s, where studies found the chief effect was to drive a few hundred girls a year to obtain abortions in neighboring states.[21] Naturally, such a destructive idea quickly spread to conservative anti-abortion lobbies and has been strongly pushed by Republicans ever since.

Former U.S. District Judge Donald Alsop of Minnesota compiled an exhaustive record showing *unanimous* opposition to the law from judges who administered it.[22] Judges reported the law's "judicial bypass" requirement that girls obtain a judge's consent in lieu of informing their parents was "absolutely traumatic" for girls, that a large majority of girls seeking abortions informed one or both parents on their own, that most who did not tell parents rightly feared violence and retribution, and that none of the 3,000 girls who applied were denied judicial authorization because "the young women were very mature and capable of giving the required consent" on their own. Indeed, no witness could document any positive effect of the law, Alsop noted in striking it down.

Then came the first of several mind-bogglingly irrational—*by their own record*—U.S. Supreme Court decisions upholding the cruelest, most extreme parental consent requirements. In *Hodgson v. Minnesota* (1990),[23] justices admitted that "many minors in Minnesota live in fear of violence of family members and are in fact victims of rape, incest, neglect, and violence;" that the law created delays imposing serious health risks on girls; that local judges had found girls mature enough to make their own decisions; that the law's requirement to notify even fathers who were abusive or had abandoned their children was unreasonable; and that no witnesses experienced with the law cited any positive effects.[24] Indeed, a National Academy of Sciences study filed with the Court reported that "parental notification and consent laws do not protect pregnant adolescents from harm. Rather, they often cause it."[25]

Then, six justices turned around and, without explanation, upheld Minnesota's extreme parental consent law as no more than a "minimal" burden on "the minor's limited right to obtain an abortion." The opinion exuded meanness. Jeannie Rosoff, then director of the Alan Guttmacher Institute, analyzed the decision and found little more than "unreasoning hostility."[26] It is as if justices and legislators saw inflicting harm on pregnant girls as a *reason* for parental consent laws.

The Court upheld the gratuitous cruelty inflicted on girls in Arkansas, Minnesota, Mississippi, and North Dakota that even long-gone, brutal, estranged fathers must be located to give consent for the abortions of daughters they abused, raped, abandoned, or had not seen in years. The Court also shrugged off laws in 22 states requiring parental consent for girls' abortions, establishing the barbaric principle that a female may be *forced* by third parties to become a mother against her will. How could any pro-choice legislator (the margin of victory of parental consent laws rests on securing votes from some lawmakers who normally support abortion rights) ratify a law that allowed forcing motherhood on adolescent girls that they would never apply to adult women?

In the August 1997 *American Journal of Public Health*, a well-designed, longer-term, multistate study by Charlotte Ellertson of the Population Council[27] dispelled both liberal and conservative phantasms about the effects of parental consent laws. The study found that teenage girls are not witless fools. Confronted with a humiliating legal barrier manufactured by adults bent on punishing them, girls seeking abortions simply travel to other states. Ellertson found the data showed that "minors who traveled out of state may have accounted for the entire observed decline" in in-state abortions. After Missouri's law took effect, abortions for Missouri minors in neighboring states rose "by over 50 percent," she concluded. Further, such laws delayed minors' abortions into more hazardous later weeks, again revealing that harming young women whose condition offends many grownups was a motivation for parental consent laws. Attempts to reach consensus on hot-button topics produces disastrous policy.

BAD CONSENSUS: PERPETUATING IDEOLOGY

Liberals' latest ideological salvo (at this writing) is sociologist Mark Regnerus's *Forbidden Fruit: Sex and Religion in the Lives of American Teenagers* (2007),[28] generously written up in *The New Yorker*.[29] Regnerus's thesis is that evangelical Protestant teenagers are more likely to have sex at earlier ages, to not use contraception, and therefore to get pregnant than non-religious or non-evangelical teenagers. Evangelical teens may *tell* surveys they believe in chastity outside of marriage, but they actually engage in earlier and riskier sex. Another bug for self-reporting surveys.

Superficially, outcome statistics would seem to back Regnerus's liberal "red sex/blue sex" hypothesis. Red states, which harbor the highest proportions of evangelical Protestants and voted the most for Republican presidential candidates, tend to have the nation's highest rates of divorce, teen pregnancy, and unwed birth. Blue states, which are more religiously diverse and voted for Democrat Obama, generally have lower rates of these outcomes. The Bible Belt stretching from Oklahoma to West Virginia and south is a map of sexual dissolution, while liberal New England is righteous. Specifically, ultra-red states such as Mississippi, Texas, Arkansas, and Oklahoma, are among the highest for divorces and pregnant teens while blue states such as Massachusetts, New Hampshire, Connecticut, and Minnesota are among the lowest.[30] Combine these outcomes with surveys indicating evangelical teens have sex more than their religious morals would seem to permit, and the red/blue theory appears to be drawing enough ants for a picnic. The evidence for the red/blue theory was summarized by *New Yorker* "Dept. of Disputation" editor Margaret Talbot:

> The red-state model is clearly failing on its own terms—producing high rates of teen pregnancy, divorce, sexually transmitted disease, and other dysfunctional outcomes that social conservatives claim to abhor. Like other American teens, young evangelicals live in a world of Internet porn, celebrity sex scandals, and raunchy reality TV, and they have the same hormonal urges that their peers have. Yet, they come from families and communities in which sexual life is supposed to be forestalled until the first night of a transcendent honeymoon.
>
> The red-state model puts couples at greater risk for divorce; women who marry before their mid-twenties . . . at the high point in the life cycle for risk-taking and experimentation . . . are significantly more likely to divorce than those who marry later. Not only do couples who marry later stay married longer, children born to older couples fare better on a variety of measures, including educational attainment, regardless of their parents' economic circumstances.

Talbot tied up Regnerus' thesis: Blue-state adults simply prepare their kids better to negotiate the temptations of pop-culture and hormones through acceptance of sexuality and sex education. Red-state adults try to stop teen sex by abstinence imprecations and enforced ignorance, producing earlier experimentation leading to earlier teen pregnancy, marriage, and divorce. Regnerus and Talbot wind up offering simply another version of standard teen-pregnancy theory blaming the other side's ideology.

Yet, the same troublesome hurdle remains: The Regnerus/Talbot thesis, like previous conservative and liberal theories, fails to control for socioeconomic status and adult behaviors. In this case, states with the biggest share of envangelicals also tend to be those with the highest rates of poverty. (The relationship between fundamentalist religion and poverty would be most productive to investigate.)

To test whether poverty or religion is the biggest factor in teen pregnancy rates, I analyzed the proportions of evangelical Protestants,[31] teen pregnancy rates,[32] and poverty rates and population statistics by state.[33] Sure enough, the analysis found that states with lots of evangelicals had lots of poverty ($r = 0.50$, $p < 0.001$), states with lots of poverty had lots of teen pregnancy ($r = 0.62$, $p < 0.001$), and states with lots of evangelicals had lots of teen pregnancy, though the relationship was weaker ($r = 0.31$, $p = 0.04$).

To make a long regression short, once youth poverty levels were factored in, any effect resulting from high proportions of evangelicals on teen pregnancy rates all but disappeared. In short, the "red state/blue state" hypothesis really amounted to a "poor state/rich state" one.

Regnerus does present the results from a limited series of regression analyses in the appendix, all of which rely on self-reported behaviors and attitudes rather than actual outcomes. The biggest predictor by far of early sex remains being black and/or having parents with less education (measures of poverty), along with going to schools where lots of kids have sex (however that was measured). Regnerus's best model winds up explaining just 25 percent of the variation in teen pregnancy rates by religious affiliation, not bad for a sociological study but still leaving three-fourths up for grabs.

Unfortunately, the Regnerus/Talbot thesis gives socioeconomics short shrift in order to invoke the same-old culture-warhorses: horny teens, pop culture, and religion. Regnerus and Talbot do not back up—or even try to back up—their claim that "America's sexed-up consumer culture" and media affect teen sex and pregnancy rates. Why do researchers and reporters rush to "culture war" explanations when there are so many more vital issues to address?

In a more intriguing vein, Regnerus does acknowledge that middle/upper-class status and its promise of higher education yield much greater teen caution with sex and much, much lower birth rates. In Regnerus's middle/upper-class teen sex paradigm, having unprotected sex is viewed as unacceptably self-destructive, "like smoking or driving a car without a seat-belt." (Note that those who believe teen brains are innately unable to reason and plan cannot explain why more affluent teens' brains apparently are.) Given the bright futures and responsibilities better-off teens headed for college and leadership roles anticipate, risking pregnancy at 16 "is not just unwise anymore; it's wrong."

In this sense, I believe, Regnerus is right. I encountered those attitudes among students I was advising at a private high school nestled in Santa Cruz's lush hills who were authoring a book on teenage dating—a broad acceptance in their culture for behaviors such as drinking, partying, and sex coupled with a strong disdain for those who took undue risks such as drinking and driving, violence, drunkenness, emotional abuse, apathy, laziness, and unprotected intercourse. Clearly, the low rates of pregnancy and STDs among more affluent teens support Regnerus's economic contention just as they weaken his evangelical thesis.

BAD CONSENSUS: SLASHING EDUCATION IS BETTER THAN RAISING TAXES

Budget cuts to schools and universities should be titled, "Teen Pregnancy Promotion" acts. By locking out poorer youth from pathways to higher education, legislators, governors, and lobbyists make early childbearing a rational alternative for impoverished youth.

In key policies, elders promote teenagers having babies. As this is written, a staggering, $2,500 tuition hike announced by the University of California Regents for 2010 is provoking massive student protests.[34] Tuition has been raised six times faster than inflation—from around $220 per year in 1969 to

$11,000 today—for one reason: the refusal of older generations, who owe much of our record affluence to the free, tax-underwritten public education we received, to pay taxes today to support the young. Taxes on Californians average 30 percent lower per dollar of income today than in 1970 as funding for schools has plummeted from among the country's highest to near its lowest. California has experienced among the most rapid racial diversification of any major state in the world. I contend it is the harbinger of white elders refusing to pay for a younger generation that approaches two-thirds nonwhite.

Again and again, whatever old or new explanation for teen pregnancy is offered—the immature teen brain, sexy media, sexed-up consumer culture, too much sex education, too much abstinence, evangelicals, sexual liberals— closer examination reveals that *socioeconomic status remains the only real issue.* Even in partisans' studies, poverty level and related measures dwarf everything else. As this book began, so it winds down: "teenage sex" and "teen pregnancy" discourses are no longer about teenagers, if they ever were. They are about aging grownups refusing to step up to the modern responsibilities and challenges of our diverse, advancing multiculture.

Chapter Twelve

KIDS TODAY

If we Americans, as a society or individuals, do not want teenagers to get pregnant, we know exactly what not to do:

- Do not raise children and teenagers in poverty and deprivation.
- Do not violently, sexually, or emotionally abuse children or allow others to do so.
- Do not deny teenagers access to media, health services, high-quality education, sexual information, economic resources, and opportunities that adults want for ourselves.

A crushing avalanche of documentation demonstrates that middle-class and richer teens, teens raised in families and communities where adults observe high standards of sexual responsibility, teens who are not sexually and violently abused during childhood, and teens afforded accurate information, health services, good schools, university access, and career pathways have far, far lower rates of early pregnancy than impoverished, abused, disadvantaged, and ignorant youths from messed up families and troubled adult communities. These strategies do not take torturous, keep-trying-till-we-find-something studies to establish. They simply work, spectacularly, everywhere tried.

It is time to stop thrashing around reciting easy ideologies invented to explain teenage behavior—the media, the culture, permissiveness, hormones, bad brains, too little supervision, too much television, too little (or too much) religion, too little (or too much) sex or abstinence education, hidden lives, pregnancy pacts—that allow us to continue evading obvious realities. It makes

214 TEENAGE SEX AND PREGNANCY

rational sense on many levels for poorer people to have babies earlier in life. The best "teen pregnancy prevention" is to build a society in which teenagers prevent it themselves. Theories of teen pregnancy that do not incorporate socioeconomic conditions (including the behavior of nearby adults) as their central theme are useless. Theories that do are overwhelmed by socioeconomics to the point that other explanations become trivial.

The sheer volume of critical issues that all sides tacitly agree to overlook so today's teen-sex debate can proceed to interests' satisfaction has wrecked reasoned discussion. The ethical standard that researchers prioritize their most significant findings was trashed for teen pregnancy studies for the simple reason that the most significant findings always go back to socioeconomics and adult behaviors. The enormous difference in teen pregnancy, birth, abortion, STD, and HIV rates along socioeconomic lines was tossed over the side. The violent and sexual abuses of hundreds of thousands of children and teens by their families were taken off the table. Once-noble initiatives to provide valuable adolescent sexual health services have degenerated into ugly, racist, sexist, new-eugenics crusades led by political and institutional demagogues abetted by poisonous news media. "Social cost" studies have been concocted, phony findings have been hyped, and promising findings have been suppressed. Made-up crises—Internet predators, sexting, media, ads, hooking up, the frightening New Girl—were trumpeted to glorify more teen-fixing programs and teen-shackling policies. Real issues like dating violence and AIDS were hijacked by exploitative lobbies and politicians pushing self-serving agendas. Everyone ignored the vital but inconvenient fact that all of the decline in teen births since 1990 occurred among married teens. No interest group even mentions the crucial effect on young people of America's burgeoning middle-aged calamities.

Adults get maddest at teens precisely when they act most like us. Teens, like adults, have sex because most who do enjoy sex; those who do not abstain because they see more problems than benefits. Teens, like adults, have babies when their economic circumstances and future prospects make parenthood a reasonable course. Teens, like adults, make mistakes with sex and parenting, suffer consequences from mistakes that grade strongly along socioeconomic lines, and benefit from good sexual information and health services. Teens, like adults, are individuals. There is no one-size-fits-all nostrum.

Privatized consensus inevitably gravitates toward pandering imbecility. The greatest shame lies with academic, agency, and institutional leaders who have succumbed to paralyzing conformity. How did phony "surveys" and "studies" blatantly designed to perpetuate profitable fabrications become acceptable "scientific" currency? What explains the complete failure of leaders to forcefully confront the disturbed malevolence of authorities and commentators who hallucinate wild orgies of seventh-grade oral sex, expose teens' private cell phone messages to brand 14-year-olds sex criminals for life, and panic in perpetual horror that teenagers experience even the mildest interactions and communications?

No major American interest that I am aware of promotes effective policies. Today's entrepreneurial climate treats teenage sex and pregnancy as *permanent commodities*, indefinitely exploitable so long as cycles of marketable images buttressed by fearsome sensationalism can be sold. If realistic measures were adopted, "teenage sex" and "teen pregnancy" would no longer be the sexy, profitable commodities exploited by interests today.

It is time for the lying, meanness, and insufferable conceit to end. Strong and secure grownups do not demean their children and teenagers as brain-damaged sluts and psychopaths. Responsible adult culture does not allow authors, privatized interests, and public-agency sycophants to popularize themselves and profit from commodifying young people with degrading myths. Caring, concerned grownups do not indulge pleasing escapisms and yuppie frettings over imaginary media and pop culture bogies to shrink from facing real-life challenges. Mature adults do not insist that media and authorities endlessly flatter our egos with unfounded praise and soothing reassurances.

My guess as to how this happened, even though it fits the best facts I can assemble, still strikes me as inadequate: I think modern American grownups are suffering maladaptive reactions against the tide of social, racial, and technological changes recent decades have brought. Stability-craving elders are hard-wired to be anxious at change ("future shock," as Alvin Toffler colorfully termed it), and we associate that anxiety with the young people who inhabit the present and future that so many grownups fear. As anthropologist Margaret Mead worried, the shift from static, traditional, homogenous cultures to modern societies of diversity and rapid change creates intense adult apprehension that, if allowed to escalate, can rip generations and societies apart.

How else can we explain the sheer irrationality of the multiple paranoias toward teenage sexuality, the return to long-debunked biological myths, the resurrection of barbaric eugenics devaluing the worth of stigmatized babies, and the alternating panic and anger toward successful girls and young women? This is not normal generational tension. Today's fear is evolutionary, the kind that accompanies dread among elders that a fundamental break in the continuity of society is rendering them obsolete.

Evolutionary fear is dangerous. Today's panics over teenage sex, pregnancy, and related youth issues holds far more troubling implications for America's social fabric and the survival of our society than now recognized. Demonizing younger generations for adult profit and enjoyment—the standard pop-media fare on sex and morals—is not about caring, concern, or even amusement. This is more than just jockeying for bucks, elections, and ratings. It is the signature of an aging America gone disastrously wrong.

THE FACE OF CHANGE

Sitting at a coffee shop in downtown Oklahoma City—where the school board fought ferociously to maintain segregated schools well into the 1960s and, when they failed, tens of thousands of whites fled for the suburbs like frightened squirrels—I see the social revolution everywhere. Most of the groups of young people, including couples, are integrated, and not just black with white, but multiracialities. This revolution astonishes my 84-year-old mother. Her generation of the 1930s and 1940s had no social contact with Negroes. Indians and Mexicans were invisible, and Asians were confined to the one Chinese restaurant in the tiny "foreign district."

Now, the population under age 25, as in most cities, is all-minority. Precinct breakdowns in the 2008 election show huge swaths of once-solidly-Republican Oklahoma City voted heavily for Democrat Barack Obama—not just African-American neighborhoods, but Hispanic, Asian, Native, and urban white populations. They were buried under 80 percent Republican votes in the city's sprawling exurbs ... countered by Obama love-ins in college districts in university-dominated Norman and Stillwater ... and reburied under Republican landslides in aging, rural Oklahoma. It is the new politics of rising youth, urban, and color versus declining old, rural, and white, and many of the latter are scared.

The key aspect of this rift is demographic: the replacement of America's white-dominated population of the past with an all-minority population, a transition visibly rising up through younger ages. In the 1950s, 90 percent of America's population age 45 and older, like 85 percent of its children and teens, were whites of European origin. That is, whites dominated, and the parents looked like the children. Now, in 2010, 75 percent of the population age 45 and older is white, but 44 percent of children and teens are Hispanic, black, Asian, Native, and other or mixed race. By 2025, the census projects more than *half* of America's children and teens will be nonwhite, harbinger of the time, around 2045, when America will have no racial majority.[1] Young parents are speeding that change. Right now, 61 percent of babies born to teenage mothers are nonwhite or mixed race, while 60 percent born to mothers age 35 and older are white.

I think unspoken anxiety over racial change underlies America's modern alarm over teenage pregnancy and related generational issues. The visibly integrated nature of younger generations creates visceral apprehension among grownups. White elders ruling nonwhite young spells trouble unless leaders, institutions, and major media discipline themselves to calm, not whip up, irrational fears, direct or coded, tied to racial change.

But it is more complex than just race. Rapid technological changes are intensifying the integration of global societies as well. Never before have humans had to deal with the triple whammy of suddenly emerging racial/ ethnic multicultures, technological advances that produce worldwide communication and information exchanges, and diverse, worldly young women. Many Americans seem unable to handle these jolting changes—even fearing, as in recent anti-health-care-reform outbursts, that this new social order intends to kill them off—while others display lesser resistances.

Myriad symbols are raised to invoke fear of change and diversity: Hispanic and Asian immigration, unclosing gays, a multiracial president, universal media presented as invading and corrupting (not informing and connecting), and any effort to invoke shared responsibility for other Americans via universal health care, low-cost education, and investment in poorer children. These fears arise in a society whose older generations view the future and children with dread and disdain. The smug senselessness that media commentators and authorities dispense about teens, sex, pregnancy, and a host of youth issues evidence an adult culture that is not up to the challenges and responsibilities of the modern age.

"The adult imagination, acting alone, remains fettered to the past," Mead warned.[2] Yet, the failure of an aging society to adapt to new realities and changes is a luxury we can't afford.

END DEMOGRAPHIC SCAPEGOATING

The devastating relic of designating demographic scapegoats to blame for the nation's troubles allows politicians, researchers, and interests to jettison modern discursive ethics and tougher research standards and to indulge primitive prejudices—selective anecdotes, wild embellishments, generalizations from rare examples, mass stigmas, easy moralizing, even outright lies and name-calling. Today, the agreed-upon demographic demon is youth, universally depicted not as the usual upstart generation with some newfangled notions, but as alien invaders bearing frightening new technologies and diversities. The culture wars, privatized social policy regimes, and make-it-up ethics repeatedly documented in this book are manifestations of a society inventing gut-grabbing moral panics to justify repressing and disowning its young people.

Demographic scapegoating sabotages America's ability to modernize institutional structures to confront its serious challenges and to serve a diverse society. This country suffers by far the worst social crises and inequities of any Western society, and most Latin American ones as well. These must be forcefully confronted, beginning with the Obama presidency, if we are to hold together as a nation. Atavistic entities like the National Campaign to Prevent Teen and Unplanned Pregnancy and the Office of National Drug Control Policy, designed to manufacture politically warped images of young people and minorities to facilitate stigma and blame, should be abolished. The popularity-attuned leadership of key agencies like the Centers for Disease Control (and its useless "adolescent risk taking" mantra), Substance Abuse and Mental Health Services Administration, National Institutes of Health, and others needs replacement by scientific, non-ideological technocrats who will deliver tough social and health realities unvarnished. The evolution of online and mobile media are providing refreshing possibilities for broadening discussion beyond the narrow parameters prescribed by current media elites.

Imagine how different our views would be if we saw the present as an improvement, not a degeneration, compared to the past. The Nostalgia Myth (see Chapter 11) obliterates progress toward building on encouraging new developments. By virtually every index we can reliably assess, today's more diverse United States is a safer, less crime-ridden, less deadly, less violent, and more educated and moral society today than at any time in our history. The chief reason is improving attitudes and behaviors among America's rapidly diversifying youth, which are more than offsetting rising drug abuse, crime, imprisonment, violent death, AIDS, and reactionary politics among their elders. Young people at the center of change seem to be handling it well, despite the best efforts of exploitative institutions to inflame alarm. The future seems likely to improve on these gains—unless older generations, acting out of ego, self-interest, detachment, and atavistic fear, decide to sabotage them.

We are approaching an endgame of intractable conflict between Americans who find participating in today's diverse, interconnected, global society dynamic and rewarding versus Americans who deeply fear today's multicultural world and seek retreat into the tribal past. The job of conservatives may be to tout traditional values, but today's Right has sunk into hypocritical meanness that regularly spreads pyschotic paranoia. The capitulation of moderates and progressives to programmatic dogma and moralizing has enabled panic over teenage sex and pregnancy to lurch backward into primitive racism and sexism, however euphemistically disguised. We Americans have the ability to identify the genuine needs of young people and the science to inform their realization. There's no reason for today's destructive, culture-war-privatized-policy-make-it-up drivel to go on any longer.

NOTES

INTRODUCTION

1. The Dos Rombos-La Comunidad Web site, http://www.forosexualidad.com/ and http://dosrombos.extremaweb.com/profile.php?mode=viewprofile&u=325 (accessed 2009).

2. Motion picture rating system, Wikipedia, http://en.wikipedia.org/wiki/Motion _picture_rating_system (accessed 2009).

3. See, for examples, M. G. Durham, *The Lolita Effect: The Media Sexualization of Young Girls and What We Can Do About It* (Overlook Press, 2008); D. E. Levin and J. Kilbourne, *So Sexy So Soon: The New Sexualized Childhood and What Parents Can Do to Protect Their Kids* (Ballantine Books, 2008); B. Kantrowitz, "Selling Advice—As Well As Anxiety," *Newsweek*, June 3, 2002, 50–52; C. Shipman, "Teens: Oral Sex and Casual Prostitution No Biggie," *Good Morning America, ABC News*, May 28, 2009; S. Azam, "Oral Sex Is the New Goodnight Kiss," http://www.thenewgoodnightkiss.com/ (accessed 2009).

4. A fine account can be found in K. Sternheimer, *Connecting Social Problems and Popular Culture* (Westview Press, 2009).

5. See any major media report on RAND Corporation study on or around November 3, 2008, such as CNN, "Study Links Sexual Content on TV to Teen Pregnancy," November 3, 2008, http://www.cnn.com/2008/HEALTH/11/03/teen.pregnancy/index.html.

6. Federal Trade Commission, "FTC Renews Call to Entertainment Industry to Curb Marketing of Violent Entertainment to Children," December 3, 2009, http://ftc.gov/opa/ 2009/12/violentent.shtm.

7. D. Denby, "Hard Knocks," *The New Yorker*, May 11, 2009, 82.

8. J. Sharlet, *The Family: The Secret Fundamentalism at the Heart of American Power* (Harper Collins, 2008).

9. Children's Internet Protection Act (2000), history and provisions detailed by The Free Dictionary, http://encyclopedia.thefreedictionary.com/Children's+Internet +Protection+Act.

10. KCBS, "Blocking Secondhand Porn in San Jose," October 20, 2007, http://www.kcbs.com/pages/1113680.php?.

11. H. Clinton, quoted in E. Mehren, "The First Lady's Family Values," *Los Angeles Times*, June 15, 1995, E1, E11.

12. C. Hansen, "To Catch a Predator," MSNBC.com, http://www.msnbc.msn.com/id/10912603 (accessed 2009).

13. J. Wolak, D. Finkelhor, and K. Mitchell, "*Trends in Arrests of Online Predators*," University of New Hampshire's Crimes Against Children Research Center, http://www.unh.edu/ccrc/pdf/CV194.pdf (accessed 2009).

14. C. Flanagan, "Babes in the Woods," *The Atlantic*, July 2007, http://www.theatlantic.com/doc/200707/myspace/3.

15. J. Wypijewski, "Through a Lens Starkly," *The Nation*, May 18, 2009, http://www.thenation.com/doc/20090518/wypijewski.

16. K. Kingsbury, "Pregnancy Boom at Gloucester High," *Time*, June 18, 2008, http://www.time.com/time/world/article/0,8599,1815845,00.html.

17. For an example of the common, absolutely bizarre attitude of treating the rape of a girl by her father as a "teen pregnancy" and using it as proof of the need for more sex education and parents talking to their kids, see L. Belton, "Story of 'Precious' Very Real," *Post & Courier*, November 15, 2009, http://www.postandcourier.com/news/2009/nov/15/story-of-precious-very-real/.

18. National Campaign to Prevent Teen and Unplanned Pregnancy, Watch now, Cougar Town, November 25, 2009 episode, cached at http://74.125.95.132/search?q=cache:TDrmu3MszTUJ:www.thenationalcampaign.org/media/watch.aspx+national+campaign+cougar+town&cd=1&hl=en&ct=clnk&gl=us.

19. S. Brown, of the National Campaign, interviewed by L. King, CNN, Larry King Live, May 6, 2009, cached at: http://www.thenationalcampaign.org/media/entertainment-media.aspx.

20. See, among many examples, D. E. Chmielewski, "Miley Cyrus' Teen Choice Performance Sparks Debate," *Los Angeles Times*, August 12, 2009, http://articles.latimes.com/2009/aug/12/entertainment/et-miley12; K. Thomson, "Miley Cyrus' Teen Choice Pole Dance," *Huffington Post*, August 10, 2009, http://www.huffingtonpost.com/2009/08/10/miley-cyrus-teen-choice-p_n_255338.html.

21. A. Adler, "The Perverse Law of Child Pornography," *Columbia Law Review*, 101(2), March 2001, 209–273.

22. J. Sharlet, "*The Family: The Secret Fundamentalism at the Heart of American Power*" (Harper Collins, 2008), 322; and J. Sharlet, "Sex and Power Inside 'the C Street House,'" *Salon*, July 21, 2009, http://www.salon.com/news/feature/2009/07/21/c_street/.

23. Wikipedia, Carrie Prejean, http://en.wikipedia.org/wiki/Carrie_Prejean (accessed 2009).

24. Wikipedia, Perez Hilton, http://en.wikipedia.org/wiki/Perez_Hilton (accessed 2009).

25. H. Fineman, "The Virtuecrats," *Newsweek*, June 13, 1994.

26. M. Raju, "Ensign Takes a Page from Vitter's Playbook," Politic.com, June 24, 2009, http://www.politico.com/news/stories/0609/24111.html.

27. M. A. Akers, "Curse of the Mark Foley Seat, Now Mahoney's," *Washington Post*, October 14, 2008, http://voices.washingtonpost.com/sleuth/2008/10/rep_tim_mahoney_d-fla_publicly.html.

28. D. Osbourne, "Newt Gingrich: Shining Knight of the Post-Reagan Right," *Mother Jones*, November 1, 1984, http://motherjones.com/politics/1984/11/newt-gingrich-shining-knight-post-reagan-right.

29. B. O'Reilly, O'Reilly Factor, Fox News, January 17, 2007, http://mediamatters.org/research/200701170009.

30. A. Mackris, Andrea Mackris, Plaintiff, Against Bill O'Reilly, Supreme Court of the State of New York, County of New York. Complaint No. 4114558, October 13, 2004, http://www.thesmokinggun.com/archive/1013043mackris1.html.

31. M. E. Dyson, *Is Bill Cosby Right?* (New York: Basic Civitas Books, 2005).

32. Wikipedia, Laura Schlessinger, http://en.wikipedia.org/wiki/Laura_Schlessinger (accessed 2009).

33. Wikipedia, Phil McGraw, http://en.wikipedia.org/wiki/Phil_McGraw (accessed 2009).

34. Wikipedia, Geraldo Rivera, http://en.wikipedia.org/wiki/Geraldo_Rivera (accessed 2009).

35. C. M. Young, "Geraldo Rivera," *Rolling Stone*, 769, September 18, 1997, 118–119.

36. D. R. Hughes, "Filters Don't Censor, They Protect Our Kids, March 27, 2001, http://www.protectkids.com/donnaricehughes/article_filtersdontcensor.htm; http://premierespeakers.com/donna_rice_hughes/bio.

37. Wikipedia, David Letterman, http://en.wikipedia.org/wiki/David_Letterman (accessed 2009).

38. C. Mitchell, *Cast Member Confidential: A Disneyfied Memoir*, Citadel (accessed 2009).

39. "Arizona Teacher on Leave for Taking Choir to Hooters," Associated Press, December 17, 2009.

40. CDC, FastStats, Marriage and Divorce, 2008, http://www.cdc.gov/nchs/fastats/divorce.htm.

41. T. Wolfe, *Hooking Up* (Picador Press, 2001), 5, 6, 8.

42. J. C. Abma, G. M. Martinez, W. D. Mosher, and B. S. Dawson Teenagers in the United States: Sexual Activity, Contraceptive Use, and Childbearing, 2002, National Center for Health Statistics, *Vital and Health Statistics*, 23(24), 2004.

43. S. J. Ventura, J. C. Abma, W. D. Mosher, and S. K. Henshaw, Estimated Pregnancy Rates for the United States, 1990–2005: An Update. *National Vital Statistics Reports*, 58(4), Hyattsville, MD: National Center for Health Statistics, 2009.

44. CDC, Division of STD Prevention, Sexually Transmitted Disease Surveillance 2008. Washington, D.C.: Department of Health and Human Services.

45. K. Bogle, *Hooking Up: Sex, Dating and Relationships on Campus* (NYU Press, 2008).

46. B. Denizet-Lewis, "Friends, Friends with Benefits and the Benefits of the Local Mall, *New York Times Magazine*, May 30, 2004; *America Anonymous: Eight Addicts in Search of a Life* (New York: Simon & Schuster).

47. C. Saillant, "Testing the Bounds of MySpace," *Los Angeles Times*, April 8, 2006, 1.

48. M. G. Durham, *The Lolita Effect: The Media Sexualization of Young Girls and What We Can Do About It* (Overlook, 2008).

49. A. Chandra, S. C. Martino, and R. L. Collins, et al., "Does Watching Sex on Television Predict Teen Pregnancy?," Findings from a National Longitudinal Survey of Youth, *Pediatrics*, 122(5) (2008): 1047–1054.

50. B. F. Whitehead, "The Failure of Sex Education," *The Atlantic*, October 1994.

51. See Center for Research on Adolescent Health and Development (2000), Dirty Campaign?, Public Health Institute, http://crahd.phi.org/dirtycampaign.html.

52. R. Maddow, The Rachel Maddow Show, MSNBC, September 9, 2009.

53. Guttmacher Institute, U.S. Teenage Pregnancy Statistics: National and State Trends and Trends by Race and Ethnicity, Updated September 2006, Alan Guttmacher Institute.

54. See R. Saul, "Whatever Happened to the Adolescent Family Life Act?" *The Gutt-macher Report on Public Policy*, 1(2), April 1998, http://www.guttmacher.org/pubs/tgr/01/2/gr010205.html.

55. California Department of Health Services' Center for Health Statistics (2009), Vital statistics query system, http://www.applications.dhs.ca.gov/vsq/default.asp.

56. B. Glassner, *Culture of Fear: Why Americans Are Afraid of the Wrong Things* (Basic Books, 2000).

57. J. Demos, "Images of the American Family, Then and Now," in B. Tufte and B. Myerhoff, *The Changing American Family* (Yale University Press, 1979), 43–60.

58. National Campaign to Prevent Teen and Unplanned Pregnancy, Parents' portal, http://www.thenationalcampaign.org/parents/default.aspx.

CHAPTER ONE: THREE REASONS WHY "TEEN PREGNANCY" DOES NOT EXIST

1. This point is rarely discussed by officials or lobbying groups, but it is clearly evident in standard pregnancy, birth, abortion, and STD statistics detailed in this chapter.

2. D. J. Landry and J. D. Forrest, "How Old Are U.S. Fathers?" *Family Planning Perspectives*, 27 (1995):159–161, 165; M. Males and K. S. Chew, "The Ages of Fathers in California Adolescent Births, 1993," *American Journal of Public Health*, 86(4) (1996): 565–568.

3. E. M. Saewyc, L. L. Magee, and S. E. Pettingell, "Teenage Pregnancy and Associated Risk Behaviors Among Sexually Abused Adolescents," *Perspectives on Sexual and Reproductive Health*, 36(3) May/June 2004; F. A. Conne, "Sexual Abuse Is a Factor in Teenage Pregnancy," in *Current Controversies: Teen Pregnancy and Parenting*, ed. Helen Cothran (Greenhaven Press, 2001); D. Boyer and D. Fine, "Sexual Abuse as a Factor in Adolescent Pregnancy and Child Maltreatment," *Family Planning Perspectives*, 24(1) (1992):4–11, 19; J. Musick, *Young, Poor, and Pregnant: The Psychology of Teenage Motherhood* (Yale University Press, 1993).

4. S. J. Ventura, J. C. Abma, W. D. Mosher, and S. K. Henshaw, "Estimated Pregnancy Rates for the United States, 1990–2005: An Update," *National Vital Statistics Reports*, 58(4), Hyattsville, MD: National Center for Health Statistics, 2009.

5. Alan Guttmacher Institute (1994), *Sex and America's Teenagers* (New York: AGI). Correlations between poverty rates and teen pregnancy rates are powerful and detailed throughout this chapter.

6. B. E. Hamilton, J. A. Martin, and S. J. Ventura, *Births: Preliminary Data for 2007*, National Vital Statistics Reports, Web release; vol. 57 no. 12. Hyattsville, MD: National Center for Health Statistics, Released March 18, 2009.

7. A good summary is by Medical University of South Carolina (2009), High-Risk Pregnancy—Pregnancy Over Age 30, at http://www.musckids.com/health_library/hrpregnant/over30.htm.

8. Landry & Forrest (1995), op. cit.

9. C. McFadden, *The Serial: A Year in the Life of Marin County* (Knopf, 1977).

10. Kidsdata.org (1999), Marin County, Demographics, Emotional and Behavioral Health, Physical Health, at http://www.kidsdata.org/data/region/dashboard.aspx?loc=217.

11. In today's say-anything climate, I recommend bypassing secondary claims and going directly to original data sources. California provides a number of useful interactive sites. Birth data by age of mother, race, ethnicity, county, and other variables can be found

at the California Department of Health Services' Center for Health Statistics (2010), vital statistics query system, at http://www.applications.dhs.ca.gov/vsq/default.asp.

12. Original international data on births, demographics, and so forth are compiled by the World Health Organization's WHOSIS detailed database search (2009) at http://apps.who.int/whosis/data/Search.jsp.

13. Original, detailed data on California demographics are tabulated by the California Department of Finance, Demographic Research Unit (2009). Demographic research data files can be found at http://www.dof.ca.gov/research/demographic/data/.

14. Poverty, income, and other social statistics are available by state, county, race/ethnicity, and other variables from the Bureau of the Census (2009). Census 2000 Summary file 3 (SF 3), with sample data and detailed tables, at http://factfinder.census.gov/servlet/DTGeoSearchByListServlet?ds_name=DEC_2000_SF3_U&_lang=en&_ts=199760803875.

15. International poverty rates are estimated in J. C. Gornick and M. Jäntti, Luxembourg income study, working paper series, "Child Poverty in Upper-Income Countries: Lessons from the Luxembourg Income Study," revised May 2009.

16. J. E. Darroch and J. J. Frost, *Teenage Sexual and Reproductive Behavior in Developed Countries: Can More Progress Be Made?* (New York: Alan Guttmacher Institute, 2001).

17. Ibid., 38, 41.

18. Original data on U.S. births by mother's age, race/ethnicity, state, county, and other details is tabulated by the Centers for Disease Control, 2009, WONDER, Natality information, live births, at http://wonder.cdc.gov/natality.html.

19. Centers for Disease Control, *Sexually Transmitted Diseases Surveillance, 2008*, data and statistics, at http://www.cdc.gov/std/stats/ (accessed in 2009).

20. Centers for Disease Control, *HIV/AIDS Surveillance 2007*, at http://www.cdc.gov/hiv/topics/surveillance/resources/reports/2007report/default.htm (accessed in 2007).

21. Kidsdata.org, 2009, teen sexual health: Selected facts, at http://www.kidsdata.org/data/topic/dashboard.aspx?cat=35.

22. Centers for Disease Control (2009), sexual and reproductive health of persons aged 10 to 24 years—United States, 2002–2007, Morbidity and Mortality Weekly Report, 58 (SS-6), July 17, 2009, 1.

23. The National Campaign to Prevent Teen and Unwed Pregnancy (2009) Web site is full of references to "teens" and links to pages that talk only about teenagers, at http://www.thenationalcampaign.org/default.aspx. However, you have to explore several links and delve into publications before finding reference to adult men's extensive role in "teen" pregnancy; the National Campaign's desire to fixate on teen girls and depict fathers as teen boys and talk only about them is palpable. See http://www.thenationalcampaign.org/resources/males.aspx.

24. A fuller discussion of this issue can be found in M. Males, *Framing Youth: 10 Myths About the Next Generation* (Common Courage Press, 1999), Chapter 6.

25. See Musick (1993), op. cit.; M. Lamb, A. B. Elster, and J. Tavare, "Behavioral Profiles of Adolescent Mothers and Partners with Varying Intracouple Age Differences," *Journal of Adolescent Research*, 1 (1986):399–408; D. Taylor, G. Chavez, A. Chabra, and J. Boggess, "Risk Factors for Adult Paternity in Births to Adolescents," *Obstetrics & Gynecology*, 89 (February 1997):199–205; K. S. Miller, L. F. Clark, and J. S. Moore, "Sexual Initiation with Older Male Partners and Subsequent HIV Risk Behavior Among Female Adolescents," *Family Planning Perspectives*, 29 (September/October 1997): 212–214.

26. Musick (1993), op. cit., 87–88.

27. Boyer & Fine (1992), op. cit.

28. Alan Guttmacher Institute, *Sex and America's Teenagers* (New York: AGI, 1994).

29. Complete, historical volumes of National Center for Health Statistics' *Vital Statistics of the United States*, Volume I (2009), Natality, from 1937–1993, providing a wealth of detail on mothers' and fathers' ages, race, marital status, and other variables, and its predecessor volume, *Birth, Stillbirth, and Infant Mortality Statistics for the Continental United States*, 1931–36, and previous vital statistics volumes back to 1890 are available for reading or download at: http://www.cdc.gov/nchs/products/vsus.htm.

30. Centers for Disease Control, "CDC Report Finds Adolescent Girls Continue to Bear a Major Burden of Common Sexually Transmitted Diseases," NCHHSTP Newsroom, November 16, 2009, at http://www.cdc.gov/nchhstp/Newsroom/STDsurveillance pressrelease.html.

31. Ibid.

32. M. Males, "Adult Liaison in the "Epidemic" of "Teenage" Birth, Pregnancy, and Venereal Disease," *Journal of Sex Research, 29* (4) (1992): 525–545.

33. M. Males, "Schools, Society, and "Teen" Pregnancy," *Phi Delta Kappan*, 74 (March 1993): 566–568; M. Males, "Poverty, Rape, Adult-Teen Sex: Why Prevention Programs Don't Work," *Phi Delta Kappan*, 75 (January 1994): 407–410.

34. Landry & Forrest (1995), op. cit.

35. See S. G. Elstein and N. Davis, "Sexual Relationships Between Adult Males and Young Teen Girls: Exploring the Legal and Social Response," Washington, D.C.: American Bar Association, October 1997.

36. P. Donovan, "Can Statutory Rape Laws Be Effective in Preventing Adolescent Pregnancy?" *Family Planning Perspectives*, 29 (January/February 1997): 31.

37. For a few years I tracked statutory rape charges under California law. There were never more than a few hundred a year, with a disproportionate tendency to concentrate on older teenage boys rather than the adult men compared to the numbers babies adult men fathered with under-18 girls.

38. M. Lait and L. Romney, "Agency Helps Some Girls Wed Men Who Impregnated Them. She's 13, He's 20. Is It Love or Abuse?, *Los Angeles Times*, September 1, 1996, A1, A34, A36; M. Lait, "Teen-Adult Weddings Draw More Criticism," *Los Angeles Times*, September 11, 1996, A1, A11.

39. S. D. Lindberg, F. L. Sonnenstein, L. Ku, and G. Martinez, "Age Differences Between Minors Who Give Birth and Their Adult Partners," *Family Planning Perspectives*, 29 (May/June 1997): 61–66.

40. M. C. Lind and N. Jones, ed., *Fighting for Girls: New Perspectives on Gender and Violence* (SUNY Press, 2010); M. C. Lind and K. Irwin, *Beyond Bad Girls: Gender, Violence and Hype* (Routledge, 2007).

41. K. Sternheimer, *Connecting Social Problems and Popular Culture: Why Media Is Not the Answer* (Westview Press, 2010); K. Sternheimer, *Kids These Days: Facts and Fictions About Today's Youth* (Rowman & Littlefield, 2006).

42. S. Montfort and P. Brick, *Unequal Partners: Teaching About Consent and Power in Adult-Teen and Other Relationships*. Expanded, Third Edition, 2007, Planned Parenthood of Greater Northern New Jersey.

43. K. Luker, *When Sex Goes to School: Warring Views on Sex—and Sex Education—Since the Sixties* (W. W. Norton & Company, 2006), 23.

44. Alan Guttmacher Institute, *U.S. Teenage Pregnancy Statistics Overall Trends, Trends by Race and Ethnicity and State-by-State Information* (New York: AGI, 2004); Alan Guttmacher Institutue, *U.S. Teenage Pregnancy Statistics. National and State Trends and Trends by Race and Ethnicity* (New York: AGI, 2006), at http://www.guttmacher.org.

45. L. T. Strauss, S. B. Gamble, W. Y. Parker, D. A. Cook, S. B. Zane, S. Hamdan, et al., *Abortion Surveillance—United States, 2003, 2000* (Atlanta, GA: Centers for Disease Control, 2006, 2003); http://www.cdc.gov/mmwr/preview/mmwrhtml/ss5511a1.htm.

46. Bureau of the Census (2000), op. cit.

CHAPTER TWO: 1915 ALL OVER AGAIN

1. See Wikipedia profiles for each president.

2. The history to follow relies on a number of compilations, including J. P. Moran, *Teaching Sex: The Shaping of Adolescence in the 20th Century* (Cambridge, MA: Harvard University Press, 2000); J. Kett, *Rites of Passage: Adolescence in America, 1790 to the Present* (New York: Basic Books, 1977); T. Hine, *The Rise & Fall of the American Teenager* (New York: Avon Books, 1999); W. Strauss and N. Howe, *Generations: The History of America's Future, 1584 to 2069* (New York: Quill, 1990); S. J. Gould, *The Mismeasure of Man* (New York: W. W. Norton, 1981); M. Hein, *Not in Front of the Children: "Indecency," Censorship and the Innocence of Youth* (New York: Hill & Wang, 2001); J. Spring, *Educating the Consumer-Citizen: The History of the Marriage of Schools, Advertising, and Media*, London: Lawrence Erlbaum Associates, (2003).

3. A. G. Spencer, "The Age of Consent and Its Significance," *The Forum 49* (1913): 407.

4. Hine (1999), op. cit., 182.

5. Kett (1977), op. cit.

6. Hine (1999), op. cit., 167.

7. G. S. Hall, *Adolescence: Its Psychology and Its Relations to Physiology, Anthropology, Sociology, Sex, Crime, Religion, and Education* (New York: D. Appleton, 1904).

8. Complete, historical volumes of the National Center for Health Statistics' (2009) *Vital Statistics of the United States*, Volume I, Natality, from 1937–1993, providing a wealth of detail on mothers' and fathers' ages, race, marital status, and so forth; its predecessor volume, *Birth, Stillbirth, and Infant Mortality Statistics for the Continental United States*, 1931–1936; and previous vital statistics volumes as far back as 1890, are available for reading or download at http://www.cdc.gov/nchs/products/vsus.htm.

9. Moran (2000), op. cit., 50–55.

10. Ibid., Chapter 2.

11. P. Cutright, "The Teenage Sexual Revolution and the Myth of an Abstinent Past," *Family Planning Perspectives*, 4(1) (1972): 24–31.

12. J. B. Martin, "Abortion," *Saturday Evening Post*, May 20, 27, and June 4, 1961. Citations are from May 20 article, 19, 21, 22.

13. National Center for Health Statistics (1931–2009) and predecessor reports, op. cit.

14. Moran (2000), op. cit., 187.

15. Ibid., 170.

16. Ibid., 182.

17. Moran (2000), op. cit., 200–201.

18. K. Luker, *Dubious Conceptions: The Politics of Teenage Pregnancy* (Cambridge, MA: Harvard University Press, 1996), 173.

19. Barson & Heller (1998), op. cit.

20. National Center for Health Statistics (1931–2009), op. cit.

21. Ibid.

22. Federal Bureau of Investigation, *Crime in the United States* (Washington, D.C.: U.S. Department of Justice, 1935–2008). Arrests by age are in Table 38, 2008, and corresponding previous annual tables, generally reliable back to 1965 or so. National Center for

Health Statistics, *Vital Statistics of the United States, Part I, Mortality* (Washington, D.C.: U.S. Department of Health and Human Services, 1937–1992). See also reference 13.

23. National Center for Health Statistics (1931–2009), op. cit.

24. Centers for Disease Control (2009), *Sexually Transmitted Diseases Surveillance*, data and statistics at http://www.cdc.gov/std/stats/.

25. Many of these trends are summarized in the Bureau of the Census *Statistical Abstract of the United States* and *Historical Statistics of the United States, Colonial Times to 1970* (2009) at http://www.census.gov/prod/www/abs/statab.html.

26. An excellent account of the new-agency survival tactics by inventing new "teenage crises" is R. L. Chauncey, "New Careers for Moral Entrepreneurs: Teenage Drinking," *Journal of Drug Issues*, 10 (1980): 45–70.

27. See R. Saul, "Whatever Happened to the Adolescent Family Life Act?," *The Guttmacher Report on Public Policy*, 1(2), April 1998, at http://www.guttmacher.org/pubs/tgr/01/2/gr010205.html.

28. Moran (2000), op. cit., 202.

29. For a comprehensive assessment, see R. Haskins and C. S. Bevan, "Abstinence Education Under Welfare Reform, Welfare Reform Academy, School of Public Policy, University of Maryland, 2009, at http://www.welfareacademy.org/conf/past/haskins2.shtml.

30. Moran (2000), op. cit., Chapter 8.

CHAPTER THREE: BABY PRICING AND THE NEW EUGENICS

1. Merriam-Webster Medical Dictionary (2009), Eugenics, at http://www.merriam-webster.com/medical/negative%20eugenics.

2. M. Sanger, *Woman, Morality, and Birth Control* (New York Publishing Company, 1922), 12; "The Eugenic Value of Birth Control Propaganda," *Birth Control Review*, October 1921, 5.

3. Planned Parenthood Affiliates of New Jersey (2009), The Truth About Margaret Sanger, at http://www.plannedparenthoodnj.org/library/topic/contraception/margaret_sanger.

4. Ibid.

5. S. J. Gould, *The Mismeasure of Man* (W. W. Norton, 1981), 168.

6. U.S. Supreme Court (1927), *Buck v. Bell*, 274 U.S. 200.

7. M R. Burt, "Estimating the Public Costs of Teenage Childbearing," *Family Planning Perspectives*, 18 (September/October 1986): 221–226.

8. A. Goreily, R. M. S. Hansen, I. B. Taylor, et al., "Activating Mutations in FGFR3 and HRAS Reveal a Shared Genetic Origin for Congenital Disorders and Testicular Tumors," *Nature Genetics*, 41 (October 2009): 1247–1252.

9. C. Murray, *Losing Ground: American Social Policy, 1950–1980*, 10th Anniversary Edition (Basic Books, 1994).

10. As is often the case, Wikipedia provides the best summary and diverse sources. See Chicago School (Sociology), 2009, Wikipedia, at http://en.wikipedia.org/wiki/Chicago_school_(sociology).

11. See the debate, moderated by J. J. Arnett, ed., Special section on the adolescent brain and risk taking *Journal of Adolescent Research*, 25(1) (2010): 3–63, at http://jar.sagepub.com/content/vol25/issue1/?etoc.

12. F. F. Furstenburg, S. D. Hoffman, and M. Foster, "Reevaluating the Costs of Teenage Childbearing," *Demography*, 30(1) (1993), 1–13.

13. Arline T. Geronimus, Sanders Korenman, and Marianne M. Hillemeier, "Does Young Maternal Age Adversely Affect Child Development? Evidence from Cousin Comparisons in the United States," *Population and Development*, 20(3) (1994): 585–609; C. G. Colen, A. T. Geronimus, and M. G. Phipps, *Getting a Piece of the Pie? Declining Teen Birth Rates During the 1990s* (Ann Arbor, MI: University of Michigan, Institute for Social Research, 2002).

14. F. F. Furstenburg, "No Silver Bullet: 30-Year Study Shows that Preventing Teenage Childbearing Won't Cure Poverty," paper presented to Council on Contemporary Families, University of Illinois, April 25–26, 2008, at http://www.contemporary families.org/subtemplate.php?ext=pregnancyandpoverty&t=briefingPapers.

15. R. A. Maynard, *Kids Having Kids. A Special Report on the Costs of Adolescent Childbearing*, Robin Hood Foundation (1996), 309.

16. For example, a 1991 U.S. Justice Department study estimated the annual costs of white-collar and corporate crime at $130 billion to $472 billion, seven to 25 times more than the costs of all personal and street crime. See S. Donziger, ed., *The Real War on Crime*, National Criminal Justice Commission (Harper Collins, 1996).

17. V. J. Hotz, S. W. McElroy, and S. G. Sanders, "Teenage Childbearing and Its Life Cycle Consequences: Exploiting a Natural Experiment, *Journal of Human Resources*, 50(3) (2005):683–715.

18. T. T. Cooper, "Contrary Take on Teen Pregnancy," *Los Angeles Times*, May 24, 1997, A1, A22–A23.

19. Public Health Institute, Teen births and costs by California counties (2007), at: http://teenbirths.phi.org/2007CountyTable.pdf. (accessed in 2009).

20. Urban Institute (2008), Kids having kids unravels the complex consequences of teen parenthood for individuals and society, at http://www.urban.org/publications/901199.html.

21. Ibid.

22. Ibid.

23. Hotz et al. (2005), op. cit., 684.

24. Ibid., 703, 708, 712–713.

25. S. D. Hoffman and L. S. Scher, Children of Early Childbearers as Young Adults-Updated Estimates, in *Kids Having Kids: Revised Edition*, R. A. Maynard and S. Hoffman, eds. (The Urban Institute Press, 2008).

26. National Campaign to Prevent Teen and Unplanned Pregnancy (2009), The public costs of teen childbearing, key data, at http://www.thenationalcampaign.org/costs/pdf/resources/key_data.pdf.

27. D. Gross, "Location, Location—Deduction: The Mortgage-Interest Deduction Costs Taxpayers Billions, But It Won't Go Away Anytime Soon," *Slate*, April 14, 2005.

28. Bureau of the Census (2009), Custodial Mothers and Fathers and Their Child Support: 2007, Washington, D.C.: US Department of Commerce, at: http://www.census.gov/Press-Release/www/releases/archives/children/014410.html.

CHAPTER FOUR: MARIE ANTOINETTE WOULD HAVE LOVED THE NATIONAL CAMPAIGN

1. See J. Trussell, "Teenage Pregnancy in the United States," *Family Planning Perspectives, 20* (1988), 262–271.

2. K. Luker, *Dubious Conceptions: The Politics of Teenage Pregnancy* (Cambridge, MA: Harvard University Press, 1996), 192.

3. Many of these points are summarized in Luker (1996), op. cit.

4. A. R. Stiffman, J. Powell, F. Earls, and L. N. Robins, "Pregnancies, Childbearing, and Mental Health Problems in Adolescents," *Youth & Society*, 21(1990)., 483–495.

5. M. Bayatpour, R. D. Wells, and S. Holford, "Physical and Sexual Abuse as Predictors of Substance Use and Suicide Among Pregnant Teenagers," *Journal of Adolescent Health*, 13 (1992): 128–132.

6. B. F. Whitehead, "The Failure of Sex Education," *The Atlantic*, October 1994.

7. B. O'Reilly, "The Birds, the Bees, and the Cell Phones," Townhall.com, May 30, 2009, at http://townhall.com/columnists/BillOReilly/2009/05/30/the_birds,_the_bees, _and_the_cell_phones.

8. National Campaign to Prevent Teen and Unplanned Pregnancy (2000), "Not Just Another Thing to Do, at http://www.thenationalcampaign.org/resources/pdf/pubs/ NotJust_FINAL.pdf.

9. R. E. Rector, K. A. Johnson, and L. R. Noyes, "Sexually Active Teenagers Are More Likely to Be Depressed and to Attempt Suicide," Heritage Foundation, Center for Data Analysis Report #03–04, June 3, 2003.

10. Alan Guttmacher Institute, *Sex and America's Teenagers* (New York: AGI, 1994).

11. Centers for Disease Control and Prevention, "Sexual and Reproductive Health of Persons Age 10–24—United States, 2002–2007," *Morbidity and Mortality Weekly Report*, 58 (No. SS-6), July 17, 2009.

12. M. Hitti, "Teen Sex May Take Emotional Toll. Girls Especially Vulnerable to Negative Emotional Aftereffects," WebMD Health News, posted September 7, 2007, at http://www.webmd.com/sex-relationships/news/20070206/teen-sex-may-take -emotional-toll.

13. S. S. Brady and B. L. Halpern-Felsher, "Adolescents' Reported Consequences of Having Oral Sex Versus Vaginal Sex," *Pediatrics* 119 (February 2007): 229–236.

14. M. A. Ott, S. G. Millstein, S. Ofner, B. L. Halpern-Felsher, "Greater Expec-tations: Adolescents' Positive Motivations for Sex," *Perspectives on Sexual and Reproductive Health* 38(2) (2006): 84–89.

15. S. S. Brady and B. L. Halpern-Felsher, "It's Not So Easy to 'Just Say No' to Sex: Social and Emotional Consequences of Refraining from Sex Among Sexually Experienced and Inexperienced Youth," *American Journal of Public Health* 98 (2008): 162–168.

16. T. M. Michels, R. Y. Kropp, S. L. Eyre, and B. L. Halpern-Felsher, "Initiating Sexual Experiences: How Do Young Adolescents Make Decisions Regarding Early Sexual Activity?," *Journal of Research on Adolescence*, 15 (2005): 583–607.

17. E. Angvall, In Western Europe, Washpost.com, posted May 16, 2006.

18. P. A. Michaud, "Adolescents and Risks: Why Not Change Our Paradigm?," *Journal of Adolescent Health*, 38(5) (2006): 481–483.

19. M. Talbot, "Red Sex, Blue Sex," *The New Yorker*, November 3, 2008, 64–69.

20. Smith, quoted in SIECUS (2009), Committee on Oversight and Government Reform holds first-ever hearings on abstinence only until marriage programs, at http:// www.siecus.org/index.cfm?fuseaction=Feature.showFeature&featureID=1144.

21. B. O'Reilly, "O'Reilly Factor," Fox News, August 2, 2006, and January 17, 2007, at http://mediamatters.org/research/200701170009.

22. A. Mackris, Andrea Mackris, Plaintiff, against Bill O'Reilly, Supreme Court of the State of New York, County of New York, Complaint No. 4114558, October 13, 2004, posted at http://www.thesmokinggun.com/archive/1013043mackris1.html.

23. H. Kurtz, "Bill O'Reilly, Producer Settle Harassment Suit," *Washington Post*, October 29, 2004, C01.

24. B. O'Reilly, "The Birds, the Bees, and the Cell Phones," Townhall.com, May 30, 2009, at http://townhall.com/columnists/BillOReilly/2009/05/30/the_birds,_the_bees,_and_the_cell_phones.

25. Wikipedia, 2009, Dick Morris, at http://en.wikipedia.org/wiki/Dick_Morris.

26. Centers for Disease Control, 2009, op. cit.

27. Centers for Disease Control, 2009, *HIV/AIDS Surveillance 2007*, at http://www.cdc.gov/hiv/topics/surveillance/resources/reports/2007report/default.htm.

28. Gayteens.about.com, 2009, "Dealing with Middle and High School," at http://gayteens.about.com/od/school/Dealing_with_Middle_and_High_School.htm.

29. See J. P. Moran, *Teaching Sex: The Shaping of Adolescence in the 20th Century* (Cambridge, MA: Harvard University Press, 2000), 205, 212.

30. Fox News, "Critics Slam 'Gay Agenda' in Public Schools," May 7, 2002, at http://www.foxnews.com/story/0,2933,52098,00.html.

31. Concerned Women for America, 2009, "CFI Panel Exposes GLSEN's Cross-Dressing Agenda," at http://www.cwfa.org/articles/498/CFI/cfreport/index.htm.

32. CNN Election Center, 2008, Ballot Measures. California Proposition 8: Ban on Gay Marriage, at: http://www.cnn.com/ELECTION/2008/results/polls/#CAI01p1.

33. Public Policy Polling, "TABOR Going Down, Gay Marriage Still Close," November 2, 2009, at http://www.publicpolicypolling.com/pdf/PPP_Release_ME_1102.pdf.

CHAPTER FIVE: THE "TEEN SEX" DEBATE UNHINGES

1. B. E. Hamilton, J. A. Martin, and S. J. Ventura, "Births: Preliminary Data for 2007," *National Vital Statistics Report*, 57(12) (2009): March 18, 2009.

2. S. J. Ventura, J.C. Abma, W. D. Mosher, and S. K. Henshaw, "Estimated Pregnancy Rates for the United States, 1990–2005: An Update," *National Vital Statistics Report*, 58(4), October 14, 2009.

3. Quoted in C. L. Allen, "Teenage Birth's New Conceptions," *Insight*, April 1990, 8–13.

4. J. P. Moran, *Teaching Sex: The Shaping of Adolescence in the 20th Century*, (Cambridge, MA: Harvard University Press, 2000), 219.

5. C. Murray, *Losing Ground: American Social Policy, 1950–1980*, 10th Anniversary Edition (Basic Books, 1994).

6. J. DeParle, "Clinton Target: Teen-age Pregnancy," *New York Times*, March 22, 1994, 11; R. Brownstein, "Welfare Reform Plan Seeks Lid on Aid to Teens," *Los Angeles Times*, March 27, 1994, 1, 19.

7. A. Cockburn, "Beat the Devil: Clinton and Teen Sex," *The Nation*, 259, Feburary 28, 1994.

8. See Cockburn (1994), DeParle (1994), and Brownstein (1994), op. cit.

9. D. Sawyer, ABC News, February 16, 1995, in L. Flanders and J. Jackson, "Public Enemy No. 1? Media's Welfare Debate Is a War on Poor Women," *Extra!* (1995) 13–16.

10. See account in M. A. Males, *The Scapegoat Generation: America's War on Adolescents* (Common Courage Press, 1996), 89–100.

11. Congressional Budget Office (1990), *Sources of Support for Adolescent Mothers*, in J. Levin-Epstein, *Understanding the Clinton Welfare Bill. Teen Pregnancy Prevention and Teen Parents*, Center for Law and Social Policy (1994) 7.

12. See Government Accounting Office in J. Levin-Epstein (1994), reference 7, and Levin-Epstein (1996), *Teen Parent Provisions in the Personal Responsibility and Work Opportunity Reconciliation Act of 1996*, Center for Law and Social Policy, November 1996.

13. C. Murray, "Does Welfare Bring More Babies?," *The Public Interest* (Spring 1994), 20, 23.

14. M. Males (1996), op. cit., 93–94.

15. Ventura et al. (2009), op. cit.

16. Hamilton et al. (2009), op. cit.

17. Everyone has their favorite research design references. Mine include the classic: T. D. Cook and D. T. Campbell, *Quasi-Experimentation: Design and Analysis Issues for Field Settings* (Houghton-Mifflin, 1979); J. J. Shaughnessy, *Research Methods in Psychology*, 8th edition, McGraw-Hill Higher Education (2008); F. F. Fowler, *Survey Research Methods*, 4the edition (Sage Publications, 2008).

18. Centers for Disease Control, "Sexual and Reproductive Health of Persons Aged 10–24 years—United States, 2002–2007 (2009); *Morbidity and Mortality Weekly Report*, 58(SS-6), July 17, 2009.

19. Center for Health Statistics (2009), Birth Public Use Files, 2002, California Department of Health Services, Electronic data sets available at http://www.cdph.ca.gov/data/dataresources/requests/Pages/BirthandFetalDeathFiles.aspx.

20. Centers for Disease Control (2009). *Sexually Transmitted Diseases Surveillance, 2008*. Data and statistics, at http://www.cdc.gov/std/stats/.

21. R. T. Michael, J. H. Gagnon, E. O. Laumann, and Kolata, G. (1994). *Sex in America. A Definitive Survey*. CSG Enterprises.

22. Kaiser Family Foundation, "*Substance Use and Risky Sexual Behavior: Attitudes and Practices Among Adolescents and Young Adults*," February 2002, at http://www.kff.org/youthhivstds/upload/KFF-CASASurveySnapshot.pdf.

23. National Center on Addiction and Substance Abuse at Columbia University, "Millions of Young People Mix Sex with Alcohol or Drugs," February 6, 2002, at http://www.kff.org/youthhivstds/loader.cfm?url=/commonspot/security/getfile.cfm&PageID=13924.

24. See M. Males, "Is Joseph Califano a Gateway Drug?," *Youth Today*, April 2002.

25. Centers for Disease Control (2008). Nationally representative CDC study finds one in four teenage girls has a sexually transmitted disease, March 11, 2008, at http://www.cdc.gov/stdconference/2008/press/release-11march2008.pdf.

26. Associated Press, "1 in 4 Teen Girls Has Sexually Transmitted Disease. Virus That Causes Cervical Cancer Most Common, Government Study Finds," March 11, 2008.

27. Monitoring the Future, *Questionnaire Responses from the Nation's High School Seniors*, Annual, 1975–2008, Ann Arbor: University of Michigan, Institute for Social Research, at http://www.monitoringthefuture.org/pubs.html#refvols (accessed in 2009).

28. Higher Education Research Institute, *The American Freshman: Forty Year Trends, 1966–2006* (Los Angeles: University of California, Los Angeles, 2009).

29. L. Remez, "Oral Sex Among Adolescents: Is It Sex or Is It Abstinence?," *Family Planning Perspectives*, 32(6), November/December 2000, at http://www.guttmacher.org/pubs/journals/3229800.html.

30. A. Jarrell, "The Face of Teenage Sex Grows Younger," *New York Times*, April 2, 2000, at http://www.nytimes.com/2000/04/02/style/the-face-of-teenage-sex-grows-younger.html?pagewanted=1.

31. L. Mundy, "Young Teens and Sex: Sex & Sensibility," *Washington Post Magazine*, July 16, 2000, 16–21 and 29–34; L. S. Stepp, "Parents Are Alarmed by an Unsettling New Fad in Middle Schools: Oral Sex," *Washington Post*, July 8, 1999, A1; L. S. Stepp, "Talking to Kids About Sexual Limits," *Washington Post*, July 8, 1999, C4.

32. K. Painter, "Sexual Revolution Hits Junior High," *USA Today*, March 14, 2002, A1.

33. A. Mulrine, "Risky Business. Teens Are Having More Sex–and Getting More Diseases. But Is Telling Them to Wait the Answer?," *U.S. News & World Report*, May 27, 2002, cover, 44; reposted at http://www.guttmacher.org/media/pdf/news2002/0528_clip.pdf.

34. P. Boyle, "Palin, Pregnancy and Sex Ed., YouthToday.org, September 12, 2008.

35. CDC WONDER (2009), Natality, 2003–2006 request. Centers for Disease Control, interactive data retrieval Web site at: http://wonder.cdc.gov/natality-current.html.

36. K. Kingsbury, "Pregnancy Boom at Gloucester High," *Time*, June 18, 2008, at http://www.time.com/time/world/article/0,8599,1815845,00.html.

37. P. Anderson, "Trio of Gloucester High Teen Moms Deny Pre-pregnancy Pact," *Gloucester Daily Times*, June 24, 2008, at http://www.gloucestertimes.com/punews/local _story_176181125.html; P. Anderson, "Sullivan Stands By View of Intentional Pregnancies; Disputes Mayor, Doesn't Recall Using Term "Pact," *Gloucester Daily Times*, June 26, 2008, at http://www.gloucestertimes.com/punews/local_story_178195452.html.

38. Office of Health and Human Services (2010), Birth Reports, Massachusetts Department of Health, at http://www.mass.gov/?pageID=eohhs2terminal&L=4&L0 =Home&L1=Consumer&L2=Community+Health+and+Safety&L3=Population+Health +Statistics&sid=Eeohhs2&b=terminalcontent&f=dph_research_epi_c_births&csid=Eeohhs2.

39. N. Reynolds, "So-Called San Marcos Miracle Actually May Be Just a Myth," *San Diego Union*, December 19, 1991, 1.

40. See Fairness and Accuracy in Reporting (2005), Mike Males, *Extra!* articles at http://www.fair.org/extra/writers/males.html.

CHAPTER SIX: GENERATION MEAN

1. K. S. Hymowitz, *Ready or Not: Why Treating Children as Small Adults Endangers Their Future—and Ours* (Free Press, 1999), 1–2.

2. J. Garbarino, *See Jane Hit: Why Girls Are Growing More Violent and What We Can Do About It* (Penguin, 2007), 30.

3. D. Elkind, *The Hurried Child: Growing Up Too Fast Too Soon*, Third Edition (Perseus Publishing, 2001, 2006), 3, 14–15.

4. D. Levin and J. Kilbourne, *So Sexy So Soon: The New Sexualized Childhood and What Parents Can Do to Protect Their Kids* (Ballantine Books, 2009).

5. M. G. Durham, *The Lolita Effect: The Media Sexualization of Young Girls and What We Can Do About It* (Overlook, 2008).

6. L. Ponton, *The Sex Lives of Teenagers: Revealing the Secret World of Adolescent Boys and Girls* (Plume, 2001), 3.

7. M. Maran, *Dirty: A Search for Answers Inside America's Teenage Drug Epidemic* (HarperOne, 2004), 65.

8. M. B. Pipher, *Reviving Ophelia: Saving the Selves of Adolescent Girls* (Riverhead Trade, 1995, 1998, 2002, 2005, 2008), 12.

9. See references, Chapter 2.

10. J. M. Twenge, *Generation Me: Why Today's Young Americans Are More Confident, Assertive, Entitled—and More Miserable than Ever Before* (Free Press, 2007), 26, 68, 70, 71, 156–158.

11. C. E. Martin, *Perfect Girls, Starving Daughters: The Frightening New Normalcy of Hating Your Body* (Free Press, 2007), 10.

12. See J. C. Abma, G. M. Martinez, W. D. Mosher, and B. S. Dawson, (2004) "Teenagers in the United States: Sexual Activity, Contraceptive Use, and Childbearing, 2002," National Center for Health Statistics. *Vital and Health Statistics*, 23(24), MMWR (1991);

"Current Trends Premarital Sexual Experience Among Adolescent Women—United States, 1970–1988," *Morbidity and Mortality Weekly Report*, 39 (51–52): 929–932; January 4, 1991.

13. Centers for Disease Control and Prevention (2009), "Sexual and Reproductive Health of Persons Aged 10–24 years—United States, 2002–2007," *Mortality and Morbidity Weekly Report*, Surveillance Summaries July 17, 2009/Vol. 58/No. SS-6.

14. Complete, historical volumes of National Center for Health Statistics' (2009) *Vital Statistics of the United States*, Volume I, Natality, from 1937–1993, providing a wealth of detail on mothers' and fathers' ages, race, marital status, and so forth; and its predecessor volume, *Birth, Stillbirth, and Infant Mortality Statistics for the Continental United States*, 1931–1936; and previous vital statistics volumes back to 1890 are available for reading or download at http://www.cdc.gov/nchs/products/vsus.htm.

15. Centers for Disease Control (2009), *Sexually Transmitted Diseases Surveillance* and previous annual reports, data and statistics, at http://www.cdc.gov/std/stats/.

16. Centers for Disease Control and Prevention (2009), *HIV/AIDS Surveillance Report, 2007*, U.S. Department of Health and Human Services, Vol. 19 and previous annual reports, at http://www.cdc.gov/hiv/topics/surveillance/resources/reports/.

17. Bureau of Justice Statistics (2010), *Criminal Victimization in the United States, 2007, Statistical Tables*, and previous annual reports, U.S. Department of Justice, at http://bjs.ojp.usdoj.gov/index.cfm?ty=tp&tid=94.

18. Federal Bureau of Investigation (2009), *Crime in the United States*, 2008, Washington, D.C.: US Department of Justice. (Arrests by age are in Table 38, 2008, and corresponding previous annual tables, generally reliable back to 1965 or so.)

19. Criminal Justice Statistics Center (1975–2008), *Crime & Delinquency in California*, California Department of Justice.

20. Institute for Social Research (1975–2008), *Monitoring the Future: Questionnaire Responses from the Nation's High School Seniors*, Annual, 1975–2005, Ann Arbor: University of Michigan, Institute for Social Research, at http://www.monitoringthefuture.org/pubs.html#refvols.

21. National Center for Injury Prevention and Control (2009), WISQARS injury mortality reports, 1980–2006, at http://www.cdc.gov/ncipc/wisqars/.

22. EPICenter (2009), California injury data online, California Center for Health Statistics, at http://www.applications.dhs.ca.gov/epicdata/content/TB_fatal.htm.

23. National Center for Education Statistics (2009), Digest of Education Statistics, 2008, U.S. Department of Education, Table 109, at http://nces.ed.gov/programs/digest/2008menu_tables.asp.

24. Higher Education Research Institute (1966–2009), *The American Freshman: Forty Year Trends, 1966–2006*, Los Angeles: University of California, Los Angeles, at http://www.heri.ucla.edu/cirpoverview.php.

25. L. Ponton (2000), op. cit., quoted on pages 3, 4, and 214.

26. D. Elkind, (2006, 2001, 1988, 1981), op. cit., quoted on pages xvii, 14–15.

27. CDC (2009), op cit., 14, 15, 16.

28. Hymowitz (1999), op cit. Quoted are pp. 1–2.

29. Centers for Disease Control (2009), op. cit., references on pages 14, 15, and 16.

30. K. S. Hymowitz, "It's Morning After in America," *City Journal*, Spring 2004, at http://www.city-journal.org/html/14_2_its_morning.html.

31. See V. Rideout, D. F. Roberts, and U. G. Foehr (2005), *Generation M: Media in the Lives of 8- to 18-Year-Olds* (Menlo Park, CA: Kaiser Family Foundation), at http://www.kff.org/entmedia/upload/Executive-Summary-Generation-M-Media-in-the-Lives-of-8-18-Year-olds.pdf.

32. Nielsenwire, "Household TV Trends Holding Steady: Nielsen's Economic Study 2008," February 24, 2009, at http://blog.nielsen.com/nielsenwire/media_entertainment/household-tv-trends-holding-steady-nielsen%E2%80%99s-economic-study-2008/.

33. Wikipedia, 2009, Gangster rap, at http://en.wikipedia.org/wiki/Gangsta_rap.

34. Pew Internet Project, 2009, "89 Percent of Teens Log in From Home," May 17, 2008, at http://blogs.zdnet.com/ITFacts/?p=14470.

35. Entertainment Software Association, "Sales and Genre Data. Economic Data. Game Player Data," at http://www.theesa.com/facts/salesandgenre.asp; GRABStats (2009), videogame statistics/video game industry statistics, at http://www.grabstats.com/statcategorymain.asp?StatCatID=13.

36. Bio-Medicine.org (2009), M-rated violent video games most popular among young teens, at http://www.bio-medicine.org/medicine-news/M-rated-Violent-Video-Games-Most-Popular-Among-Young-Teens-23938-1/.

37. Media Education Foundation (2009), Videos, at http://www.mediaed.org/cgi-bin/commerce.cgi?display=home.

38. Rideout et al. (2005), op. cit., 14, 24, 37, 39.

39. C. K. Olson, L. A. Kutner, D. E. Warner, et al. (2007), "Factors Correlated with Violent Video Game Use by Adolescent Boys and Girls," *Journal of Adolescent Health*, 41(1):77–83.

40. Levin & Kilbourne (2009), op. cit., 139, 162.

CHAPTER SEVEN: SAME OLD RACISM

1. National Campaign to Prevent Teen and Unplanned Pregnancy (2009), About the National Campaign, at http://www.thenationalcampaign.org/about-us/default.aspx.

2. Guttmacher Institute, U.S. teenage pregnancy statistics: National and state trends and trends by race and ethnicity, Updated September 2006, Alan Guttmacher Instititute.

3. S. J. Ventura, J. C. Abma, W. D. Mosher, and S. K. Henshaw, (2009), Estimated pregnancy rates for the United States, 1990–2005: An update. National vital statistics reports, 58:4, Hyattsville, MD: National Center for Health Statistics.

4. Innocenti Research Centre (2001), Teenage births in rich nations, Florence, Italy: UNICEF, July 2001.

5. National Campaign to Prevent Teen Pregnancy (1997), *Whatever Happened to Childhood? The Problem of Teen Pregnancy in the United States*, quoted on pages 11–13, 16.

6. National Campaign to Prevent Teen Pregnancy (2009), Resources and briefs: Racial and ethnic disparities, at http://www.thenationalcampaign.org/policymakers/res_racial_ethnic_disparities.aspx.

7. The National Campaign to Prevent Teen and Unplanned Pregnancy (2009), *The Fog Report*, at http://www.thenationalcampaign.org/fogzone/.

8. L. B. Finer and S. K. Henshaw (2006), "Disparities in Rates of Unintended Pregnancy in the United States, 1994 and 2001," *Perspectives on Sexual Reproductive Health*, 38:90–96.

9. S. Singh, D. Wulf, R. Hussain, A. Bankole, and G. Sedgh, *Abortion Worldwide: A Decade of Uneven Progress*, Guttmacher Institute, October 13, 2009.

10. R. B. Russell, N. S. Green, C. A. Steiner, et al., "Cost of Hospitalization for Preterm and Low Birth Weight Infants in the United States," *Pediatrics*, 120 (July 2007): e1–e9.

11. CDC WONDER (2009), Natality request, Figures are average for 2003 to 2006, at http://wonder.cdc.gov/natality-current.html.

12. M. Males (2007), Fact checking Obama on "youth violence." *GBMNews*, November 5, 2007, at http://www.gbmnews.com/articles/1848/1/Fact-Checking-Obama-on-Youth-Violence/Page1.html.

13. M. Males (2004), "With Friends Like These. Black Youth Stereotyped by Progressive Columnist Bob Herbert," *Extra!*, January/February 2004.

14. S. Steele, The double bind of race and guilt, November 15, 2004, at http://blackinformant.wordpress.com/2004/11/15/the-double-bind-of-race-and-guilt-commentary-by-shelby-steele/.

15. J. Williams, *Enough: The Phony Leaders, Dead-End Movements, and Culture of Failure That Are Undermining Black America* (Three Rivers Press, 2006), 10, 108, 114, 193, 206.

16. M. E. Dyson, *Is Bill Cosby Right? (Or Has the Black Middle Class Lost Its Mind?)* (Perseus Basic Books, 2005).

17. Dyson (2005), op. cit., quoted on pages viii–ix, 39.

18. C. Page (2002), Essay: Poverty's Children, PBS.org, Online Newshour, May 6, 2002, at http://www.pbs.org/newshour/essays/jan-june02/poverty_5-06.html.

19. C. Brown, *Manchild in the Promised Land* (Signet, 1965).

20. M. Porter (2007), *Rap and the Eroticizing of Black Youth*, African American Images.

21. Porter (2007), op. cit., quoted on pages viii, 17, 27, 40, 51, 53, 54, 83, 85, 100, 101.

22. Federal Bureau of Investigation (2009), *Crime in the United States*, 1970–2008. Washington, D.C.: US Department of Justice, at http://www.fbi.gov/ucr/ucr.htm#cius.

23. Bureau of Justice Statistics (2009), *Criminal Victimization in the United States*, 1973–2006, Statistical Tables, Washington, D.C.: U.S. Department of Justice.

24. Bureau of the Census (2009), Census 2000 Summary file 3 (SF 3) - Sample data, detailed tables, at http://factfinder.census.gov/servlet/DTGeoSearchByListServlet?ds_name=DEC_2000_SF3_U&_lang=en&_ts=199760803875.

25. Dyson (2005), op. cit.

26. National Center for Injury Prevention and Control (2009), WISQARS injury mortality reports, 1980–2005, a http://www.cdc.gov/ncipc/wisqars/.

27. Criminal Justice Statistics Center (1980–2008), *Crime & Delinquency in California*. California Department of Justice.

28. W. J. Sabol, H. C. West, and M. Cooper, *Prisoners in 2008*, and previous annual reports, *Bureau of Justice Statistics Bulletin*, December 2009.

29. Centers for Disease Control (2009), *HIV/AIDS surveillance 2007*, and previous annual reports, at http://www.cdc.gov/hiv/topics/surveillance/resources/reports/2007report/default.htm.

CHAPTER EIGHT: SAME OLD SEXISM

1. National Center for Education Statistics (2009), Digest of Education Statistics, U.S. Department of Education, Chapters 2, 3, at http://nces.ed.gov/programs/digest/2008menu_tables.asp.

2. Bureau of the Census (2009), Current Population Survey. Income statistics, at http://www.census.gov/hhes/www/income/incomestats.html#cps; Bureau of the Census (2009); Census 2000 Summary file 3 (SF 3)—Sample data, detailed tables, at http://factfinder.census.gov/servlet/DTGeoSearchByListServlet?ds_name=DEC_2000_SF3_U&_lang=en&_ts=199760803875.

3. These estimates are calculated from CNN (2008), Exit Polls, CNN Election Center, at http://www.cnn.com/ELECTION/2008/results/polls.main/, National Student/Parent Mock Election (2008), at http://www.nationalmockelection.org/viewresults.html.

4. An outstanding compilation of popular articles and cultural images depicting American teenagers from the 1930s to the 1960s can be found in M. Barson and S. Heller, *Teenage Confidential: An Illustrated Story of the American Teen* (Chronicle Books, 1998).

5. M. B. Pipher, *Reviving Ophelia: Saving the Selves of Adolescent Girls* (Riverhead Trade, 1995, 1998, 2002, 2005, 2008), 208, 247.

6. R. Wiseman, *Queen Bees and Wannabes: Helping Your Daughter Survive Cliques, Gossip, Boyfriends, and Other Realities of Adolescence* (Three Rivers Press, 2002).

7. C. E. Martin, *Perfect Girls, Starving Daughters: The Frightening New Normalcy of Hating Your Body* (Free Press, 2007), 4.

8. D. Offer, 1997, Personal letter to author.

9. M. Pipher, 1998, *Reviving Ophelia* (video), Media Education Foundation, at http://www.mediaed.org/.

10. A good summary is by the Office of Juvenile Justice and Delinquency Prevention (2009), Break the cycle of violence by addressing youth victimization, abuse, and neglect, at http://www.ojjdp.ncjrs.gov/action/sec5.htm. National Victim Center (1992); *Rape in America* (Arlington, VA); see also M. Bayatpour and M. D. Wells, "Physical and Sexual Abuse as Predictors of Substance Use and Suicide Among Pregnant Teenagers, *Journal of Adolescent Health*, 13 (1992), 128–132.

11. C. Dellasega and C. Nixon, *Girl Wars: 12 Strategies that Will End Female Bullying* (New York: Simon and Schuster, 2003), 93.

12. M. Pipher, 1995, reference 4, 246.

13. Institute for Social Research (1975–2008), *Monitoring the Future: Questionnaire Responses from the Nation's High School Seniors*, Annual, 1975–2005, Ann Arbor: University of Michigan, Institute for Social Research, at http://www.monitoringthefuture.org/pubs.html#refvols.

14. Higher Education Research Institute (1966–2009), *The American Freshman: Forty Year Trends, 1966–2006*, Los Angeles: University of California, Los Angeles, at http://www.heri.ucla.edu/cirpoverview.php.

15. J. M. Twenge, *Generation Me: Why Today's Young Americans Are More Confident, Assertive, Entitled—and More Miserable Than Ever Before* (Free Press, 2007). This book is a mess. My own review is at http://www.youthfacts.org/twenge.html.

16. M. Pipher, 1998, op. cit., 208, 247.

17. M. G. Durham, *The Lolita Effect: The Media Sexualization of Young Girls and What We Can Do About It* (Overlook, 2008).

18. D. E. Levin and J. Kilbourne, J., *So Sexy So Soon: The New Sexualized Childhood and What Parents Can Do to Protect Their Kids* (Ballantine Books, 2008), 22–23.

19. M. Males, "Have Girls Gone Wild?," in *Fighting for Girls: New Perspectives on Gender and Violence*, ed. M. C. Lind and N. Jones (SUNY Press, 2010).

20. R. C. Hendrickson, *Youth in Danger: A Forthright Report by the Former Chairman of the Senate Subcommittee on Juvenile Delinquency* (Harcourt, Brace, 1956).

21. *The O.C.* (2003), Fox Television, Episode 16, Season 3, which may be viewed at http://www.youtube.com/watch?v=mzuRjAGLlWc.

22. T. Hoff, L. Greene, and J. Davis, 2003, *National Survey of Adolescents and Young Adults: Sexual Health, Knowledge, Attitudes and Experiences*, Henry J. Kaiser Foundation, see Table 32, at http://www.kff.org/youthhivstds/upload/National-Survey-of-Adolescents-and-Young-Adults.pdf.

23. B. Albert, ed., et al., 2003, 14 and younger: The sexual behavior of young adolescents, National Campaign to Prevent Teen Pregnancy, at http://www.thenationalcampaign.org/resources/pdf/pubs/14summary.pdf.

24. Centers for Disease Control and Prevention (2009), Sexual and reproductive health of persons aged 10–24 years—United States, 2002–2007, *Mortality and Morbidity Weekly Report*, Surveillance Summaries July 17, 2009/Vol. 58/No. SS-6.

25. S. J. Ventura, J. C. Abma, W. D. Mosher, and S. K. Henshaw, Estimated pregnancy rates for the United States, 1990–2005: An update, *National vital statistics reports*, 58(4), Hyattsville, MD: National Center for Health Statistics, 2009.

26. B. E. Hamilton, J. A. Martin, and S. J. Ventura, (2009), Births: Preliminary data for 2007, *National Vital Statistics Reports*, Web release; 57(12), Hyattsville, MD: National Center for Health Statistics, released March 18, 2009.

27. United Nations Statistics Division (2009), *Demographic Yearbook 2007* and previous annual volumes, United Nations, Natality, at http://unstats.un.org/unsd/demographic/products/dyb/dyb2.htm.

28. Levin & Kilbourne (2008), op. cit., quoted on pages 142, 143, 145, 146, 147, 150, 158.

29. Office of Juvenile Justice Delinquency Prevention (2009), and National Victime Center (1992), op. cit.

30. M. J. Blythe, J. D. Fortenberry, M. Temkit, W. Tu, and D. P. Orr, "Incidence and Correlates of Unwanted Sex in Relationships of Middle and Late Adolescent Women," *Archives of Pediatric & Adolescent Medicine*,160 (2006):591–595.

31. National Center for Injury Prevention and Control (2009), WISQARS injury mortality reports, 1980–2006, at http://www.cdc.gov/ncipc/wisqars/.

32. B. Kantrowitz, "Selling Advice—As Well as Anxiety," *Newsweek*, June 3, 2002, 50–52.

33. Federal Bureau of Investigation (2009), op. cit.

34. J. Garbarino, *See Jane Hit: Why Girls Are Growing More Violent and What We Can Do About It* (New York: Penguin Press, 2006), 15.

35. D. Prothrow-Stith, and H. Spivak, *Sugar and Spice and No Longer Nice: How We Can Stop Girls' Violence* (San Francisco: Jossey-Bass, 2005). 48.

36. D. Steffensmeier, J. Schwartz, H. Zhong, and J. Ackerman, "An Assessment of Recent Trends in Girls' Violence Using Diverse Longitudinal Sources: Is the Gender Gap Closing?," *Criminology*, 43(2) (2005): 355–405; M. Zahn, ed., *Delinquent Girls: Findings from the Girls Study Group* (Temple University Press, 2007).

37. Federal Bureau of Investigation (1975–2009), Uniform Crime Reports for the United States, 2007, U.S. Department of Justice (1964–2008), at http://www.fbi.gov/ucr/ucr.htm#cius, Table 40, Arrests, females by age, at http://www.fbi.gov/ucr/cius2007/data/table_40.html.

38. For a fuller discussion of the myth of an increase in girls' violence, see Males (2010), op. cit.

39. Martin (2007), op. cit., 4.

40. A. Quart, *Branded: The Buying and Selling of Teenagers* (Cambridge, MA: Perseus Publishing, 2003), 115, 120, 126.

41. Plastic Surgery Research.info. (2009), Cosmetic Plastic Surgery Research, Statistics and Trends for 2001–2007, at http://www.cosmeticplasticsurgerystatistics.com/statistics.html.

42. Pipher (1995), op. cit., 28.

43. Prothrow-Stith & Spivak (2006), op. cit., 48.

44. Dellasegga & Nixon (2003), op. cit., 35.

45. Garbarino (2006), op. cit., 35.

46. C. E. Martin, "Underneath Pop Star Scandals Is a Serious Message About Young Women and Addiction," *Huffington Post*, June 7, 2007.

47. See, for example, New American Media, *California Dreamers: A Public Opinion Portrait of the Most Diverse Generation the Nation Has Known*, University of California, Office of the President, April 25, 2007.

48. See CNN Election Center (2008), reference 3, Edison/Mitofsky (2007), Exit Poll, November 7, 2004, presidential election, CNN, at http://www.cnn.com/ELECTION/ 2004/pages/results/.

CHAPTER NINE: PANICS DU JOUR

1. J. Dobson, *Washington Monthly*, April 12, 2009.

2. L. S. Stepp, *Unhooked: How Young Women Pursue Sex, Delay Love, and Lose at Both* (New York: Riverhead Books, 2007), quoted on front flap and pages 4, 25, 70, 71, 116, 224, 228, 230, 233.

3. Monitoring the Future (2009), *Questionnaire Responses from the Nation's High School Seniors*. Annual, 1975–2008, Ann Arbor: University of Michigan, Institute for Social Research, at http://www.monitoringthefuture.org/pubs.html#refvols.

4. Bureau of the Census (2009), Census 2000 Summary file 3 (SF 3) - Sample data, detailed tables; marital status by sex, age, 2000 and previous decennial censuses, at http:// factfinder.census.gov/servlet/DTGeoSearchByListServlet?ds_name=DEC_2000_SF3_U &_lang=en&_ts=199760803875.

5. H. M. Karjane, B. S. Fisher, and F. T. Cullen, *"Campus Sexual Assault: How America's Institutions of Higher Education Respond,"* Final report to the National Institute of Justice, October 2002, 2.

6. L. R. Taylor, "Has Rape Reporting Increased Over Time? *National Institute of Justice Journal*, 254 (July 2006), at http://www.ojp.usdoj.gov/nij/journals/254/rape _reporting.html.

7. Bureau of Justice Statistics (2009), *Criminal Victimization in the United States, 2006*, Previous reports, 1973–2005. Washington, D.C.: U.S. Department of Justice, available at http://www.ojp.usdoj.gov/bjs/abstract/cvusst.htm#full.

8. K. Bogle, *Hooking Up: Sex, Dating, and Relationships on Campus* (NYU Press, 2008), 1, 5.

9. A. Landers, *Ann Landers Talks to Teenagers about Sex*, Crest (1965).

10. Norval Glenn and Elizabeth Marquardt, *Hooking Up, Hanging Out, and Hoping for Mr. Right: College Women on Dating and Mating Today*, Institute for American Values, 2001, quoted on pages 4, 6, at http://www.americanvalues.org/Hooking_Up.pdf.

11. Criminal Justice Statistics Center (2009), *Crime & Delinquency in California*, annual reports, 1986–2008, California Department of Justice.

12. National Association of Attorneys General; Resolution in support of teen dating violence education; Adopted, Summer Meeting, June 17–19, 2008, Providence, RI.

13. American Bar Association (2006), Teen dating violence initiative, at http://www .abanet.org/unmet/teendating/facts.pdf.

14. S. Catalano, *Intimate Partner Violence in the United States*, Washington, D.C: Bureau of Justice Statistics, U.S. Department of Justice, revised December 19, 2007.

15. S. Catalano and H. Snyder (2009). Female Victims of Violence. Bureau of Justice Statistics. At: http://bjs.ojp.usdoj.gov/content/pub/pdf/fvv.pdf.

16. W. H. James, C. West, K. E. Deters, and E. Armijo, "Youth Dating Violence," *Adolescence*, 35 (139), Fall 2000, 455–465.

17. Liz Claiborne Inc. (2008), New research indicates that significant numbers of children as young as 11 are engaging in sexual activity and that dating violence and abuse are part of their relationships, press release, July 8, 2008, Washington, D.C.

18. Teen Research Unlimited, Liz Claiborne Relationship Study (tweens), Fielded January 2–18, 2008, Table 9.1, obtained by author from reporter.

19. C. Wetzstein, "Youthful Indiscretion, Tweens' Pairing Up Worrisome," *Washington Times*, February 27, 2008.

20. For some good reviews, see M. O'Keefe and S. Lebovics, "Adolescents from Maritally Violent Homes," *The Prevention Researcher*, 12 (1) (2005): 3–7; J. E. Samuels, An Update on "the Cycle of Violence," Research in brief, National Institute of Justice, February 2001; Violence against Women Office (2000), Children and youth, U.S. Department of Justice, Office of Justice Programs.

21. A. L. Myers, "Man Accused of Posting Sex Assault Live on Web," Associated Press, June 3, 2009.

22. MSNBC Dateline (2009), To catch a predator, at http://www.msnbc.msn.com/id/10912603.

23. D. McCollam, "The Shame Game: "To Catch a Predator" Is Propping Up NBC's Dateline, but at What Cost?," *Columbia Journalism Review*, January/February 2007, at http://www.cjr.org/feature/the_shame_game.php.

24. *Dateline NBC* (2006), Most teens say they've met strangers online. New nationwide survey reveals teens interact with strangers on the Web, aired April 27, 2006, at http://www.msnbc.msn.com/id/10912603.

25. University of New Hampshire's Crimes against Children Research Center (2009), at http://www.unh.edu/ccrc/.

26. J. Wolak, D. Finkelhor, and K. Mitchell, 2009, Trends in arrests of "online predators," Crimes Against Children Research Center, University of New Hampshire, at http://www.unh.edu/ccrc/pdf/CV194.pdf.

27. J. Wolak, D. Finkelhor, D., and K. Mitchell (2007), "1 in 7 youth: The statistics about online sexual solicitations," Crimes against Children Research Center, University of New Hampshire, at http://www.unh.edu/ccrc/internet-crimes/factsheet_1in7.html.

28. Administration on Children, Youth and Families (2010), *Child Maltreatment 2008*. U.S. Department of Health and Human Services.

29. M. Hughes, "Molly Is a Teenage Girl Who Likes Hannah Montana, Lily Allen and Pink (or So the Covert Investigator Who Plays Her Would Like Internet Pedophiles to Think)," *The Independent*, London, October 30, 2009.

30. John Jay College of Criminal Justice, *The Nature and Scope of the Problem of Sexual Abuse of Minors by Catholic Priests and Deacons in the United States*, February 27, 2004, at http://www.bishop-accountability.org/reports/2004_02_27_JohnJay/index.html.

31. The Commission to Inquire into Child Abuse (2009), *Final Report of the Commission*, at http://www.childabusecommission.ie/.

32. D. D. Wishnietsky, "Reported and Unreported Teacher-Student Sexual Harassment," *Journal of Educational Research*, 3 (1991): 164–169.

33. C. Shakeshaft and A. Cohan, "Sexual Abuse of Students by School Personnel," *Phi Delta Kappan* (1995): 513–520.

34. M. Irvine and R. Tanner, "Sexual Misconduct Plagues U.S. Schools," Associated Press, October 20, 2007, at http://www.newsvine.com/_news/2007/10/20/1037899-ap-sexual-misconduct-plagues-us-schools.

35. American Association of University Women (2001, 1992), *Hostile Hallways: Bullying, Teasing, and Sexual Harassment in School*, quote from 1993 report is on page 24; from 2001 report on page 5; the 2001 report is at http://www.aauw.org/research/upload/hostilehallways.pdf.

36. B. Witte, "More than 100 Could Be Victims of Pediatrician," Associated Press, December 23, 2009, at http://my.earthlink.net/article/us?guid=20091223/3a021e0c-4824-4283-a763-ebcef99b43f7.

37. Reverbiage (2009), at http://reverbiage.com/find/sexting.

38. National Campaign to Prevent Teen and Unplanned Pregnancy (2009), Sex and tech: What's really going on, at http://www.thenationalcampaign.org/sextech/.

39. L. Quaid, "Think Your Kid Is Not 'Sexting'? Think again," Associated Press, December 3, 2009, at http://www.foxnews.com/story/0,2933,579025,00.html?mep.

40. A. Lenhart, *Teens and Sexting*, Pew Internet, December 15, 2009, at http://www.pewinternet.org/Reports/2009/Teens-and-Sexting.aspx.

41. Press Watch, *Youth Today* (2008), "Teen dating abuse on the rise, experts say," May 2008 (from *Daytona Beach News-Journal*, April 6, 2008); "Teens get more exposure than they intended," (from *San Francisco Chronicle*, August 5, 2008).

42. See, among many examples, M. J. Quadrel, B. Fischhoff, and W. Davis (1993); "Adolescent (In)vulnerability," *American Psychologist*, 48(2): 102–116; D. Offer (1987), "In Defense of Adolescents," *Journal of the American Medical Association*, 257: 3407–3408; D. Offer and K. Schonert-Reichl, "Debunking the Myths of Adolescence: Findings from Recent Research," *Journal of American Academy of Child & Adolescent Psychiatry*, 31(6) (1992): 1003–1014.

43. J. Wypijewski, "Through a Lens Starkly," *The Nation*, May 18, 2009, at http://www.thenation.com/doc/20090518/wypijewski.

44. A. Chandra, S. C. Martino, R. L. Collins, et al., "Does Watching Sex on Television Predict Teen Pregnancy? Findings from a National Longitudinal Survey of Youth," *Pediatrics*, 122(5) (2008): 1047–1054.

45. K. Masters, "Teens, sex and TV: A risky mix?," All Things Considered, National Public Radio, December 2, 2008, at http://www.npr.org/templates/story/story.php?storyId=97637718.

46. L. Tanner, "Teen Pregnancies Tied to Viewing Sexy TV Shows," Associated Press, November 3, 2008; R. Stein, "Study First to Link TV Sex to Real Teen Pregnancies," *Washington Post*, November 2, 2008; A. Park, "Sex on TV Increases Teen Pregnancy, Says Report," *Time*, November 3, 2008, at http://www.time.com/time/nation/article/0,8599,1855842,00.html.

47. Research: Report Roundup, "Teens, TV and Sex," *Youth Today* (December/January 2009).

48. B. Albert, "TV and Teen Pregnancy. National Campaign to Prevent Teen and Unplanned Pregnancy," November 3, 2008, at http://blog.thenationalcampaign.org/pregnant_pause/2008/11/tv-and-teen-pregnancy.php.

49. R. Stein (2008), op. cit.

50. J. L. Singer and D. G. Singer, "Family Experiences and Television Viewing as Predictors of Children's Imagination, Restlessness, and Aggression," *Journal of Social Issues*, 42(3) (1986): 107–124.

51. M. J. Bradley, *Yes, Your Teen Is Crazy!: Loving Your Kid Without Losing Your Mind* (Harbor Press, 2003), quoted on every page.

52. M. Maran, *Dirty: A Search for Answers Inside America's Teenage Drug Epidemic* (HarperOne, 2004), 56–57, 150.

53. K. Sternheimer, *Connecting Social Problems and Popular Culture: Why Media Is Not the Answer* (Westview, 2009).

CHAPTER TEN: WILL SEX-ED SAVE THE DAY?

Portions of this chapter are reproduced from M. Males, "Youth Health Services, Development Programs, and Teenage Birth Rates in 55 California Cities," *Californian Journal of Health Promotion*, 4(1) (2006): 46–57. Used by permission.

1. J. E. Darroch and J. J. Frost, *Teenage Sexual and Reproductive Behavior in Developed Countries: Can More Progress Be Made?* (Alan Guttmacher Institute, 2001).

2. Get Real About Teen Pregnancy, & California Adolescent Health Collaborative (2004), Teen birth rate declines, but challenges loom for California cities, 55 cities get "Reality Check," September 22, 2004, at http://www.letsgetreal.org/nr_RealityCheck Cities_2004.htm.

3. K. Bender, "California: Birth Rate for Teens in Berkeley a State Low," *Oakland Tribune*, September 23, 2004, B1.

4. L. Lambert, Berkeley High: A Sex Ed Success Story, Planned Parenthood, January 27, 2005, at http://www.plannedparenthood.org/pp2/portal/files/portal/webzine/ newspoliticsactivism/fean-050127-berkeley.xml.

5. My complete analysis is found in M. Males, "Youth Health Services, Development Programs, and Teenage Birth Rates in 55 California Cities," *Californian Journal of Health Promotion*, 4(1) (2006): 46–57, at http://www.csuchico.edu/cjhp/4/1/46-57-males.pdf.

6. Males (2006), op. cit.

7. Males (2006), op. cit.

8. Center for Health Statistics (2009), Birth profiles by ZIP code, California Department of Health Services, at http://www.cdph.ca.gov/data/statistics/Pages/BirthProfiles byZIPCode.aspx.

9. National Campaign to Prevent Teen Pregnancy (2009), PWWTW, at http://www .thenationalcampaign.org/resources/works/PWWTWabout.aspx.

10. Advocates for Youth (2005), Teen pregnancy, at http://www.advocatesforyouth .org/teenpregnancy.htm.

11. Sexuality Information and Education Council of the United States (2009), Fact sheets, adolescent sexuality, teen pregnancy, comprehensive sexuality education, at http:// www.siecus.org/index.cfm?fuseaction=page.viewpage&pageid=619&grandparentID=477 &parentID=612.

12. NARAL (2009), Sex education, at http://www.prochoiceamerica.org/issues/ sex-education/.

13. California Adolescent Health Collaborative (2005), Pregnancy, STI overview, at http://www.californiateenhealth.org/pregnancy_sti_overview.asp.

14. N. A. Constantine and C. R. Nevarez, No Time for Complacency, Teen Births in California, Public Health Institute, March 2003, 1, 15, at http://teenbirths.phi.org/ TeenBirthsFullReport.pdf.

15. The California Wellness Foundation (2009), Teen pregnancy prevention campaign aims its messages at adults, at http://www.calwellness.org/pub_portfolio/2000/ winter/pages/teenage_pregnancy_prevention.htm.

16. Alan Guttmacher Institute (2001), Five-country study points to ways the United States could further decrease teenage pregnancy and STD rates, Press Release, November 29, 2001, at http://www.guttmacher.org/media/nr/nr_euroteens.html.

17. D. Kirby, *Emerging Answers: Research Findings on Programs to Reduce Teen Pregnancy*, Washington, D.C.: National Campaign to Prevent Teen Pregnancy, 2001.

18. D. Kirby, *Emerging Answers 2007: Research Findings on Programs to Reduce Teen Pregnancy and Sexually Transmitted Diseases*, National Campaign to Prevent Teen and Unplanned Pregnancy.

19. W. D. Mosher, A. Chandra, and J. Jones,(2005). Sexual behavior and selected health measures: Men and women 15–44 years of age, United States, 2002, *Advance Data from Vital and Health Statistics*, 362. National Center for Health Statistics. September 15, 2005.

20. Family Research Council (2009), Human Sexuality, at http://www.frc.org/human-sexuality.

21. T. Perkins, Teen birth rate increase demonstrates need for authentic abstinence education, Family Research Council, December 6, 2007, at http://www.frc.org/get.cfm?i=PR07L02.

22. M. G. Pardue, More evidence of the effectiveness of abstinence education programs, Heritage Foundation, May 5, 2005; C. Kim and R. Robert, Abstinence Education: Assessing the Evidence. Heritage Foundation, Backgrounder #2126, April 22, 2008, at http://www.heritage.org/Research/Welfare/bg2126.cfm.

23. G. Denny and M. Young, "An Evaluation of an Abstinence-Only Sex Education Curriculum: An 18-Month Follow-Up, *Journal of School Health*, 76(8) (2006): 414–422; E. A. Borawski, E. S. Trapl, L.D. Lovegreen, N. Colabianchi, and T. Block, "Effectiveness of Abstinence-Only Intervention on Middle School Teens," *American Journal of Health Behavior*, 29(5) (2005): 423–434; J. B. Jemmott III, L. S. Jemmott, and G. T. Fong, "Abstinence and Safer Sex HIV Risk-Reduction Interventions for African American Adolescents: A Randomized Controlled Trial, *Journal of the American Medical Association*, 279, 19 (1998): 1529–1536.

24. S. Weed, *Another Look at the Evidence: Abstinence and Comprehensive Sex Education in Our Schools. Institute for Research and Evaluation*, 2009, at http://instituteresearch.com/docs/Another_Look_at_the_Evidence_(IRE,_05-13-09).doc.

25. D. Kirby, 2007, op. cit., 6, 15, 16, 17, 20, 21.

26. S. Weed, 2009, op. cit.

27. National Campaign to Prevent Teen and Unplanned Pregnancy, 2009, *What Works 2008: Curriculum-Based Programs that Prevent Teen Pregnancy*.

28. P. K. Kohler, L. E. Manhart, and W. E. Lafferty, "Abstinence-Only and Comprehensive Sex Education and the Initiation of Sexual Activity and Teen Pregnancy," *Journal of Adolescent Health*, 42 (2008): 344–351.

29. J. Russell, "Abstinence-Only and Comprehensive Sex Education and the Initiation of Sexual Activity and Teen Pregnancy," *Youth Today*, May 2008, 27.

30. Centers for Disease Control (2009), WONDER, Natality information, live births, at http://wonder.cdc.gov/natality.html.

31. K. Luker, *When Sex Goes to School: Warring Views on Sex—and Sex Education—Since the Sixties* (W. W. Norton, 2006).

CHAPTER ELEVEN: THE CALAMITY OF CONSENSUS

1. B. Obama, *Dreams from My Father: A Story of Race and Inheritance* (Three Rivers Press, 1995), xii, 229, 233–234, 242, 246.

2. Wikipedia, 2009, Ann Dunham, at http://en.wikipedia.org/wiki/Ann_Dunham.

3. B. Obama, *The Audacity of Hope: Thoughts on Reclaiming the American Dream* (Vintage Books, 2006), 222–223, 303, 394, 408.

4. An especially cogent analysis is found in M. Mead, *Culture and Commitment: A Study of the Generation Gap* (Panther, 1970, 1977).

5. Wikipedia, 2009, Entries for *Father Knows Best*, Robert Young, Lauren Chapin, and Elinor Donahue; *The Patty Duke Show*, Patty Duke; *I Love Lucy*, Lucille Ball and Desi Arnaz, at http://en.wikipedia.org/wiki/Main_Page.

6. American Academy of Pediatrics (2009), National day to prevent teen pregnancy is May 7, at http://www.aap.org/advocacy/releases/apr08teen.htm; National School Boards

Association (2009), Celebrate the national day to prevent teen pregnancy. at http://www.nsba.org/MainMenu/SchoolHealth/Updates/National-Day-.aspx; National Campaign (2009), Pregnant pause, at http://blog.thenationalcampaign.org/pregnant_pause/national-day-to-prevent-teen-p/.

7. B. Strauch, *The Primal Teen: What the New Discoveries About the Teenage Brain Tell Us About Our Kids* (Anchor, 2004), xi–xiv, 67.

8. See, among many examples, M. J. Quadrel, B. Fischhoff, and W. Davis, "Adolescent (In)vulnerability," *American Psychologist*, 48(2) (1993):102–116; D. Offer, "In Defense of Adolescents," *Journal of the American Medical Association*, 257 (1987): 3407–3408; D. Offer and K. Schonert-Reichl, "Debunking the Myths of Adolescence: Findings from Recent Research," *Journal of American Academy of Child & Adolescent Psychiatry*, 31(6) (1992): 1003–1014.

9. Quoted in R. Kotulak, "Teens Driven to Distraction," *Chicago Tribune*, March 24, 2006, 1.

10. L. Steinberg, "Risk-Taking in Adolescence: New Perspectives from Brain and Behavioral Science," *Current Directions in Psychological Science*, 16 (2007): 55–59.

11. H. L. Petri, *Motivation: Theory, Research, and Applications*, Third Edition (Belmont, CA: Wadsworth Publishing, 1990).

12. Public Broadcasting System (2002), Inside the teenage brain, Interview, Kurt W. Fischer and Daniel Siegel, at http://www.pbs.org/wgbh/pages/frontline/shows/teenbrain/interviews/todd.html.

13. S. Jayson, "Teens Driven to Distraction: Nature or Nurture?," *USA Today*, September 26, 2007.

14. R. Epstein and J. Ong, "Are the Brains of Reckless Teens More Mature than Those of Their Prudent Peers?," *Scientific American*, August 25, 2009, at http://www.scientificamerican.com/article.cfm?id=are-teens-who-behave-reck; R. Epstein, *The Case Against Adolescence* (Quill, 2007), 201.

15. G. S. Berns, S. Moore, and C. M. Capra, "Adolescent Engagement in Dangerous Behaviors Is Associated with Increased White Matter Maturity of Frontal Cortex," *PLoS ONE* 4(8) (2009): e6773.

16. T. Lu, Y. Pan, S. Kao, C. Li, I. Kohane, J. Chan, and B. Yankner. "Gene regulation and DNA damage in the ageing human brain," *Nature* AOP, published online June 9, 2004.

17. H. Sercombe and T. Paus, "The "Teen Brain" Research: Implications for Practitioners," *Youth and Policy*, 103 (Summer, 2009), 25–38.

18. J. J. Arnett, "Special Section on the Adolescent Brain and Risk-Taking," *Journal of Adolescent Research*, 25(1) (2010): 3:63, at http://jar.sagepub.com/content/vol25/issue1/?etoc.

19. The Pew Research Center for the People & the Press, Support for abortion slips, October 1, 2009, at http://people-press.org/report/549/support-for-abortion-slips.

20. California General Exit Poll (2009), How did you vote today on Proposition 4?, Edison/Mitofsky, November 5, 2008, at http://media.sacbee.com/smedia/2008/11/05/18/abortion.source.prod_affiliate.4.pdf.

21. V. G. Cartoof and L. V. Klerman, "Parental Consent for Abortion: The Impact of the Massachusetts Law," *American Journal of Public Health*, 76 (1986), 397–400; R. Blum, M. Resnick, and T. Stark, "The Impact of Parental Notification Laws on Adolescent Abortion Decision-Making," *American Journal of Public Health*, 77, (1987): 619–620.

22. D. Alsop (1986), *Hodgson v Minnesota* (1986) 646 FS up 756, Minnesota Digest.

23. U.S. Supreme Court (1990), *Hodgson v Minnesota*, 497 US 417.

24. P. Donovan, "Judging Teenagers: How Minors Fare When They Seek Court-Authorized Abortions," *Family Planning Perspectives*, 15 (1983), 259–267; Ed., "Factors Associated with the Use of Court Bypass by Minors to Obtain Abortions," *Family Planning Perspectives, 22*, (1990): 158–160.

25. J. O'Keefe and J. M. Jones, National Academy of Sciences, "Easing Restrictions on Minors' Abortion Rights," *Issues in Science and Technology*, 7 (Fall 1990): 1.

26. J. I. Rosoff, "The Supreme Court Retreats Another Step on Abortion," *Family Planning Perspectives*, 22 (August 1990): 183.

27. C. Ellertson, "Mandatory Parental Involvement in Minors' Abortions: Effects of the Laws in Minnesota, Missouri, and Indiana," *American Journal of Public Health*, 87 (1997) 1367–1374.

28. M. D. Regnerus, *Forbidden Fruit: Sex and Religion in the Lives of American Teenagers* (Oxford University Press, 2007).

29. M. Talbot, "Red Sex, Blue Sex," *The New Yorker*, November 3, 2008, 64, 66, 67, 69.

30. Details on U.S. births are tabulated by the Centers for Disease Control (2009), WONDER, Natality information, live births, at http://wonder.cdc.gov/natality.html .Centers for Disease Control (2009), *Sexually Transmitted Diseases Surveillance, 2008*, Data and statistics, at http://www.cdc.gov/std/stats/.

31. Association of Statisticians of American Religious Bodies (2009), U.S. congregational membership: State reports, at http://www.thearda.com/mapsReports/reports/selectState.asp.

32. Alan Guttmacher Institute (2006), *U.S. Teenage Pregnancy Statistics. National and State Trends and Trends by Race and Ethnicity* (New York: AGI, 2006) at http://www .guttmacher.org.

33. Bureau of the Census (2009), Census 2000 summary file 3 (SF 3) - Sample data, detailed tables, at http://factfinder.census.gov/servlet/DTGeoSearchByListServlet?ds _name=DEC_2000_SF3_U&_lang=en&_ts=199760803875.

34. For a variety of university fiscal measures, see California Postsecondary Education Commission (2009), Fiscal profiles at http://www.cpec.ca.gov/FiscalData/FiscalSnapshot Menu.asp.

CHAPTER TWELVE: KIDS TODAY

1. Bureau of the Census, "U.S. Population Projections: 2009 National Population Projections" (supplemental), http://www.census.gov/population/www/projections/2009 projections.html (accessed in 2010).

2. M. Mead, *Culture and Commitment: A Study of the Generation Gap* (Natural History Press, 1970), 73.

INDEX

Puritanism, 3, 6, 8, 13, 14, 16, 22, 44–46, 68, 71–73, 75, 78, 91, 98, 107, 110, 117, 124–25, 137–38, 149, 151–52, 158, 177, 180, 183, 186, 199, 205, 207, 208–11
Lifetime Movie Network, 93, 94. *See also Pregnancy Pact* (film)
Lolita Effect, The (book), 97, 139–41. *See also* Durham, M. Gigi
Los Angeles Times, 12
Losing Ground (book), 45, 78. *See also* Murray, Charles
Luker, Kristen, 37, 66, 194. *See also When Sex Goes to School*

Mackris, Andrea, 72–73. *See also* O'Reilly, Bill
Maddow, Rachel, 14, 15, 150, 180
"Make-It-Up" ethic, 19, 114, 171, 180
Maran, Meredith, 96, 177
Marin County, California, 25–27, 29, 82, 193
Martin, Courtney, 98, 131, 145. *See also Perfect Girls, Starving Daughters*
Matthews, Ross, 76
McCain, John, 71, 75
McFadden, Cyra, 25; *The Serial*, 25
Mead, Margaret, 215, 217
Mean Girls (film), 94
Media, "New," 111–13. *See also* Internet, growth of; information source for teens
Media, violence and sex. *See* Abuse and violence, in media and popular culture; Internet, sexually explicit content; Intimate Partner Violence; Rape and sexual violence, fears of popular culture and
Media Education Foundation (MEF), 13, 95, 99, 110–12, 137. *See also* Kilbourne, Jean
Mexico, teenage sex and pregnancy, 2, 14, 15, 26, 27, 65
Miscarriage, 28, 29, 37, 42, 101, 113, 117, 124
Monitoring the Future (MTF), 89, 105–06, 133, 135–36, 153–55
Moran, Jeffrey, 43, 51. *See also Teaching Sex*
Morris, Dick, 7, 14

Mother Jones (magazine), 152
Moynihan, Daniel Patrick, 45
MSNBC, 8, 14, 73, 125, 150, 163–64, 180. *See also To Catch a Predator*
MTV, 5, 138, 147, 170
Murray, Charles, 45, 57, 78. *See also Losing Ground*
Musick, Judith, 33, 66
MySpace, 12, 23, 141, 147, 172

Nation, The, 78, 142
National Abortion Rights League (NARAL), 185
National Association of Attorneys General, 158
National Association of Christian Educators, 74
National Campaign to Prevent Teen and Unplanned Pregnancy (National Campaign): derelictions and distortions of, 4, 14, 18, 32, 33, 68, 78, 80–81, 83, 117–19, 121–23, 170, 174, 183–84, 202, 217; new eugenics of, 58–61, 63–64, 118–19, 123, 199; sex education study by, 188–94; surveys by, 68, 83, 119, 141, 170
National Center for Health Statistics, 28, 101
National Crime Victimization Survey (NCVS), 104–05, 159. *See also* Bureau of Justice Statistics
National School Boards Association, 202
National Survey of Family Growth (NSFG), 99–100
National Violence against Women Survey, 156
NBC News, 150
"New girl," 129–47; troubling achievements, 129–30, 215; disturbing assertiveness, 11–12, 68–69, 74, 84, 99, 134, 136, 173, 215; infuriating optimism, low risks, 25–26, 69, 82, 84–85, 89, 100, 105–6, 130–36, 146–47, 155, 159, 161, 174, 188, 194; myths and fears toward, 5, 8–10, 23, 28, 40, 49, 68–69, 88–89, 92–96, 109, 125, 128, 129–32, 136–46, 153–55, 160–61, 172–75, 200–01, 206–8, 214; popular culture seductions presumed, 76, 78, 110–11,

About the Author and Editor

MIKE A. MALES is senior researcher for the Center on Juvenile and Criminal Justice, San Francisco, and the online information service, YouthFacts.org, and section editor for the *Californian Journal of Health Promotion*. He served for five years on the advisory board of Teen Pregnancy Prevention Initiative of the California Wellness Foundation. Dr. Males earned his Ph.D. in social ecology from the University of California, Irvine, taught sociology at UC Santa Cruz for six years, and has published four books on youth issues: *The Scapegoat Generation*, 1996; *Framing Youth*, 1999; *Smoked*, 2000; and *Kids & Guns*, 2004. Dozens of his research papers have appeared in professional literature, and he has given scores of keynote addresses at conference presentations around the country.

JUDY KURIANSKY, PhD, is an internationally known, licensed Clinical Psychologist and an adjunct faculty member in the Department of Clinical Psychology at Columbia University Teachers College and in the Department of Psychiatry at Columbia University College of Physicians and Surgeons. At the United Nations, she is an NGO representative for the International Association of Applied Psychology and for the World Council for Psychotherapy, and is an executive member of the Committee of Mental Health. She is also a Visiting Professor at the Peking University Health Sciences Center, a Fellow of the American Psychological Association, cofounder of the APA Media Psychology Division, and on the board of the Peace Division and U.S. Doctors for Africa. A certified sex therapist by the American Association of Sex Educators and Counselors, she is a pioneer in the field of sexuality. An award-winning journalist, she hosted the popular LovePhones syndicated call-in radio show for years, was a feature reporter for WCBS-TV and CNBC, and regularly comments on news and current events on television worldwide. Her wide-ranging expertise in interpersonal and international relations is evident in her books ranging from *The Complete Idiot's Guide to a Healthy Relationship* and *Sexuality Education: Past, Present and Future* to *Beyond Bullets and Bombs: Grassroots Peacebuilding between Israelis and Palestinians*. Her Web site is www.DrJudy.com.